Bad Faith

Bad Faith

A Spiritual Humanist Alternative
for Christianity and the West

TOM DRAKE-BROCKMAN

RESOURCE *Publications* • Eugene, Oregon

BAD FAITH
A Spiritual Humanist Alternative for Christianity and the West

Copyright © 2019 Tom Drake-Brockman. All rights reserved. Except for brief quotations in critical publications or reviews, no part of this book may be reproduced in any manner without prior written permission from the publisher. Write: Permissions, Wipf and Stock Publishers, 199 W. 8th Ave., Suite 3, Eugene, OR 97401.

Resource Publications
An Imprint of Wipf and Stock Publishers
199 W. 8th Ave., Suite 3
Eugene, OR 97401

www.wipfandstock.com

PAPERBACK ISBN: 978-1-5326-7349-8
HARDCOVER ISBN: 978-1-5326-7350-4
EBOOK ISBN: 978-1-5326-7351-1

Manufactured in the U.S.A.   JANUARY 17, 2019

Unless otherwise indicated, bible quotations are taken from New International version copyright © 1973, 1978, 1984 by Biblica, copyright ©1986 Zondervan Publishing House

Contents

Introduction | 1

1. Christian History: how metaphysical faith eclipsed *hesed* humanism | 19
    From Jewish Christianity to Christian anti-Judaism | 21
    From the Dark Ages to the Enlightenment | 26
    Bad faith gravitates towards a secular black hole | 32

2. The Word Was *Hesed* | 40
    The political context of *hesed* in Christ's mission | 42
    The unacknowledged centrality of *hesed* in the Gospels | 48
    Hesed e'meth in Matthew and John | 53
    Racist reservations | 56

3. The Baseless Fabric of Paul's Messianic Visions | 63
    Paul's metaphysical visions and Judaic realities | 64
    Good news and fake news | 67
    Isaiah's suffering servant was not Paul's sacrificial Christ | 71
    Paul's Flawed Sacrificial Typology | 74
    The primacy of atoning repentance over the sacrificial cult | 79
    Paul's grace negates free will and aligns him with Christ's mortal enemies | 84

4. Jesus Reveals the Purpose of Human Existence: Spiritual Evolution | 94
    God is Elohim, Adam is YHWH—and Jesus | 96
    One life is not enough: Jesus and reincarnation | 105
    Christians can go to hell | 111

5. Christian Humanist Theopraxis | 119
    Christ's humanized approach to worship, faith and prayer | 120
    New social/spiritual frontiers of compassion | 125
    New social and political priorities | 128

Conclusion | 142

Bibliography | 151

Index | 173

Introduction

JUST A FEW DECADES ago, the Western democracies were buoyant. Freedom and capitalism had triumphed in the Cold War and to some it seemed like the "end of history,"[1] a new age of peace and the triumph of Western civilization. Now the worm has turned. The new century seems destined to belong to authoritarian China and Russia and in the West, there is growing anxiety. Pathological evil has become a norm and another world war now looms as a real possibility. Mutually assured destruction (MAD) has kept the nuclear beast tethered so far; but there is a chilling acceptance that those tethers could be all too easily broken. Economies are stagnant or shrinking. Mass unemployment seems a likely flow on from the coming robotics revolution; and traditional pillars of stability—like the middle classes and two parent families—are dwindling. Add to this declining education standards, endemic crime and unsustainable health and welfare costs, and the result is building to a perfect storm.

Creative efforts to grapple with such problems are dogged by a deeper postmodern malaise. There is a breakdown of core values, most evident in the proliferation of divisive identity politics. Instead of pursing traditional goals of justice and equality, various grievance groups now seem more interested in venting their victimhood and receiving ongoing recognition of their special status. This has taken us from a consensus on broad humanist goals into a miasma of atomized self-obsessions.

This political tribalism is found on both sides of the political spectrum and has resulted in new levels of hostility as culture warriors now regard politics as intensely personal. Civic discourse and reasoned debate have been major casualties and democratic processes are threatened with

---

1. This term was coined by US political science author Francis Fukuyama in his 1992 book, *The End of History and the Last Man*

gridlock. Populism of the right appeals to less affluent (especially 'white') elements who see themselves as shunned by multicultural, global elites. The response of the Left has been to double down, empathizing with minority groups that see the enemy as 'white', 'male' and 'privileged'. As a result, much of the Left now regards hallowed traditions of Western culture like the Enlightenment and even democracy itself, as Eurocentric and supremacist.

If secular humanism has come to this parlous juncture, it is surely time to consider its alternative: spiritual humanism. Some progressive Christians claim to have latched onto this idea; but their perspective seems to yield little more than a rehashed social gospel.[2] Yet there is a more substantive tradition of spiritual humanism that stretches far back in time and it could provide a deeply healing balm for our fractured world. It reached a high water-mark in the European Renaissance though it was also a feature of many world religions and civilizations long before then.

In her book, *The Great Transformation*, Karen Armstrong examines a fascinating period of relative enlightenment known as the 'Axial Age'. Spanning the centuries from 900 to 200 BCE, it saw the establishment of the great spiritual and philosophical traditions that have profoundly impacted humanity through to the present day—Confucianism and Daoism in China, Hinduism and Buddhism in India, monotheism in Israel and philosophical rationalism in Greece. Armstrong also includes the teachings of Jesus and Mohammed as 'latter-day flowerings of the Axial age.' In their search for transcendence, the founders of these traditions relied less on the heavens than human wisdom and reason. They provided new insights into morality and ethics, particularly in relation to notions of ego sublimation, compassionate empathy and theosis; and their revelations became the gold standard that on-coming generations used for guidance in times of spiritual and social crisis.[3] These are all rich spiritual humanist veins worthy of exploration; and it is the Judeo-Christian one that is explored in this book.

The life and teachings of Jesus distilled the essence of a latent Judaic humanism and moulded it into an elaborate system of ethical faithfulness. But like all its religious bedfellows, Christianity became institutionalized and ritualized and never seriously embraced the revolutionary humanist teachings of its founders. Otherworldly concerns and faith abstractions

---

2. Olson R.E, 2012. *A Christian Humanist Manifesto*. For example, no attempt is made to reconcile this Christian humanist version of an interventionist God of faith with the basic humanist insistence on absolute human autonomy.

3. Armstrong K, 2006, p xi-xviii.

Introduction

came to dominate and, over the millennia, these can be seen to have degraded all religions to a point where, today, for many, they have all but lost their credibility. But with Western civilization also at a low ebb, it may be time to consider whether the spiritual humanism of the Jewish Jesus can be rediscovered, displacing metaphysical faith to become, belatedly, the centrepiece of a humanized Christianity and the matrix of a revitalized Western culture. This is a radical proposition but both Christianity and the West are fast running out of options.

Both Christians and humanists have long seen themselves as mutually exclusive—but they operate on hackneyed assumptions. The vision of Jesus that emerges here cuts through conventional stereotypes, providing an alternative, humanistic way of imaging him, his God, our relationship with both and our basic world view. While others appended lofty titles to Jesus—Lord, Christ (Messiah)[4], Son of God, etc—the only title Jesus himself claimed was the 'Son of Man'. Chapter Four of this book presents a new understanding of that title and suggests that while Jesus did not see himself as God, he may yet have been semi-divine. However, it will be shown how even this imposing spiritual dimension would not necessarily disqualify him from being a humanist.

Humanists of course reject the very notion of God, though what they mainly object to is the idea of an interventionist God that impinges on human autonomy. While Jesus certainly believed in God, it will be argued that neither he nor his 'Father' envisaged anything more than a minimal intervention in human affairs and one that never impeded the operation of free will. To do other would inevitably curtail human freedom and autonomy—which may well have been the whole point of creation in the first place. Far from signalling any intent to redeem the world as a 'once and for all' sacrificial oblation (Heb 10:10), Jesus used the brief time he had on earth to impart a wisdom that might help us find our own redemption. His departure still left humanity adrift in the universe, needing to plot its own destiny but now equipped with some very specific spiritual and ethical guidelines. Jesus was seen as a Messiah by his own disciples who called him the 'Christ'. He himself was more reticent and the only time he pro-actively referred to himself as 'the Christ' was in the context of being an enlightened rabbi or teacher (Mt 23:10 & Jn 4:25–26), thus implying it was through his teachings that we might seek redemption, not his mystical persona.

---

4. The name Jesus Christ was given to Jesus after his crucifixion by his followers who claimed he was the Messiah.

It is in that sense, as a messianic teacher, that the title 'Christ' is used interchangeably with 'Jesus' throughout this book. That may ruffle the feathers of Jesus scholars who like to make a clear distinction between 'the Jesus of history and the Christ of faith'. But the Christ that emerges here did not rely on faith. By his own reckoning, he is both a celestial and historical figure who appeals not so much to faith as faithfulness and human reason. This depiction throws out a direct challenge to mainstream Christian theology which still insists Jesus was the Messiah whose sacrificial death redeemed the sins of the world; and that makes the man first responsible for establishing this spurious personality cult, Paul of Tarsus, a prime target of this book.

Nietzsche's sarcastic observation that there was 'only one Christian and he died on the cross', contains more than a grain of truth. Soon after Christ's death, Paul took control of his legacy and the teacher of wisdom quickly morphed into the iconic Christ of faith. Christian theology continued to uphold Christ's social and ethical teachings, but became so fixated on Paul's faith dogmas as to lose sight of their revolutionary social and political implications. At the core of Christ's teachings was the Hebraic notion of *hesed*.

Hesed was the covenantal loyalty God promised to humanity and expected to be reciprocated. It was the bedrock of Judaic monotheism. Established as a core principle from the outset in Genesis, it went on to become the focal point of all the covenants God made with his 'nations'—but particularly with his 'chosen people', the Jews.[5] *Hesed* is most often translated as 'mercy' and refers to God's steadfast, loving kindness towards humanity. But it was never a one way transaction. As well as reciprocating this loyalty in their monotheism, Jews came to understand God as obliging them to replicate His loving kindness in their dealings with each other. That was especially mandated in the relationships between the weak and the strong. Just as the *hesed* relationship between God and humanity was asymmetrical, its social expression was understood mainly in terms of the more powerful helping the weakest and most vulnerable.[6] This spiritual ethic was first practiced within the family unit and then found expression at a wider social level. It may well have been the origins of the principle that later became known as *noblesse oblige*.

---

5. Elazar D, 1996. *Covenant as the Basis of the Jewish Political Tradition.*
6. Knowles M.P, 2012, p129.

Introduction

The scriptures make it clear that God chose the Jews as his main conduit for transmitting this seminal ethic to the world (Gen 18:18; Deut. 4:5–8; Isa 2:3–4 &49:6; Mic 4:2–3; Zech 8:23).[7] *Hesed* expressed divinely sourced love in a variety of ways–merciful forgiveness, compassionate empathy, charity, loving kindness, grace, all characterized by unwavering, steadfast commitment and encapsulated in the Hebrew word *emunah*: faithfulness.[8] Over the centuries of the Axial age, the Jewish prophets and sages extolled the virtues of *hesed* and extended its scope beyond interpersonal relationships. They resoundingly affirmed *hesed* to also include God's passion for justice and especially social justice (*tzedakah*).[9] Their appeals for basic *hesed* justice were invariably couched in biblical and historical accounts of political and religious leaders promoting justice or, conversely and more commonly, committing acts of cruel injustice.[10]

Not only in Jewish scripture but also in the ancient mystical literature of the Kabbalah, *hesed* is nominated as the supreme attribute of God to be emulated in human relationships.[11] Through *hesed*, the prophets and sages affirmed that humanity could pursue one of the other great quests of the Axial age—theosis. This was the desire to actually know God (Hos6:6; Jer 22:16–17; 31:33–34; & Isa 58:1–10) by imitating his *hesed* qualities, a seminal, spiritual humanist ideal that was later expressed by the Latin phrase *imitatio dei*. That aspiration is given credence in the first chapter of the first book of Genesis where God is said to have created humanity in his own image (Gen 1:27). The ancient Prophets and Psalmists affirmed the pathos of God in terms of *hesed*, the practice of which would enable people to 'know and love' God (Hos 6:6; Jer 31:34). In other words, they proclaimed that epistemic faith was attainable, not through any adopted, a priori metaphysical belief, but only through *hesed* faithfulness, acted out in this world.

---

7. Sachs J, 2014, *Yitro (5774)—A Nation of Leaders*. For a detailed exposition of this divinely ordained role, see Tzadok A.B, 2013. *Israel: the Mission*.

8. Shapiro R.M, 2013, p89–90.

9. Hayes J.H, 2013, p289–9. Also Zion N.2013, p6.

10. Houston W.J, 2018. *Social Justice and the Prophets*.

11. Leiberman S. 2000, *Kabbala #12: Chesed and Gevurah*. The Kabbalah was/is the corpus of Judaic theosophic teachings about the nature of life, originating in ancient Judaism and continuing through to today. Though the Kabbalah only became a formal belief system in the Middle Ages, Jews tend to use the name to refer to the mysticism of early Judaism (and especially the Zohar of the 2nd century CE, on which the later Kabbalah was based.

Thus in the Judaic covenantal theology, 'faith' became indivisible from—indeed, even synonymous with—faithfulness expressed through *hesed*. There was no strong reliance on divine grace because the religious experience was deemed to be grounded in *hesed* ethics and morality for which Jews held themselves basically responsible, both as individuals and collectively, by virtue of free will. Christ's brother James famously declared that "faith without works is dead" (Jas 3:18-19), implying faith was meaningless and ineffectual without the kind of *hesed* works that reflected God's love of humanity. For James, not faith as belief but works faithfulness was pivotal and his strident rejection of bad faith, "faith alone" (Jas 2:24), was aimed squarely at Paul.[12]

Thus in early Judaism, God was not so much a metaphysical idea as a human ideal and faith stemmed from what were perceived to be his actions in the world, the steadfast covenant he forged with the Jews and his justice in rewarding or punishing human moral behaviour. To that extent it was empirically based and involved a high level of trust. The word for faith most commonly used in the Hebrew bible was *emunah* which translates mainly as faithfulness, trust and confidence inspiring faith in action. But *emunah* also conveyed a specific kind of faithfulness that involved practicing all the key attributes of *hesed*—trust, steadfastness, justice and compassion.[13] God could be understood and 'known' through imitating his *hesed* in our social interactions and this *emunah* faithfulness is basically what constituted 'faith' in mainstream early Judaism.

It is here that the disjunction between the Jewish Jesus and the subsequent emergence of bad faith Christianity actually began. The New Testament record of Jesus and the early church was written in Greek which had by then become the lingua franca. However, the closest Greek word the Jewish authors of the Gospels could find to convey *emunah*, was *pistis*—which actually means faith as a belief in metaphysical ideas about God.[14] Accordingly, while they used the word *pistis*, what they usually meant to convey was the Hebrew concept of *emunah*.[15]

However as will be shown in Chapter Three, Paul was aligned with a Jewish minority who conceived of faithfulness in terms of *pistis*, ritualistic

---

12. Vermes G, 2000, p114-115. See also Wilson AN, 1992, p37.

13. Shapiro R.M, 2013, p89-90. Also Andrews D.2008, p45-46. Christ's references to 'faith' are examined in more detail in chapter five

14. Bible Study Tools: *Pistis*.

15. Werner D, 2017, p46-48. Wright N.T.1997, p 160.

legalism rather than ethics. Thus, when Paul's Jewish covenantal loyalty with superseded by a new, inchoate belief in Christ as a sacrificial Saviour, *pistis* more precisely suited his intent—faith as a kind of unknowing, unquestioning belief in the mystical idea of universal salvation through Christ crucified.[16] On the other hand, it will be argued that Jesus rarely called for unquestioning belief but preferred to evoke *emunah*. Thus *pistis* in the Gospels is strongly linked to the faithfulness of his healing miracles, with empirical observation of them being a striking manifestation of God's *hesed*, alleviating human suffering and thereby 'bringing great glory' to God (Jn 11:4; Mt 5:16).

All of Christ's teachings recorded in the Gospels can be seen to pivot on *emunah* faithfulness. But following Paul's emphasis on *pistis*, Christian theologians struck out in a different direction, generally failing to grasp the centrality of *hesed*.[17] Their overriding focus on gentiles and the new faith abstraction of a crucified Saviour, tended to deflect consideration of the basic Judaic spiritual priorities enshrined in *emunah*. *Imitatio dei* became more of a distant ideal, only attainable through faith in Jesus as Redeemer and the grace supposed to flow therefrom. Paul's pessimistic view was of a humanity so compromised by Adam's sin that God's grace was indispensable. Yet once received, he believed this grace could magically transform people into a saintly 'new creation' (Gal 6:15). It was not long before the debauched behaviour of his Corinthian flock soon dispelled such pipe dreams.[18]

Jesus was clearly more realistic. He knew most people, like his disciples, were "of little faith."[19] He regretted this but fully understood human limitations. It was not divine grace per se that would transform them into obedient automatons but a thorough understanding of and steadfast commitment to *hesed*. Thus he devoted virtually his entire mission teaching his followers the ramifications of *hesed*—particularly the importance of compassion, humility and forgiveness—and how to cultivate an empathetic disposition. He knew, as the Jewish prophets affirmed, that *emunah* was the only way to 'know' God. His miracles of healing made this tangible and verifiable.

16. McConville J.G, 2002, p145.
17. Evans C.A (ed), 2004, p302.
18. Chidester D, 2000, p37.
19. In all the gospels, Jesus constantly berated his disciples for their lack of faith, probably in terms of both *emunah* and *pistis,* with the latter dependant on the former.

Christians have been too mesmerized by 'faith' and gratuitous 'grace' to countenance this alternative notion of *emunah* with its deep spiritual and human connections. They like to believe, as Paul did, that loving kindness will arise from faith in a doctrinal belief. But for the vast majority of Christians, that has never happened, at least not to the extent that Jesus clearly desired. No one could overlook the enormous outpouring of love and charity that attended Christ's mission and these virtues have always been cherished by Christianity. That has been both admirable and salutary—but it could have been vastly more so if Christ's specific commitment to *hesed* had become Christianity's lodestar. Charity is excellent but not enough. It does not encompass *hesed* imperatives of justice and non-violence which have all too often been absent from Christian humanitarianism or merely articulated as platitudes.

Today, justice initiatives are largely restricted to social gospel 'progressives' who emphasise Christ's 'preferential option for the poor', a phrase coined by, Gustavo Gutierrez, one of the founders of 'Liberation Theology' in the late 20th century. But by failing to tap into the unique *hesed* insights of Jesus, the liberationists fell between two stools. Instead of demanding a radical and distinctive Christian response to gross injustice and suffering, liberation theology chose to operate within the constraints of Christian faith, while also often tying itself to Marxist agendas and ideologies. These basically conflicted with that faith and history would soon show them to be deeply flawed. As a result, Liberation Theology has become passé and overtaken in Latin America by a more populist (and reactionary) Pentecostal Christianity.[20]

Such theological confusion has actually impeded prioritization of the poor. The Greek word for poor is *penes* but in the Gospels, the word Jesus used was *ptochos*, meaning poorest of the poor. It was the most desperate and vulnerable sections of humanity that he reached out to,[21] those he called "the least of these brothers and sisters of mine" (Mt 25:40). That was entirely consistent with the generally asymmetrical nature of *hesed* relationships—the strong helping the weak—referred to above. Failure to prioritize the *ptochos*, most notably the millions of helpless children who

---

20. Gale T. 2005. *Pentecostal and Charismatic Christianity.*
21. Crossan J.D, 1998, p321-2.

are hungry and abused, above lesser, more modish secular causes[22] (or even just church dogma itself), has long had the effect of diffusing and compromising Christian activism.

There are certainly plenty of Christian humanitarians who uphold the principles of *hesed*, often heroically. But the primary commitment to faith tends to pull many of them back towards a default position of quietism.[23] There is in fact a fundamental contradiction between conventional faith and Christ's *hesed* commitment to this world. The inescapable reality is that faith in immanent salvation is as likely to induce a compassionate sensibility as inheriting billions would promote a dynamic work ethic. Faith tends to divert people from the problems of this world by offering salvation as a "free gift" in the next. (Rom. 5:15) With its worship rituals and abstruse dogmas, it is more conducive to complacency, tokenism, relativism and even amorality. Paul himself soon confronted this problem in the licentiousness of his followers in Corinth and had to tailor his message accordingly.[24]

But while Paul propounded this kind of spurious faith, it was not long before the Gospels appeared, virtually ignoring Paul's sacrificial dogmas[25] and loudly proclaiming Christ's *hesed* faithfulness. Thus, from the outset, Christian history oscillated between these two poles with distinctly chequered results. Christian faithfulness anchored in *imitatio dei*, can be seen to have inspired some of the greatest achievements of Western civilization, not only in the creative arts but in fostering the emergence of human rights, modern democracy and the rule of law.[26] On the other hand, the deceptions of Christian faith often inspired bigotry, facilitating, abetting and even perpetrating a litany of monstrous evils—inquisitions and crusades, patriarchal misogyny, anti-Semitism and, more recently, clerical pedophilia.

While it may still be argued that Christianity has produced more good than harm, it seems certain that had the religion grounded itself on Christ's *hesed* instead of Paul's metaphysics, human history might have taken a very different and better course. But people are more repelled by the evil men

---

22. Lomborg B, 2018. *Climate-change policies may be making world hunger worse.* Lomborg argues most climate-change policies are prohibitively expensive, yield negligible results and exacerbate world hunger.

23. A spiritual attitude of withdrawal from worldly concerns to focus purely on the divine.

24. Chidester J,2000, p37

25. Finlan S, 2005, p109. This will be argued at length in chapters two and three.

26. Wolfe G,2011. *Is culture more powerful than politics?* Also Carroll V & Shiflett D. 2002. *Christianity On Trial.*

do than they are attracted by the good, especially when the good is hidden under a bushel of opaque faith instead of shining brightly as "the light of the world"(Mt 5:14). So today, Christianity is being shunned by a more informed populace, all too aware of its gross and ongoing historical lapses.

Christianity is floundering in its Western heartlands. In traditionally devout Ireland, church attendance dropped by 25% between 1975 and 2004 and has continued to drop in Dublin so steeply that by 2030 the churches there may be empty.[27] Throughout Europe, the situation is comparable. In France, the Netherlands and Sweden, Christian Sabbath observance has plummeted to a mere 10% of the population.[28] In Australia, people identifying as Christians have decreased by nearly a third over the past 15 years and are now a minority of the population.[29] Americans see themselves as the world bastion of Christianity but the proportion of the American population that can be classified as Christian declined from 86 per cent in 1990 to 70 % in 2015 (and 43% of these lapsed Christians were under the age of 35).[30] Importantly in the US, it is youth and the elites who have mainly exited the churches and they tend to lead public opinion.[31]

Within the shrinking corpus of Western Christianity, only Pentecostal fundamentalism is bucking the trend.[32] In the underdeveloped World, where Christianity is actually growing, Pentecostal and charismatic influences are also at the forefront. But regrettably, these brands put a premium on mystical faith and tend to be reactionary. They are known to inspire superstition, mass hysteria and a bigoted attitude to non-believers,[33] as well as homophobia and misogyny.[34] Churches take some solace in the growth of Christianity in the underdeveloped world, but it is likely this kind of Christianity will serve as a useful vehicle—or as Marx called it, 'opiate'—for social control by corrupt, opportunistic ruling castes.[35] This third world

---

27. Zwartz B, 2009. *Losing our Religion*; & McGarry,2016. *Mass attendance in Dublin to drop by one-third by 2030.*

28. Zwartz B, op cit.

29. Knox N, 2005. *Religion takes a back seat in Western Europe.*

30. Buchanan P, 2015. *The Decline of Christian America.*

31. Sheridan G, 2017. *Is God Dead?*

32. Wallis J, 2008, p30-32.

33. The Economist, 2006. *Pentecostals: Christianity reborn.*

34. Alves M.2012. *Hate speech and the rhetoric against criminalization in homophobic discussion by religious leaderships in Brazil.*

35. Rocha J.L. *The Third Horseman of Neoliberalism: The Neo-Pentecostals.*

INTRODUCTION

Christianity is shaping as depressing rerun of the blind faith primitivism that the European world endured for centuries.

Instead of asking what might be wrong with a theology so easily bent to such perverse causes, Christian churches in the West have been busy digging themselves into a deeper hole, one that could easily become their final resting place. Their handling of clerical child abuse in recent decades speaks of a Church more intent on protecting degenerate priests, and their own reputation, than helping their devastated victims.[36] Instead of isolating and bringing these predatory monsters to justice, church authorities often just shifted them to new parishes exposing yet more children to their depredations. The Catholic Church has been particularly culpable and it was this that triggered a mass exodus of German Catholics in 2010.[37] In the same year it was revealed that in Belgium, less than twenty percent of pedophile priests had faced any retribution for their heinous acts.[38]

Yet even in the teeth of world condemnation, the Catholic Church response was to double down on its own depravity. Also in 2010, the Vatican decided to elevate the 'sin' of ordaining women priests by equating that 'iniquity' with child abuse in Catholic cannon law.[39] While Catholic apologists insist canon law is separate from moral law, the implied equivalence betrays a crass insensitivity if not indifference to child abuse, not to mention a thinly veiled misogyny. Thus we find Catholic dogmatists simultaneously degrading women who aspire to the priesthood and upgrading child abusers, so that both end up inhabiting the same 'legal' if not moral strata. Compounding this Catholic abomination was an ensuing stampede of 50 Anglican priests to the male-only cloisters of Catholicism in protest against the growing Anglican acceptance of female ordination.[40]

The Russian Orthodox Church has sunk to even lower depths of depravity. It has supported new laws that virtually legalize spousal abuse and aligned itself with Vladimir Putin, the tyrant 'strong man' who has systematically destroyed democracy in Russia while plundering billions of dollars from his own people, that may now rank him as one of the wealthiest men

---

36. Shields J, 2015. *Lawyers accuse Catholic Church of 'push back' against victims of child sex abuse.*

37. Ross T, 2010, p14.

38. Sydney Morning Herald, 2010. *Belgian priest tells of 300 sexual abuse cases.*

39. Hooper J, 2010. *Vatican makes attempted ordination of women a grave crime.* Also Bates S, 2010. *Church of England parish sings battle hymns as it plans move to Rome.*

40. Jones J.W, 2010. *Catholic Church to welcome 50 Anglican clergy.*

on the planet.[41] In its craven submission to Putin's state, the church has never even acknowledged the bulging catalogue of war crimes Russia is said to have committed in Syria.[42]

Here is bad faith at its worst, the moral dereliction of a perverted Christian theology displayed in all its ugliness. Thus has faith theology now brought Christianity to its knees, not in remorseful prayer but stricken by its own reckless, self-inflicted blows. In an age of sectarian madness where terror stalks the earth, patience with such lunacy is wearing thin.

Christianity is far from alone in affording evil the safe harbours of faith. All the major religions of faith have had shocking track record in recent times, assimilating psychopaths and violent extremists. Islam is the most blatant but by no means only example of this. Hindu 'nationalists' in India and hard line Buddhists in Sri Lanka and Myanmar have also promoted hatred and sanctioned violence against minority groups. Christianity may be relatively benign in terms of inciting violence these days, but it has a disgusting record of instigating and sanctifying brutality over the centuries. Desecrations like Christian anti-Semitism, which will be given particular attention throughout this book, still lurk in the shadows of the recent past.

The basic problem is not hard to identify. Since the end of the Axial age, all major religions have evolved to preference abstract notions of faith, symbolic ritual and prayer, above what Jesus called "the more important matters . . . justice, mercy (*hesed*) and faithfulness"(Mt 23:23). These are the core values lie at the heart of all the great religious traditions[43] and It would be salutary if they would all examine their origins in a similar way to what is undertaken here. Only then can they strike at the source of their problem: faith theology. For Christianity, this originated with St Paul whose personal 'voices' and 'visions' convinced him that Jesus' real purpose was to atone for original sin by dying on the cross. Two thousand years of reiteration and convoluted theorizing has arrived at multiple variations of Paul's atonement theology and cloaked it with sham legitimacy. But the 'baseless fabric' of his vision melts away under closer scrutiny. Chapter Three provides such scrutiny, but some preliminary observations might be made here.

---

41. Ellis G & Kolchyna V, 2017. *Putin and the 'triumph of Christianity' in Russia.* Also, May R. 2018. *Putin: From Oligarch to Kleptocrat.*

42. Amnesty International Report, 2018. *Syria: Relentless bombing of civilians in Eastern Ghouta amounts to war crimes.*

43. Armstrong K, 2006, p xiii-xiv.

Introduction

First it should be understood that original sin was basically Paul's idea.[44] The Jewish Christ and his disciples, had no clear concept of original sin and might have been the first to wonder how Paul could saddle all humanity with damnable guilt for the actions of the first human who God made in his own image. Today, many would also wonder why God would wish to forbid his human charges from eating the fruit of the 'tree of knowledge'—ie, wanting to discover 'truth' and wisdom—and then to punish us so severely for doing so? How could that be such a heinous sin that only a brutal crucifixion could atone for it? Even if God rated disobedience as so reprehensible, conducive to evil and suffering in his creation, he would have foreseen Adam's rebelliousness which would surely make him more than an accessory to it. And that of course, begs the ultimate theological conundrum of theodicy which has always been religion's Achilles heel.

Christian 'true believers' are content to just shrug off these anomalies as 'mysteries of faith'. But surely the real mystery is exactly how a rational human mind is supposed to have faith in, let alone a 'personal relationship' with, such a strange and perverse deity, in whose image we are purportedly made. Chapter four will examine all these confected 'mysteries' more closely and propose some radically new, rational and humanist interpretations of Genesis that could go to the heart of our life purpose and even resolve the theodicy enigma.

In recent years a 'new perspective on Paul' (NPP) has disputed the precise nature of Paul's atonement theology and this will be discussed in Chapter Three. But the predominant view still holds that God's anger had to be assuaged.[45] Just like the imperious gods that caused our cave dwelling ancestors to cower in fear, this *YHWH* also demanded a blood sacrifice. But in a curious twist, Paul's God chose to become the sacrifice himself. He sacrificed Jesus his 'Son', as an act of love, thereby somehow appeasing himself and getting us off the hook—even though God had previously forbidden any human sacrifice (Deut 12:30-31 & Jer 19:4-6).

This is all, prima facie, nonsensical; but 'faith' requires Christians to accept it on the word of Paul and his patriarchal successors, worshipping a 'jealous', punitive God, to be home free for eternity. Evidently the true believers have never paused to wonder what species of narcissistic deity

---

44. Vermes G, 2012, p100. Some theologians argue that original sin originated with Augustine who developed the idea and expanded it into an elaborate doctrine of faith. But the basic postulates—Adam's 'fall' and ensuing human sinfulness—were clearly established by Paul.

45. Peterson D, 2009. *Atonement in Paul's Writings*.

would crave 'worship' in the first place, or why Jesus himself never seems to have bothered with ritual worship?[46] Nor do many of them seem interested in where Paul's faith soteriology[47] would leave the vast majority of the human race, who have little or no concept of the weird Christian salvation scenario?

It is hardly surprising that some of these questions have remained barely considered, as the bible itself was restricted to clerical elites until fairly recent times. Perhaps it was a growing realization of their vulnerability to a more educated and aware populace, that made the gatekeepers of Christian orthodoxy declare the basics of their pot-holed theology to be off limits long ago, a closed book, a *kerygma*[48] beyond revision. They were content to rest on the laurels of 2000 years of tortuous intellectual sophistry, paraded as scholarly intellectualism, despite all its inherent contradictions and inexplicable 'mysteries.'

But sacred cows cry out to be slaughtered. What are such self-serving rationalizations if not bad faith? The Christian humanist theology unpacked here has no such oddities. It does not rely on inscrutable mysteries or unfathomable paradoxes and is consistent with the teachings of Jesus in virtually every chapter and verse of the Gospels. Conversely, it should become increasingly evident that gross inconsistency is a hallmark of Christian faith theology.[49]

It is time for a thorough overhaul of all faith constructs. Radical theological remodelling would be analogous to what the West did with its political ideologies; and though it took several centuries, the democratic, pluralist systems that finally evolved now provide a reasonably effective safeguard against the worst forms of human rights abuse. It is incumbent on any civilised, moral human being to embrace belief systems like liberal democracy that promote the pursuit of happiness and minimise the possibility of harm to others. Such ideals should eschew all kinds of dogmatic

---

46. Though the Gospels relate how Jesus visited synagogues and the Temple, they show him engaged in teaching, healing and protesting, not worshipping.

47. soteriology is a theological doctrine of salvation

48. *kerygma* is presented by Christian theologians as the distilled essence of apostolic proclamation: the doctrine of salvation through Jesus Christ.

49. Some Christian scholars like to make fine distinctions between Paul's Christianity and that which later developed—Luther's faith alone theology for example. But few if any serious scholars of Christianity see Luther as anything other than entirely consistent with Paul or dispute that Paul was the original and seminal proponent of indispensable grace (Eph 2:8–9). This will be discussed further in Chapter Three

INTRODUCTION

faith and hierarchical structures that mirror authoritarianism and tend to attract psychopaths and deviants. Thus faith should only be viable if it is conditional and rational, the product of a belief system that is logical, coherent and unequivocally ethical. Ideally it should also have some empirical basis. The Christian humanist theology proposed here, seeks to satisfy all these criteria.

Modern democracy sprouted in the fertile pastures of the 18th century Enlightenment which also produced the first major challenges to traditional Christology,[50] providing much of the groundwork for theological revision. However, while political theories emerged to overturn once undisputed assumptions like the divine right of monarchs and heredity privilege, corresponding insights eluded the deeply flawed tenets of Christian theology. The Christian humanism that flows from this book, constitutes a belated attempt at reconstructing Christianity in a way that could have salutary spinoffs for the wider world.

The case for a spiritual humanist Jesus is strong and its singular importance is apparent if two key propositions are accepted: firstly, that the basic problem afflicting our world is a dearth of compassionate empathy; and secondly, that such empathy may only become effective if it is given the kind of spiritual dimension provided by Jesus. Of course nearly everyone endorses compassion and research psychologists have even claimed some progress in teaching it.[51] But it seems unlikely that anything much will change in the human psyche or the real world unless compassion is embedded as a religio-cultural norm, practiced as a discipline and nuanced by the spiritual and ethical insights of Jesus and other great mystics. That, it will be suggested, was the entire purpose of Christ's mission and its full scope is elaborated throughout the book; but two particularly salient aspects of it should be highlighted at the outset.

Firstly it is well known that compassion can too easily lapse into what is sometimes called 'bleeding heart do-goodism,' and it will be shown that Jesus certainly understood this. It is very likely he was well acquainted with the Kabbalah[52] where the effusive love of *hesed* is counterbalanced by the restraint of detached judgment described as *geruvah*, to produce a synthe-

---

50. Christology is theology that is focused on the person, nature and role of Christ.

51. Ladwig J,2013. *Brain can be trained in compassion, study shows.* This will be discussed at greater length in Chapter five.

52. More precisely the Zohar on which much of the later Kabbalah was based. See Simmans G, 2007, p164-167. Also Keizer L,2010, p9-11; & Wippler M.G, 2018.*The Christian Kabbalah*

sis known as *tiferet*.⁵³ Thus strictly speaking, it might be more exact to use the term *tiferet* rather than *hesed* as Christ's goal. But *hesed* is the 'thesis' in this dialectic process and since *hesed* was the only one of these *sefirots*⁵⁴ referenced in the ancient scriptures and the Gospels, that term is used throughout this book, with the proviso that Jesus, and Kabbalistic Jews, would have understood it to have the more complete meaning of *tiferet*.

Secondly, and importantly given the special role he accorded to it, Christ saw human forgiveness as pivotal to *hesed*, which is probably why it is most often translated as 'mercy'. Jesus actually established forgiveness as prerequisite for *hesed* empathy and in the Gospels, he uses forgiveness and *hesed* interchangeably (Mt 5:7 & Mt 6:14–15). His mission of forgiveness was essentially a humanist project but after Paul connected it to original sin, it was given a metaphysical dimension which came to overshadow the humanist one. Christ's real message of forgiveness was that only through a deep commitment to forgiving others, is it possible to forgive oneself and be capable of expressing *hesed* love. Without a steadfast desire to forgive, self-righteous anger is likely to prevail in the human psyche and render mercy (*hesed*) an empty shell. This pivotal role of human forgiveness as a core spiritual value, and its key importance in enhancing human empathy and reducing conflict, was central to Christ's mission and will be expanded further in ensuing chapters.

The propositions and arguments advanced in this book are provocative and some have scarcely been aired before. They include the following:

- Faith theology has led to countless atrocities and has now made Christianity and religion generally an object of derision, more profane than sacred. Christianity must reinvent itself if it is to survive, particularly in the West.

- There is little or no Gospel basis for the notion that Christ's purpose was to make himself a sacrificial act of atonement. That idea was entirely the product of St Paul's 'voices and visions'.

- Christian theology derives from St Paul whose faith nostrums in turn derived from the Jewish faith fanatics who plotted Christ's death.

- Jesus, like the prophets, psalmists and most of his fellow Jews, was far less interested in faith than faithfulness—our efforts to convert

---

53. Prophet E.C, Spadaro P.R & Steinman M.L, 1997, p13.
54. Sefirots are divine emanations or virtues expounded in the Kabbalah

- compassion into action to improve this world, making it more worthy of its creator.
- Such a goal went beyond vague appeals to love or charity and mandated the nurturing of deep human empathy and a passion for justice, all enshrined in the Judaic covenantal imperative of *hesed*.
- Jesus sought to establish *hesed* as the basis of a universal ethic of compassion requiring spiritual evolution over multiple reincarnated lifetimes-and that can be taken as the purpose of human existence.
- In his elaboration of this existential purpose, Jesus may have also provided an explanation to the theodicy conundrum.
- Jesus was not God but he was semi-divine. He may well have been the prototype human that God created as Adam. As the 'Son of Man', he may have continued to oversee the creation as *YHWH*, the lesser, errant God of the Old Testament who ancient Gnostics regarded as a demiurge.
- The future not only of Christianity but Western civilization and the world in general, may hinge on the kind of spiritual humanism inherent in *hesed* which is probably also latent in the other great religious traditions.

If even a few of these assertions are correct, the implications would be seismic. But the evidence for all of them is strong and the logic is persuasive, if not compelling. They should not be blithely dismissed without at least providing a feasible, equally coherent alternative that is capable of yielding transformative results. To do so is wishful thinking at best and self-deception and at worst, bad faith perpetuating a bad faith. If accepted, such propositions would mandate nothing less than a total overhaul of Christianity as it has been conceived and practiced hitherto. As humble servants of God dedicated to *hesed* empathy, a renewed Christian West might find new purpose, wisdom and resolve. Here is a fresh, authentic and robust humanism, beside which the time worn, secularist version looks decidedly hollow.

Ultimately of course, the proof of the pudding would be in the eating; and here, unlike all traditional religions, Christian Humanism would adopt the rational yardstick of Jesus himself and present itself be judged entirely on its results, what Jesus called its "fruit" (Mt7:15–17). Christianity to date has produced both good and toxic fruit; but if a religion is to have credibility as the manifestation of a divine will, it should tend to produce only the former. Our world desperately needs such fruit and both our temporal and our eternal fate may hinge on it. So far we have managed to blunder through without fully embracing the liberating truths of Jesus —though to continue on the same track could be an extremely high risk option.

This Christian Humanism did not arise out of any epiphany on the road to somewhere. It took shape in the process of a deliberate, even painstaking attempt to exegete from the teachings of Jesus, a theological system that was worthy of him, one that was entirely comprehendible, rational and positive, attuned to human needs and conducive to human advancement. The end result is an alternative Christian humanist theology, one that is, arguably, more plausible than either the discordant tenets of conventional Christianity or the nihilistic deconstructions of postmodernist scholars, be they Christian or secular. What might make it infinitely more appealing, if not conclusive, is its symmetry with the grandeur and nobility of purpose that could be expected to emanate from a moral giant such as Jesus Christ and a divine plan for this world.

1

Christian History

HOW METAPHYSICAL FAITH ECLIPSED *HESED* HUMANISM

> More than anything else, *hesed* humanizes the world.[1]
> RABBI J SACHS

PAUL CAN CERTAINLY TAKE much credit for the establishment of Christianity—even if the downside was a distortion of Jesus' teachings.[2] But crucially, the chief medium of those teachings was not lost. In the decades following Paul's death (67CE), when Christ's original Jewish followers had also died or been dispersed, the Synoptic Gospels[3] emerged, recording in elaborate detail, as Paul did not, Christ's ethical teachings and social and political activism.

Thus, while Pauline faith became Christianity's lynchpin, Christ's social exhortations, so prominent in the Gospels, could not be ignored. Paul expected that his faith would conduce to 'works' faithfulness which

---

1. Zion N.2013, p8.
2. Butz J.J, 2005, p172.
3. Mark, Matthew and Luke are called Synoptic (a term derived from Greek words 'seeing' and 'together') as their subject matter was broadly similar. The scholarly consensus is they were written (probably) in that order, between 65 and about 90CE. John's Gospel came later (between 90-110 CE) and has a distinctly different, more mystical style and tone and professing a 'higher Christology', that Jesus was coterminous with God.

might objectify and validate the subjective faith.[4] However as one steeped in faith, he seems to have had no idea of the *hesed* based, *emunah* form of faithfulness that Jesus espoused. In prioritizing faith over works, Paul was putting the cart before the horse. Instead of arriving at Jewish *emunah*, Paul's faithfulness was expressed as a generalized concept of brotherly love and it remained almost as nebulous as his doctrines of faith. Faithful works might obviously involve charity and kindness, but just exactly how that would be any different to pagan charity, in character and extent, was far from clear. Was good works more or less important than prayer and worship? These questions remained unanswered then as they still do today and consequently, most Christians have simply relied on Paul's constant reiteration of faith as sufficient for salvation and in so doing, have tended to set the 'good works' bar fairly low. That much will shortly become clear

But the light of *hesed* shone strongly during the first century of the new religion. The Apostles continued Christ's devotion to the poor and the sick while continuing to resist the oppressive Temple elites and their Roman overlords. They and their successors also strongly upheld the sanctity of human life, opposing capital punishment and deprecating military service;[5] and many Christians risked their lives to relieve the suffering of plague victims, even though most were non-Christians.[6] Such strong ethical purpose and commitment has been identified as "the most potent single cause of Christian success."[7] But from about the middle of the second century, the rot began to set in.[8] Without *hesed* as a firm moral compass and with only the vagaries of 'faith' to guide them, clerical officeholders ballooned and became increasingly attuned to the expediency and amorality of state power.

Fortunately, at key times over ensuing centuries, individual luminaries were able to rekindle the spark of *hesed* and inspire some of the finest achievements of Western civilization. But it must be said that, for the most part, *hesed* was effectively dormant, leaving faith at the helm to either ignore or abet a monstrous tally of historical crimes. Indeed, Christianity even perpetrated more than a few of its own under the banner of abstract faith.

---

4. Maston J, 2009, p210.
5. Sider R (ed), 2012. *The Early Church on Killing.*
6. Moore C.E. *Pandemic Love.*
7. Chadwick H, 1967, p56.
8. White P, 2014. *The Doctrine of the Trinity.*

CHRISTIAN HISTORY

The starting point of this lamentable story was a growing hostility between Jews and Christians that began with Paul's push for gentile converts, but soon gathered a momentum of its own. What follows is an outline of the chequered history of Christianity to the present, where its bondage to bad faith may have finally caught up with it.

FROM JEWISH CHRISTIANITY TO CHRISTIAN ANTI-JUDAISM

> After my departure there will arise the ignorant and the crafty, and many things will they ascribe unto me that I never spake, and many things which I did speak will they withhold.[9]
>
> THE WORDS OF JESUS ACCORDING TO THE GNOSTIC GOSPEL OF THE HOLY TWELVE

Hesed might have become the bedrock of both Judaism and Christianity had both religions not been hijacked by faith intoxicated zealots. Paul could readily be identified as one of these—but he was not alone. It is surely an indication of how theological correctness has overshadowed historical reality that so little attention is paid to a group of first century Jewish faith fanatics known as Shammaites,[10] even though these fringe elements had come to dominate Judaic officialdom and had even taken control of its cultic center, the Jerusalem Temple.[11] The Gospels make it very clear that it was they who were responsible for Christ's crucifixion.

But these Jewish faith bigots did not dominate first century Judaism itself. Rather, it was the theological undercurrents of *hesed* that predominated and these were widely perceived as the leitmotif of the *Tanakh*.[12] *Hesed* was passionately embraced by moderate groups like the Hillelite Pharisees as well as influential sages like Ben Sira[13] and authors of 4 Ezra and the

---

9. *The Gospel of the Holy Twelve*.
10. The nefarious role of Shammaite Pharisees will be fully examined in the next chapter.
11. Falk H,1990, p347.
12. *Tanakh* is the Hebrew bible which formed the basis of the Old Testament
13. Theissen G,1977, p.83.

Book of Enoch.[14] It was also the guiding beacon of John the Baptist and at least one major faction of the Dead Sea Scrolls community.[15] Thus, after the destruction of the Jewish nationalists and their Temple stronghold in the war with Rome in 70 CE, *hesed* became the sheet anchor of a new rabbinic Judaism that arose under the leadership of Rabbi Yohanan ben Zakkai.[16]

Hesed was also, of course, the dominant ethos of the earliest (Jewish) Christians who, guided by the Apostles, had established themselves in Jerusalem under the leadership of Christ's brother James.[17] They focused on helping the sick and the poor and confronting the hostile, oppressive religious establishment (Acts 2:44-45 & 5:12-21), exactly as Christ had done. Thus Jewish Christianity and rabbinic Judaism were both animated by *hesed* in the late first century; but, sadly, they were unable to converge. The upheavals of 70 AD dispersed Jews and Jewish Christians alike and accelerated the triumph of Paul's faith based, gentile Christianity. Rabbinic Judaism was also swamped by a new wave of religious extremists who resurfaced in the early second century under the self-proclaimed Messiah, Bar Kokhba.

The historical record in the Acts of the Apostles understates the differences between the Jewish Christians and Paul's increasingly gentile Christianity.[18] The former believed that Christ's redemptive purpose was not fulfilled in his crucifixion and would only be completed in his second coming.[19] Their chief priority was to attain a higher level of personal sanctity in preparation for that anticipated return. They may have interpreted his prioritization of *hesed* as a means of expediting this, regarding it as a prerequisite 'interim ethic',[20] even though Christ probably had a much longer time frame in mind. In the meantime, as devout Jews they continued to practice the Law[21]—including observance of the traditional Jewish Day of

---

14. Wills L.M & Wright B.G,2005, p91.
15. Gruber E.R & Kersten H, 1995, p194-196.
16. Nunnally W.E, 2012, p299.
17. Vermes G,2000, p113-114.
18. Vermes G,2000, p143. This divergence will be expanded further in subsequent chapters.
19. Butz J.J, 2005, p151
20. Vermes G, 2000, p134. Jews regarded practicing *hesed* as one of the surest means of repentance and atonement. This will be explained further in Chapter three.
21. Jewish Law was a set of religious rules for ethical behaviour, ritual and day to day piety.

Atonement,[22] which in Paul's new soteriological scheme would have been redundant.

Drawing on Judaic sacrificial conventions, Paul rationalized the crucifixion as an atoning sacrifice to heal the breach between God and humanity caused by Adam's 'original sin'.[23] This was quite a novel proposition, not the least because Jesus had never made any such an assertion. Nor had the Jews read Genesis in that way.[24] But Paul was adamant that simple faith in 'Christ crucified' as a sacrificial, messianic Redeemer, was all that sufficed for salvation to become a 'free gift' of God's grace. There was no need for irksome initiation rites like circumcision and most, like Paul, were happy to overlook the fact that their Saviour had ruled out easy options and free rides (Lk 9:33 & Mt 16:24–26). Social justice, human forgiveness and compassion for suffering, so prominent in Christ's mission, were ideals barely mentioned by Paul and regarded as of secondary importance. He bracketed such things as 'works of the law' which carried no inherent benefits in terms of ultimate salvation. At best, he might have seen them as among a range of felicitous bi-products of the grace that might be expected to flow from the primary commitment to faith in the sacrificial Christ (1 Cor12: 7–11).

The Church fathers who succeeded Paul and bore his torch aloft, now sought to distance themselves from Judaism. That was problematic as the two religions were, paradoxically, both mutually exclusive and inextricably linked. The early patriarchs of the Church sought to appropriate Judaism's past (reading into the Hebrew Bible multiple prophesies of Jesus as the coming Messiah), while diminishing its presence. Bishop Irenaeus attempted to enforce orthodoxy by instituting an 'apostolic tradition' to assert the primacy of Paul's gentile orientated faith over the Jewish Christian *emunah* of James and his group.[25]

By the end of the first century, Jewish Christianity had waned and the stage was set for a mounting friction between Pauline Christianity and a new Rabbinic Judaism. In this, the fault line between the two religions could be found midway between the primacy of grace *vis a vis* human works and implicitly, divine verses human agency. This rivalry became

---

22. Powel F.F,2009, p7–8 & p68. See also Oliver I.W,2012, p448. As discussed in chapter Three, it is likely they observed Yom Kippur by fasting rather than participating in the animal sacrifices of the Temple.

23. Catholic Encyclopedia: *Original Sin*.

24. Collins J.J, 2014, p76.

25. Pagels, 2003, p.34, p148; & Valantasis R, 1997, p.73-4.

increasingly heated and by the early second century, church leaders like Justin Martyr were espousing a virulent anti-Semitism that would grow to become a cancer at the very heart of Christendom.

The early Christian heresies that emerged to confront Pauline orthodoxy had distinct Judaic overtones. The first of these was Gnosticism and although Christian Gnostics were themselves anti-Jewish, they shared the core Judaic belief that salvation was achieved not only by God's grace but also by human effort. Some claimed to have actually received esoteric knowledge from Jesus himself, a gnosis that was not imparted to many of his disciples. Arianism was another heresy that split the Church by rejecting trinitarianism and emphasising Jewish monotheism, prompting Emperor Constantine to call the Council of Nicaea in 325 AD to reach a settled Christian position. There, Pauline faith was extended into iron-clad dogma with Jesus being officially anointed the mystical 'third person of the Trinity'. But Arianism would not go away and yet another threat arose in the form of Donatism.

The Donatists also had strong Jewish 'works' proclivities, contending that Christian priests had to be of the highest moral probity in order to administer Church sacraments. North African Bishop Augustine opposed the Donatists by arguing that priests were merely conduits for the transmission of divine grace and that their moral state was therefore irrelevant. However Augustine's tolerance of licentious priests, and even Bishops, in the bosom of the church, was too much for a visiting British monk called Pelagius who now mounted a full scale assault on the increasingly corrupt Church citadel of faith.

Pelagius was the product of a distinctive 'Celtic Christianity' that had its earliest roots in the legacy of the Desert Fathers, the first Christian monks who aspired to *imitatio dei* by following the social and spiritual directives of Jesus.[26] Accordingly, Pelagius made a concerted attempt to reassert early Judaic Christianity by loosening Paul's shackles of faith and reprising *hesed*. The monk was a conspicuous Judeophile and his clashes with Augustine brought to an explosive climax, the differences that began with James and Paul. In his epistle entitled *On the Christian Life*, Pelagius submitted that the Jews had been chosen by God and consequently, it was crucial "we should know how he taught them."[27] His letter cited James in asserting the primacy of "works righteousness" over faith, and did so in a

---

26. Boyce J,2014, p23–27.
27. Pelagius, *On the Christian Life*, 8,1.

manner that clearly presumed the former did not inevitably proceed from the latter. He flatly rejected the notion of Adam's original and eternal sin and asserted the Christ's death was less important than his moral teachings and especially, his example of *imitatio dei*.[28]

In countering Pelagius, Augustine really pushed the faith envelope. To give his pessimism about the fallen human condition more theological clout, he jettisoned any lingering notions of free will and rediscovered his earlier Manichean[29] gloom about the depravity of all material existence.[30] Humanity was thus deserving of damnation; but because of Christ's sacrifice and God's 'mysterious' grace, a predetermined and unknowable few could expect to be saved in arbitrary dispensations of divine mercy.[31] Grace was purely a vehicle for salvation, dispensed at God's pleasure, with no guaranteed flow on benefit to this world. Moral rectitude became irrelevant to salvation—saints and sinners were now indistinguishable—and so Augustine deemed the church to be morally "invisible."[32] So much for Christ's insistence in the Beatitudes that it should be the "world's light ... for all to see" (Mt 5:15). So much even for Paul's vision of a 'new creation' (2Cor 5:17–20).

Pelagius managed to awaken many in the Church to Augustine's excesses and his ideas persisted, particularly in Britain.[33] They also gained traction in France thanks to the influence of fellow monk John Cassian, who adopted a 'middle' more moderate position that allowed for some human initiative in salvation apart from grace.[34] But Augustine had effectively carried the day and American Rabbi, Ben Zion Bosker has not been alone in observing that his legacy

> introduced into culture a morbid outlook toward all natural life ... (and) a guilt feeling toward sex. It fostered a quietism and resignation concerning the real evil in man and society. It blunted the passion of the Hebrew prophets, who continually challenged

---

28. Ferguson J, 1956, p164–5.

29. Manicheanism was a third century gnostic movement led by the Iranian prophet, Mani.

30. Fitzgerald A.D & Cavadini J, 1999, p.341.

31. Ferguson J, 1956, p100.

32. McGrath A.E.(ed), 2011, p412.

33. Boyce J, 2014, p24–28.

34. Cassian J, 1985, p27.

their people toward moral activism, to abandon the lowly aspirations and pursuits, to strive to be better and to do better.[35]

Inexorably, these doctrinal faith/works divisions enflamed anti-Jewish feelings and there was a mounting state harassment of Judaism and Jews. Augustine added fuel to recurring accusations that the Jews were guilty of deicide in crucifying Jesus;[36] and spurred on by the hateful diatribes of John Chrysostom, Church patriarchs pressured succeeding emperors into fierce anti-Jewish reprisals.[37] Instead of the benign grace that Paul had anticipated, faith was now inspiring bigotry and hate, leading Pelagius to quite reasonably conjecture on the basis of Christ's own criteria, that with so much "bad fruit" (Lk 6:43), the Christian tree might have bad doctrinal roots.[38]

Pelagius testified to the fact that the all-consuming humanity of Jesus, so evident in the Gospels, could not be suppressed. For every bigot like Chrysostom and Augustine, there would always be a heretic like Pelagius who was animated by Christ's spirit of selfless humility and compassionate love. That the former remain 'saintly' pillars of the church while Pelagius is still despised and ostracized, speaks volumes for the bad faith and ongoing perversion of Christianity.

FROM THE DARK AGES TO THE ENLIGHTENMENT

> As body is clad ... in skin ... so are we, soul and body, clad and enclosed in the goodness of God.[39]
>
> *JULIAN OF NORWICH, C1393*

> How comes it then that I, a poor stinking maggot sack ...[40]
>
> *MARTIN LUTHER, 1522*

35. Ben Zion Bokser, 1967, p335.
36. Michael R, 2006, p2.
37. Safrai F, 1969, p353–4.
38. Chadwick H, 1967, p227.
39. Julian of Norwich. *Revelations of Divine Love* (c. 1393).
40. Cortright C.L, 2009, p217.

With barbarians at the gates of the Roman Empire, Augustine's bleak idea of a small, invisible, predetermined elect was not helpful in rallying the faithful. Many Christians still gleaned from Christ's teachings, the notion of latent human goodness and some of the genial currents of *hesed* continued to course through the arteries of the Church. St Patrick seems to have absorbed the more humanistic Celtic Christianity of Pelagius[41] and by the 7th century, Pope Gregory re-asserted the Church's responsibility to provide active pastoral care for the sick and the needy.[42] This struggle between the darker side of Christianity and its better angels had now become a recurring pattern, but the former was maintaining its overall ascendancy. Faith-bigotry reached a high point in the violence of the Crusades and the scandal of Papal Indulgences which fraudulently offered divine favours for money, signalling the ongoing corruption of Church power.

The Gothic and Renaissance periods swung the pendulum strongly back towards *hesed*, marking a resurgence of *imitatio dei* in Christian Europe and firing the creative imagination to take human civilization to one of its highest peaks.[43] How this originated is intriguing but many of its intellectual roots can be traced to a new humanistic and scholastic theology that developed in the monasteries and cathedral schools of Western Europe. The monasteries in particular were re-ordered, disciplined and entrenched under the aegis of St Benedict, who was in turn, strongly influenced by Pelagius' protégée, John Cassian.[44] *Imitatio dei* was the core principle and it inspired the quite unique belief that the mysteries of theology and the natural world must be accessible to human investigation because they were the product of God's rationality.[45]

This movement away from faith abstraction to the humanization of the divine was accentuated by early medieval Christian mystics like Hildegard of Begin, Meister Eckardt, Julian of Norwich and St Francis of Assisi.[46] In their humility, humanity and attribution of feminine qualities to God and indeed, to Jesus,[47] these luminaries seem to have rekindled the 'feminine principle' which became one of the most powerful motifs of the entire

41. Boyce J,2014, p23–25.
42. Chidester D, 2000,p181.
43. Stinger C.L,1998, p316.
44. Chadwick H,1967, p182–3.
45. Stark R,2005, p11–15.
46. Boyce J, 2014, p47-54; & Clark K, 1977, p74-77.
47. Beer F, 1992, p152.

Renaissance period.[48] Female equality is implicit in the original creation story (Gen 1:27) and woven into the *hesed* teachings of Jesus. He regarded *hesed* as the essence of the Holy Spirit (Lk 4:18)[49] and the Hebrew word for spirit, *ruah*, is feminine. In the Gospel of Thomas, Jesus actually depicts the Holy Spirit as feminine.[50] In fact Jesus recognition of women as equals was completely unique and revolutionary in the ancient world.[51]

The net result of this spiritual humanism was an "intensification of existence,"[52] the outpouring of a creative brilliance unparalleled in human history. Perhaps nowhere was this sublime genius more evident than in Michelangelo's masterpiece of divine/human compassion, the *Pieta*, an artistic statement of *hesed* that seems to embody the intense Christian humanist character of the Renaissanc.

Humanism was articulated by several renaissance scholars who drew inspiration both in art and philosophy, from the ancient Judaic, Greek, Roman world as well as the Islamic world of the Middle Ages.[53] The Jewish mysticism of the Kabbalah, where *hesed* is esteemed as the highest virtue—indeed as the original purpose of creation[54]—was particularly evident in the writings of Marsilio Ficino as well as Giovanni Pico. The latter's *Oration on the Dignity of Man* was one of the most important Renaissance affirmations of Christian humanism.[55] But because of Pico's interest in the Jewish humanist roots of Christianity, the Pope banished him as a heretic. The most prominent theological humanist of that time was Desiderius Erasmus, who tried to purge the Catholic Church of corruption, emphasising faithfulness rather than just faith and free will and ethics rather than total reliance on grace.[56]

But Erasmus' efforts were in vain and the Renaissance was brought to an untimely and violent end by the Reformation with its strident reassertion

---

48. Davies,1986, p1. Also Rose G.B, 1906, p395.

49. Durland W,2010. p66.

50. Pagels E, 1979, p74. The Gospel of Thomas is regarded as a legitimate fifth gospel by many scholars—see Butz J.J, 2005, p16.

51. Crossan J.D, 1998, p371-2. See also Eisler R, 1987, p126-127; Pagels E, 1979, p81-82 & Pagels E, 2003, p159.

52. Clark K, 1977, p33 & p74-77.

53. Chidester D.2000, p319-325.

54. Miller M, 2012. *Chesed, Gevurah, & Tiferet*.

55. Chidester D.2000, p325.

56. Ibid, p341-2.

of *sola fide* (faith alone), human depravity, and abject dependence on preordained dispensations of divine grace. Luther's Reformation unleashed bully boy philistines to destroy glorious works of art and it plunged Europe into more than a century of religious warfare. On the upside, John Calvin in Geneva introduced pioneering social reforms in health, education and welfare, not because he believed he should emulate Jesus, but as a means of signalling the virtue that supposedly accrued to those who saw themselves as a preordained elite.[57] But other 'fruits' of the Reformer's faith were much less congenial. Calvinism spawned a puritanism that supressed the joy and spontaneity of life. It sanctioned the drowning of single pregnant women along with persecutions and violent witch-hunts, even by Calvin himself.[58] It exported a malign elitism and bigotry to Ulster and southern Africa that blighted those places for centuries.[59]

The ill wind of the Reformation did have the salutary effect of weakening the power of the Catholic Church and, particularly in England, the resulting fillip to intellectual freedom facilitated the Scientific Revolution and the age of Enlightenment. But the roots of both had already been well established in the monasteries and universities of Catholic Europe.[60] Calvin and Luther's reassertion of 'justification by faith' carried Augustine's 'morbid outlook' to its ultimate conclusion, relieving Christians of any real responsibility for bettering this world. In the peasant uprisings of 1524, Luther's fellow Reformationist Thomas Muntzer, led the peasants' revolt to ruin by asserting a proto-Pentecostal faith that a militant Holy Spirit would spring to their side against a vastly superior state army. Luther for his part, had already turned his back on the peasants and thrown his support behind the oppressive feudal aristocracy, bequeathing to Germany a legacy of authoritarian servitude that would culminate in the horrors of the Third Reich.[61]

Nazism found plenty of traction in Luther's own anti-Semitic bigotry which became viral in Germany as a result of his Reformation there.[62] In his diatribe *On the Jews and their Lies*, Luther fulminated:

---

57. *Christianity Today*,1990. *1536 John Calvin Publishes Institutes of the Christian Religion*.
58. Viola F, 2015. *Shocking Beliefs of John Calvin*.
59. Boyce J, 2014, p76–81.
60. Stark R,2005, p12–16.
61. Shirer WL, 1960, pp91–2.
62. Michael R.2006, pp. 105–151.

> What then shall we Christians do with this damned...race of Jews?...first, to set fire to their synagogues...schools and...houses.[63]

What other than worlds such as these, could Christ have had in mind when he said: "... it is what comes out of the mouth, this defiles a man"(Mt 15:11). Who else but the likes of Luther would Christ be referring to when he warned: "Beware of false teachers . . . . . . By their fruits, you shall know them?" (Mt 7:15-23).

The Reformation and its bloody aftermath is a classic example of how religion becomes perverted by a faith cut loose from humanist and rationalist moorings: "Faith must trample under foot all reason, sense, and understanding,"[64] Luther ranted. It is yet another instance of Christian bad faith that most Protestants are still in denial about the vile consequences of Luther's hateful actions and pronouncements. That their theology owes so much to a man who facilitated the most satanic crime in human history, should itself constitute a sufficient indictment of that theology. Luther, as the author of 'faith alone' Christianity, also serves as the epitome of everything rotten in it.

Apart from setting his misanthropic time-bombs, Luther's sola fide was bad news for the poor in other respects. It tended to sanction, to use Rabbi Bosker's phrase, a 'quietism and resignation' towards the gross exploitation and oppression of the impoverished masses in the ensuing industrial age. And it would not be long before more rational souls began to draw the appropriate conclusion that such an intrinsically inhuman, other-world view could only have dangerously negative ramifications for humanity in the world of here and now. These free thinkers and heretics, who were the children of the 18th century Enlightenment, would later become known as humanists.

The Enlightenment eventually crystallized humanism as a distinctly secular philosophy, even though it owed so much to the Judeo-Christian ethos, and especially the notion of individual dignity and human rights inherent in *hesed* and *imitatio dei*.[65] This was perhaps most pronounced in Britain, which, despite its recent Reformationist orientation, sustained a far deeper legacy of Celtic Christianity that reached back to Pelagius and early

---

63. Williams S, 1993. *The Origins of Christian anti-Semitism*.
64. Kaufmann W, 1958, p307.
65. Wolfe G, 2011. *Is culture more powerful than politics?* Also Carroll V & Shiflett D, 2002. *Christianity On Trial*.

Celtic monasticism.[66] Due to the efforts of the semi-Pelagian John Cassian, a similar ethos had permeated the monastic precursors of Enlightenment thought in France. Thus it can readily be concluded that modern Western liberal democracy arose from these Judeo-Christian humanistic impulses and became fully articulated by Christian and Deist Enlightenment thinkers like Locke and Hume, Rousseau and Montesquieu.[67]

Deists were religious rationalists who rejected traditional theology and clericalism in favour of 'natural religion'. Non conformists, they preferred to seek God personally by way of reason and innate moral intuition. Many now simply regarded Jesus as entirely mortal and a prophet of benign social ethics. The rise of capitalism further boosted these liberal tendencies and Adam Smith's non-deterministic, free market vogue gave free will an enduring edge over predestination theology.[68] In this more fluid setting, the evangelical John Wesley even managed to briefly bring Pelagius in from the cold;[69] and in the 19th century, Darwinist evolutionary science further dimmed Augustine's star in the Christian firmament, by making his Genesis theories look childish.[70]

During the 19th century, these humanist impulses drove a host of biblical scholars to attempt to rationalize religion and they sought to interpret the supernatural episodes in the Gospels in more mundane, human terms, beginning a 'quest' for the human Jesus that continues today. Emanating mainly from Protestant Germany, an outpouring of liberal renditions or 'lives of Jesus' depicted him as a quasi-divine beacon of virtue, dispensing homilies that accorded nicely with precepts of 19th century bourgeois liberalism. Despite their trite idealism, they gave new currency to Christ's ethical teachings and spawned wave of social gospel liberalism. At its crest were reformers like Wesley who positioned Christianity at the forefront of many of the political and social reform movements of the 19th and 20th centuries. Wesley's most illustrious convert, William Wilberforce, played a decisive role in the abolition of slavery.

---

66. Boyce J,2014, p23–27

67. Lezard N, 2015. *Inventing the Individual: the Origins of Western Liberalism by Larry Siedentop—review.*

68. Boyce J, 2014, p121–127.

69. Boyce J, 2014, p115.

70. ibid, p144–146.

BAD FAITH GRAVITATES TOWARDS A SECULAR BLACK HOLE

> What did we do when we unchained this earth from its sun? Where is it moving now? ... Aren't we perpetually falling? ... Is there any up or down left? Aren't we straying as through an infinite nothing? ... Do we not hear anything yet of the noise of the gravediggers who are burying God? ... God is dead. God remains dead. And we have killed him.[71]
>
> FRIEDRICH NIETZSCHE,1882.

Despite these liberal, humanistic influences, basic Christian theology remained impervious to change. Unlike its liberalization of political doctrines, humanism was never able to deeply penetrate and rationalize Christianity. 'Good works' too often degenerated into tokenism and platitudinous virtue signalling. Without the theological underpinning of *hesed*, 'social gospel' initiatives were often tainted or remained confined to charity, playing second fiddle to the virtuoso of faith and serving as an optional adjunct to the larger salvific purpose of Christianity. In the post Reformation/ Enlightenment world, any hint of 'justification by works' was often regarded as a throwback to the discredited Catholic indulgences of the middle ages.

Heirs to Luther's legacy, 19th century liberal Protestants often tended to be anti-Semitic and for them, the perceived 'works' excesses of Catholicism were equated with Judaic 'legalism'—circumcision, purity rituals, etc[72]—which Christ was thought to disdain. That itself was incorrect as it is now accepted that the Jewish Jesus endorsed many of the *halakhah* laws, especially insofar as they were linked to social justice and compassion.[73] What he opposed was their elevation above "the more important matters of the law" which he identified as *emunah* faithfulness (Mt 23:23). He especially abhorred the pedantic and obsessive way the Laws were interpreted and practiced by his Judaic fundamentalist opponents. However such subtleties were lost in the anti-Semitic hothouse of 19th century Christianity.

---

71. Friedrich Nietzsche,1882. *The Gay Science, sect125, The Madman.*
72. Allen C,1998, p168–69.
73. Crossan J.D, 1998, p580–84.

By the second half of the century, secularism had gathered unstoppable momentum and liberal rationalism was increasingly being overshadowed by dogmatic scientism and rabid nationalism. Modernism was leaving both the Enlightenment and Christianity in its wake and Nietzsche was proclaiming the death of God. His pessimism seemed to be justified by the carnage of the Great War which exposed the dark underbelly of the human condition and left a spiritual vacuum that would be filled by *carpe diem* hedonism.

Imitatio dei now seemed a distant, faded dream and there was a realist backlash amongst Christian scholars and theologians, known as 'neo-orthodoxy'. Two of its leading protagonists were Reinhold Niebuhr and Karl Bath, both erstwhile theological liberals who were now intent on getting 'back to basics'. Just as their United States sought political refuge in inward looking isolationism, *sola fide* navel gazing returned with a vengeance. The curse of original sin seemed borne out by the horrors of the war and any social aspirations would now have to be rooted in a theology of redemption and acceptance of complete human dependence on God. Though concepts of human 'depravity' and 'predestination' were not emphasised, subjective, personalized faith was; and Christianity would be even more tightly bound to it in the twentieth century than it was in the nineteenth.

This strong conservative reaction was reflected in Albert Schweitzer's *Quest for the Historical Jesus*, a landmark book published in 1906. Here Christ was portrayed as an 'eschatological prophet' with a first century Judaic agenda that could only be relevant to Christians if they chose to see Jesus through a prism of faith, a human cipher who God used to fulfil a deeper, divine salvific purpose. Whether Christians accepted or rejected that idea, the only conclusion to be drawn from Schweitzer's book was that the human, historical Jesus was largely irrelevant to the modern world and his full immersion in first century Judaism—bereft of *hesed*—meant he could have no practical relevance to it. Consequently, interest in the historical Jesus waned and conservative, faith based Christianity regained ascendency.

In 1970s, 'Liberation Theology' emerged in Latin America and South Africa, with the aim of harnessing Christianity to the cause of social justice and even revolutionary socialism. But its strong Marxist orientation rendered it more a partisan, secular ideology than a radical alternative to conventional Christianity, to which, indeed, it remained doggedly attached.[74]

---

74. Segovia F.F,1999, p302–3.

Because it was so closely associated with communism, liberation theology was repudiated by the Christian establishment and tended to recede when Marxism itself fell from grace at the end of the Cold War.[75] In South Africa, under the sway of Bishop Desmond Tutu, it played a very constructive role in helping to end apartheid with reconciliation instead of a bloodbath; but it tended to subside thereafter. With social gospel Christianity devoid of any specific ethical direction or theological rigour, its faith-based flagship now faced a withering onslaught, not only from radical atheists and anti-Western culture warriors but from the broad masses repulsed by clerical pedophilia.

In this setting, a 'New Quest' for the historical Jesus emerged. Born aloft by archaeological discoveries like the Dead Sea Scrolls and the Gnostic gospels of Nag Hammadi, historians were enticed by the prospect of clearer picture of Jesus in his Jewish world. But New Quest theologians were still wedded to Schweitzer's earlier revelations and even more inclined to magnify his mortal limitations and brush aside any transcendent attributes. Trapped in a web of historical space and time and viewed through the deconstructive prism of postmodernism, these new profiles limned Jesus as distinctly fallible and chronically inconsistent.

To the delight of atheists and secularists, his pronouncements were presented as confused hotchpotch of apparent contradictions and double standards. Stripped of any divine prescience, this reconstituted Jesus of history is often impulsive, vacillating between flashes of sublime wisdom and reckless misjudgement. The revisionist scholars rarely concede that some of his variability might be explained by the practical necessity of needing to assimilate deeply ingrained prejudices. For example, Jesus is accused of negating his strong egalitarian principles in having an all-male troupe. But in the intensely patriarchal society of his time, such a sexist recourse may have been unavoidable if he wished to be taken seriously. In pandering to that element, Jesus, as noted above, still managed to introduce a variety of radical 'feminist' initiatives that were unprecedented in the ancient world,[76]

---

75. Now it has had a rebirth of sorts in the person of Pope Francis. However his idea of liberation theology includes handing final authority over his church in China to the Chinese Communist Party with its track record of gross abuse of human rights and even genocide. See Oriel J, 2018. *The Pope Caves in to Church's Old Enemies*.

76. Crossan J.D, 1998, p371-2. See also Eisler R, 1987, p126-127; Pagels E, 1979, p81-82 & Pagels E, 2003, p159. These feminist principles established by Jesus will be discussed further in Chapter Five.

and this actually started the long, tortuous process of undermining sexist attitudes.

Schweitzer's portrait has now become the template for a diminished Jesus who was consumed with the same apocalyptic mania that gripped so many of his Jewish contemporaries, a longing for immanent divine intervention to liberate Israel and reinstate God's dominion on earth. Perhaps as the sacrificial 'lamb of God', some may regard a sheep-like mentality as appropriate for Jesus. Many Christians now accept that as a deluded Messiah who thought he was the catalyst for Israel's deliverance, he sacrificed his life to secure this deliverance for all. In other words, Christ was an apocalyptic firebrand whose expectations about the imminent 'end days' turned out to be pathetically wrong.[77] But for many faith-filled Christians, if his blunder still resulted in our eternal salvation, his delusions can be reconciled with Pauline theology, justified and celebrated.

Such a depleted individual now stands as the personification of equally conflicted church dogmas that can be marshalled to any spurious 'Christian' cult or cause. For some liberal Christians, the deconstructed Jesus forms the centrepiece of a quasi-secular faith, one in which both Christ and God are expendable. According to self-confessed 'atheist Christian' minister Gretta Vosper,

> stripped of the designation of God's only begotten, complete with its requisite claims of salvation, there is nothing that (Jesus) said or did that we must take more seriously than anything said by anyone else.[78]

Jesus as the 'Son of Man' established the principles of a spiritual and moral enlightenment that lasted over 2000 years. As the earthbound, patchwork construct of revisionist theologians and post-modern progressives, he will surely become much less durable.

This debasement of Christianity has involved Legions of scorched earth scholars trawling over the Gospels and discarding much of the original material as unreliable and inauthentic. Again, many Christians may be quite relaxed about this as for them, the truth of the New Testament

---

77. Sanders E.P. 1993, p78. Those who hold Jesus was an eschatological zealot seem to overlook the fact that he actually sketched pre-end day scenarios that stretched far into the distant future (Mt 24). While he does suggest this will all happen before 'this generation will pass away', that can be explained in terms of reincarnation which is explored more fully in Chapter 4.

78. Vosper G, 2008, p238.

lies in Paul's writings, rather than the Gospels. But diminution of the Gospels ultimately threatens the entire Christian enterprise, since they are the only real biographical record of Christ and his teachings. They are also the foundation of the Christian humanist position unfolded in this book and accordingly, a more critical examination of this scholarship is called for.

There are of course many obvious discrepancies in the Gospel accounts and this has provided one of the main excuses for Gospel evisceration. But the divergences are overstated. They are confined to relatively inconsequential details and do not necessarily impugn the Gospels' basic integrity. Matthew's Jesus is described as launching a more vehement attack on the Pharisees than the other three, but that is at most, only a minor difference of degree. Mark doesn't mention Christ's birth while Matthew and Luke elaborate on Christ's lineage and stress the virginal nature of his birth, probably for propagandistic reasons. Both Matthew and Luke say Jesus was born in Bethlehem to connect his Messiah with Old Testament prophecies. Matthew says he lived there while Luke claims he lived in Nazareth. Both also differ by ten years on the time of Christ's birth.

So much time and energy has been expended on such issues, but from a humanist Jesus standpoint, rather than a 'Jesus as God', faith one, it is of little import where Jesus was born or even if his conception was a carnal event. Scholars argue persuasively that many Gospel references to Old Testament prophecies—like the birthplace of Christ, or that he was Isaiah's prophesied 'servant Messiah'—were not "history prophesied" but "prophecy historicised." The key point is that such factual improbabilities and inconsistencies do not carry over to the Gospel accounts of Christ's actual teachings, which is really what the Gospels are all about.

There is little doubt that the Gospel writers were intent—as indeed was Christ himself—on disseminating a vital message and that goal took precedence over strict historical accuracy or consistency. Their narratives are often historicised prophecy. Locations, chronological sequences and even actual events may have been erroneous—even deliberately so. But wherever Christ himself speaks directly and cites Old Testament prophecy, it is invariably to extract the grace and truth, the *hesed e'meth*[79] of its Judaic social teachings. In expounding those *hesed* teachings, Jesus was entirely consistent in every verse of the Gospels.

---

79. *hesed e'meth* is a recurring phrase in the OT used to describe God's essential nature. As will be shown, the phrase carries great significance in Christ's teachings

Some scholars have attempted to discredit the Gospels on this basic level as well, but here they fail dismally. The example they most often select is itself quite illuminating. Several have alluded to the apparent contradiction between Jesus' professed exclusive focus on the Jewish people and other statements about taking his message to 'all nations' (Mt 28:19 & 8:11–12). Even the renowned Jesus scholar, Geza Vermes finds Matthew's Jesus quite 'schizophrenic' in this regard.[80] But again, the problem is that academics are captive to the conventional wisdom that Christ's mission was essentially spiritual, concerned with abstract redemption from sin. Otherwise it might occur to them that Christ chose to focus on the Jews for the same reason they were chosen as 'God's elect' in the first place: they were intended to serve as an ethical/spiritual exemplar for humanity in general, the "light of all nations."[81]

Thus, by confining his mission to the Jews, Christ was intending to universalize the sacred ethic of Hebraic *hesed* compassion and social justice. Once that is accepted, the much touted contradictions evaporate. In the next chapter, will be shown how his central purpose can be discerned as establishing *hesed*, as a supreme, universal moral law, the very lifeblood of his 'new covenant'. *Hesed* was rooted in the original ethos of the Temple[82] which was intended as "a house of prayer for all nations" (Mk 11:17) as well as a sanctuary for the oppressed;[83] so it was entirely logical that Christ's *hesed* mission was restricted to the Jews and dedicated to attacking an oppressive Temple leadership that was now asserting its chauvinistic exclusivity and perverting that sacred ethos for its own advantage.[84]

Other scholarly eviscerations can be put down to dubious methodology or the overly exacting standards of postmodern deconstruction. So often literary criticism of the Gospels involves such minutiae that the forest is lost in the trees. For example, painstaking efforts have been made to disqualify verses on the basis of deviant or uncharacteristic terminology—words that don't closely match Christ's overall linguistic style or 'signature'. But such dissonance might have resulted from the Gospel writers—or

---

80. Vermes G, 2000, p217.

81. Sachs J, 2014. *Yitro (5774)—A Nation of Leaders*. For a detailed exposition of this divinely ordained role, see Tzadok A.B, 2013. *Israel: the Mission*. This role is broadly affirmed in Gen 18:18; Deut. 4:5–8; Isa 2:3–4 &49:6; Mic 4:2–3; Zech 8:23.

82. Crossan J.D, 2002, p221.

83. Evans D.A, 2018, p325.

84. This will be examined in some detail in the next chapter.

earlier primary sources—paraphrasing Christ, even though they may have professed to quote him directly. Another test of authenticity is the so-called criteria of 'limited attestation'—a saying or event being mentioned in only one or two Gospels. That may reflect the partiality of a Gospel author but it is surely a flimsy basis for summary expurgation.

One of the most widely used—and abused—tools of biblical scholars is redaction criticism. This presumes a bias, often a theological agenda of the authors, perhaps reflecting the dominant concerns of the decades later period in which they wrote, that may have coloured their accounts. But detecting a motive does not establish automatic guilt of bias. There probably was some degree of selective editing; but if scrupulous avoidance of retrospective bias was to become a prerequisite for historical inquiry, little history would have any value.

Some scholars are also hoist by their own methodological petards, J.D Crossan being a notable case in point. The next chapter will show how, wishing to eliminate any trace of biblical anti-Semitism, Crossan has used redaction criticism to downplay recorded clashes between Jesus and the Jewish religious authorities, even though these are by far the most multiply attested incidents in the Gospels.

Given that these tools of biblical criticism are far from reliable, this exegesis largely avoids them. Instead it relies mainly on historical criticism which is more objective and evidence based. Using *hesed* and historical context—rather than a sacrificial mission—as the central point of reference, there is little if anything contradictory in the Gospel accounts and there is no reason why virtually all of Christ's recorded teachings and actions cannot be taken as a basically accurate and consistent record. As may now be obvious, and should become progressively moreso, this book does not extend such confidence to the remainder of the bible[85] which is far less coherent and is often diametrically opposed to what Christ taught. Multiple glaring anomalies are also evident in the Gospels when they are pressed into the service of Pauline exegesis. In fact Paul is kneecapped in such comparative endeavours. For example, Luke does not even raise the notion of Jesus as a sacrificial Messiah and John never even uses the word 'faith'—except in reference to the 'doubting Thomas' story, which may be the only clear instance of Gospel redaction.[86]

---

85. Acts and Epistle of James can probably be bracketed with the Gospels, as the only books of the Bible that can be seen as relatively consistent and historically reliable.

86. Pagels E, 2003, p58. This will be discussed in more detail in Chapter five.

The Christian humanism presented here owes much to scholars like J.D Crossan and Marcus Borg who have both correctly discerned a Christ seeking to revitalise existing Judaism by putting it more in touch with its rich ethical roots. Without referencing *hesed*, Borg still reveals how Christ tapped into the prophetic and wisdom traditions of Judaism, reasserting its ethos of compassion and establishing enduring principles of social justice by attacking and subverting the oppressive power of the religious and colonial elites. Similarly, Crossan describes Jesus as a social revolutionary, again intent on promoting the egalitarian and justice principles of the Jewish tradition.[87] However, enmeshed in their respective worlds of postmodern deconstruction and Christian progressivism, neither Crossan nor Borg dared to take these observations to their natural conclusion. Upholding faith and grace as the central feature of Christianity, both exude a theological correctness, propounding a time-worn, vapid kind of social gospel liberalism.

Crossan actually muddies the historical waters with his post-colonialist slant, making the Romans the bad guys, blaming them for Christ's death and deflecting attention from the machinations of the Judaic religious elites, detailed so expansively in the Gospels. The net result is that he has failed to detect what might otherwise be obvious, that compassion and justice are the central motifs of the Gospels, conflated into *hesed* and framed in the clash between Christ and the Jerusalem Temple. While both he and Borg regard Jesus as a social revolutionary figure, they are blandly disinterested in the seismic theological implications of this. Instead, Crossan lapses into fashionable cynicism, denigrating his revolutionary Jesus as a "peasant nuisance nobody,"[88] a derision which carries even more negative overtones for a Christian humanist, than the grandiloquent 'Lord and Redeemer' title.

It is almost as though postmodern scholars are intent on kneecapping the colossus, reducing him to insignificance, as if to confirm the ironic comment in John's Gospel that 'nothing good' could come from Nazareth (Jn1:46). What is perhaps more apposite is that little can come from such bleak deconstructions other than perhaps the ultimate extinction of Christianity. With its historical skeletons now well out of the closet, that process is gathering pace and unless some degree of uniqueness and transcendence is restored, the precious life and teachings of the human Jesus are likely to become as barren and moribund as the mythical Christ of faith.

---

87. Crossan J.D, 1998, p203–4.
88. Crossan J.D, 1995, p117.

2

The Word Was *Hesed*

The world is built with *chesed*.[1]

PSALM 89:2

IN THE ANCIENT WORLD where the merciful compassion was seen more as a human weakness,[2] the Jewish prophets and sages had enshrined it in *hesed* and made it the cornerstone of Judaic faithfulness. But the prophets and the Laws grounded in *hesed* were renowned for going unheeded and Jesus saw it as his primary goal to change this: "I have come not to abolish them but to fulfill them" (Mt 5:17). *Hesed* evolved from Mosaic Law but was not mandated as part of the Law because *hesed* was seen as transcending it. It was a moral, not a legal obligation, one that arose from an innate human propensity to reciprocate kindness. Tracing its social origins to family kinship, *hesed* was "the gift of love that begets love."[3] It was the loving spirit of God that permeated the Jew's covenant with God, making it a dynamic spiritual and social reality.[4]

Humans could not achieve the sublime levels of divine *hesed* and some were content to simply resign themselves to this and rely on God's

---

1. This is the translation Jews often give to Psalm 89:2—see Leiberman S, 2000. *Kabbala #10: Chesed*. Note, *hesed* and *chesed* are interchangeable spellings. The former is used here because it is more widespread but Jews usually prefer the latter.
2. Tuckness A & Parrish J.M, 2014, p87.
3. Zion N, 2013, p11.
4. Elazar D,1996. *Covenant as the Basis of the Jewish Political Tradition*.

unilateral *hesed*. But others who aspired to *imitatio dei*, accepted the challenge implicit in *hesed* to try to imitate God's loving kindness by replicating it in human relationships.[5] For devout Jews, this meant seeking a higher state of holiness through human empathy, going beyond the basic letter of the Law[6] to access its holy spirit.[7] Indeed, as already shown, Jesus actually identified *hesed* with the Holy Spirit. In this quest for mutuality, *hesed* was particularly esteemed by charismatic holy men known as *hasidim* (*hesed* men) and it came to be widely regarded as the spiritual heartbeat of the Law.[8]

It is in this Judaic spiritual/ethical (rather than religious) context, that a more coherent image of the Jewish Jesus begins to take shape. The Gospels are invariably read through a Pauline lens where Christ's 'saving death' overshadows their far more compelling testimony to his compassionate life. Even his healing miracles are mainly viewed as projections of divine power, with their function as simple, beautiful acts of human compassion seldom acknowledged and their intensely political character, even less so. But when the Gospel accounts are placed in their historical context and read from a more detached, humanist perspective, a very different interpretation emerges—one that turns conventional Christianity on its head.

Christ takes on the mantle of a *hasid* teacher but one who preaches a message of *hesed* for everyone, not just the spiritual elites, or even the Jews. Viewed in this light, his healing miracles then form the humanitarian platform from which he launches this message of compassionate love. With the focus shifted from the Easter events to Christ's teachings and actions, the Gospels begin to crystallize his mission into a campaign for human solidarity and social justice. As a devout Jew, Jesus could not have seen himself as God;[9] but he did see himself as an image of God in human form, prepared to give his life to implant the spiritual humanism of *hesed* in a world so desperately in need of it. Viewed from this perspective, his mission becomes simple, clear and comprehensible: to make *hesed* the cornerstone of a New Covenant that could bring shards of the 'Kingdom of Heaven' down to

•

5. Finkle A, 1994, p74.

6. Goodman L.E, 2008, p16. See also Elazar D, 1996 op cit; & Zobel H.J, 1986, p49–50.

7. Elazar D, 1996, op cit.

8. Zion N, 2013, p10.

9. Vermes G, 2000, p207.

earth, a new world oriented spirituality acted out, not in temples, churches or rituals, but in the real world of human suffering and political conflict.

THE POLITICAL CONTEXT OF *HESED* IN CHRIST'S MISSION

> The Spirit of the LORD...has anointed me...to proclaim freedom for the prisoners...give sight to the blind and free the downtrodden from their oppressors.
>
> LUKE 4:18–19

Christian theology is overwhelmingly focused on Christ's death and resurrection even though these passages comprise only about 15% of the Gospel content. The remainder is essentially devoted to his compassionate teachings and his confrontations with the Temple over their hostility to those teachings. Such concerns were recurrent throughout the Old Testament, especially in the protest voices of the prophets. With Jesus, this is no different. Even when he is not making his own explicit, direct references to *hesed*, his mission is strongly anchored in the *hesed* prophets and their cognate social and political agendas.[10]

The primacy of *hesed* is clearly established at the outset of Christ's mission. Against a background of land dispossession, his opening statement in Luke's Gospel (above) resonates with prophetic conviction. In a liberating declaration of compassion and justice, the Holy Spirit is equated with *hesed*.[11] This passage in Luke is taken from Isaiah (Isa 61:1) which was also a direct reference to the Old Testament proclamation of the Jubilee year that, according to inveterate Judaic traditions, retired debt and redistributed the land to the poor every 50 years.[12] As well as proclaiming his compassionate empathy with those who suffered, Jesus was targeting a primary cause of that suffering—the dispossession of small peasant landholders by wealthy aristocratic landowners who included the Sadducean priesthood of

---

10. Hayes J.H, 2013, p289-9. Also Zion N, 2013, p6. Also Borg M,1997, pxii.

11. Durland W, 2010, p66. To be more precise, the Holy Spirit is associated with 'righteousness' in the Isaiah 61 verses that Christ is drawing on and righteousness (*tsdeq*) and *hesed* are used interchangeably in Hebrew scripture. See Torrance T.F, 1996, p16–17.

12. Borg M, 1987, p136.

the Jerusalem Temple. The Temple in fact derived much of its wealth from taxing and dispossessing indebted peasants[13] and Jesus was intent to expose its cruel injustices.

Christ's opening words in Luke mark the beginning of an ongoing campaign against the Temple elites that would culminate in his crucifixion. Many Jesus scholars blame the Romans who controlled Judea and feared civil unrest might destabilize their rule,[14] and these claims will be assessed at the end of this chapter. But according to the Gospels, the initiative came not from the Romans but the Temple religious leaders who had been plotting to eliminate Jesus for some time. History is strongly on the side of the Gospels.

By the first century CE, the Temple was being usurped by a group of kleptocratic priests and religious extremists. Its sacrificial rites had become a major commercial activity with animals being sold and slaughtered on an industrial scale.[15] At the apex of its hierarchy was a Saducean priesthood that was enriching itself by taxing small farmers, driving them into debt and seizing their land to form large estates.[16] This travesty was particularly rife in Galilee where Christ had located his mission.[17] There were frequent uprisings and first century Jewish historian Josephus, relates that in one of these, the first act of rebels was to seize the Temple and destroy records of debt that were kept there.[18] It was the impoverished victims of this dispossession that made up the bulk of Christ's followers[19] and their plight became a prime focus of his mission.

Ptochos was the Greek word used in the Gospels to depict these people as utterly destitute.[20] Jesus also called them "poor in spirit" (Mt 5:3) because their poverty took a heavy psychological toll. Dispossessed of their land, they were effectively cut off from their families by being either forced to work as slaves or itinerant day labourers. They were also wrenched from

---

13. Freyne S, 1980, p169-199.

14. A case for this view is outlined in J.D Crossan's book *Who Killed Jesus?* which will be evaluated later in this chapter

15. Ghose T, 2013. *Animal Sacrifice Powered Ancient Jerusalem's Economy.*

16. Vearncombe E.K, 2010, p201. See also Gottwald N. K, 2008, p128; Freyne S, 1980, p169-170 & p199; & Fiensy D, 1991, p75-132.

17. Borg M and Wright NT, 1999, p44.

18. Josephus. *The Wars of the Jews*, 2.427.

19. Horsley R.A, 2010, p105-6. See also Crossan J.D, 1994, p60-62.

20. Witherington III B, 2009, p135.

their cultural and spiritual roots, because they believed the land belonged to God and was held by them in sacred trust.[21] But perhaps most devastating was a crushing sense of guilt caused by the prevailing social stigma that poverty was God's punishment for sinfulness.[22] Traditionally such guilt neurosis could be alleviated through public absolution via the sacrificial offerings of the Temple; but these had become expensive and difficult to access,[23] leaving the impoverished 'sinner' cast adrift. As well as being burdened by such anxieties—indeed, probably because of them—these destitute multitudes were often also afflicted with sickness and disability.

Jesus was well aware that this stigma of sin was conducive to a smugness and judgmental vanity that compounded suffering and negated any sense of *hesed* empathy. That was the lesson of the adulteress stoning episode (Jn 8:2–11) where those 'without sin' were invited to cast the first stone. In the midst of this repressive, judgmental culture, forgiveness was critically important and all Christ's *hesed* teachings pivoted on it. Throughout the Old Testament, *hesed* is mainly translated as 'mercy', and forgiveness is the precondition for mercy. In the fifth Beatitude, Jesus declares mercy (*hesed*) will be reciprocated and then, in the Lord's Prayer, he also underscores forgiveness as reciprocal (Mt 6:14–15). He demanded unstinting forgiveness "not seven times, but seventy seven times" (Matt 18:21); and he reaffirmed forgiveness as a core social ethic in several parables including the Prodigal Son (Lk 15:11–32), the Good Samaritan (Lk10:25–37) and the Unmerciful Servant (Matt 18:21–35).

Thus forgiveness was central to Christ's mission—not the divine forgiveness Paul spoke about but salutary human forgiveness that was indispensable to the nurturing of compassionate empathy between people. With his intensive focus on forgiveness, Christ contrasted the callous vindictiveness of the Temple cult. Yet it was the abstract, faux forgiveness of Temple sacrifice that would be taken by Paul as the template for the new Christian faith.

Several Judaic sects like the Essenes and the followers of John the Baptist, had broken with the corrupted Temple, offering alternative, cheaper

---

21. Crossan 1995, p41. See also Routledge R, 2008, p241.

22. Nolan A, 1991, p22–26. See Also Grant M,1977. p51; Romer J,1988, p85; & Vermes G, 2000, p232.

23. Crossan J.D, 1991, p231. Also Crossan J.D, 1994, p34; & Argubright J, 2003, p18–19.

and simpler rituals of forgiveness, like baptism.[24] The Temple bristled at John's baptismal ritual of forgiveness as unwelcome competition[25] and when John was eventually arrested and decapitated by King Herod, it seems highly likely Herod acted at the behest of the Temple priesthood with whom he had very close links.[26] But Christ's unique kind of forgiveness was much more problematic for the priesthood. He was able to fully heal people and with the ailment gone, the sin purportedly causing it was implicitly forgiven. His healing miracles therefore re-empowered the afflicted and gave them new hope, while leaving the Temple looking impotent and shonky. Here was real forgiveness that had the potential to put 'Temple Inc' and its sacrificial rites, out of business.

Linked with the corrupt Temple priesthood were religious extremists. These were a clique of Pharisees who belonged to the Shammaite school, and like-minded scribes. Jesus referred to them as "thieves," *lēstōn*, (Mt 21:13 Mk 11:17; Lk 19;46), the same derogatory term used by the Romans to describe nationalist political fanatics and brigands known as Zealots.[27] It is now clear that the Zealots had close connections with the Shammaites[28] and combined, they formed a distinct faction, probably the one referred to by Josephus as "the fourth philosophy."[29]

The Shammaites were opposed by moderate Hillelite Pharisees with whom Jesus was clearly aligned. Both he and Hillel were *hasidim*[30] and though Jesus differed with Hillelites on the issue of divorce,[31] his central message of *hesed* was strongly endorsed by that sect.[32] Hillelite Pharisees were probably more popular but when Hillel died around 10CE, the Shammaites had gained the ascendency.[33] Dogmatic and fiercely nationalistic,

24. Romer J,1988, p179. See also Crossan J.D, 1991 p231.

25. Horsley R & Thatcher T, 2013, p111.

26. Horsley R.A, 2010, p124.

27. Regev E, 2010, p152.

28. Jastrow M and Mendelsohn S, 2002. *Bet Hillel and Bet Shammai.*

29. Tabour J.D, 2015. *Ebionites & Nazarenes: Tracking the Original Followers of Jesus.* Also, Hezakiah4, 2010. *Jesus the Pharisee.*

30. Glatzer N, 2009, p59.

31. Both Jesus and the Shammaites opposed divorce though their reasons would have differed dramatically. Jesus knew that marriage was one of the few legal protections women and children had in those times; while for the Shammaites, marriage would have been seen as a means of patriarchal control.

32. Falk 1990, p347. Also Finkle A,1994, p74.

33. Falk, H,1990, p347.

they occupied key positions of power and sought to establish clear demarcations between Jews and Gentiles. They insisted Jews had no wider social responsibility beyond their own race and regarded Gentiles as infidels.[34] Steeped in the fanaticism of their Maccabean forebears,[35] they were paranoid about the intrusion of Hellenistic culture which, under Roman rule, was becoming pervasive—and nowhere more so than in Galilee,[36] the 'ground zero' of Christ's mission. Shammaites were determined to insulate 'God's chosen people' from what they perceived as insidious and corrupting foreign influences. In all this they bore more than a passing resemblance to today's Islamist fanatics.

To foster Jewish exclusivity, Shammaites relied on intrusive purity laws and it took them to pedantic excess.[37] They insisted that all 'undefiled' Jews observed the complex, stringent rules of Leviticus, previously reserved for priests.[38] Purity rules had been intended as a means of inducing piety. But they were now functioning more as a mechanism for imposing guilt and shame to shore up the authority, status and wealth of the Temple hierarchy.[39] The underlying assumption was that those who were poor, typically peasants made landless by a rapacious priesthood, were inherently impure and unworthy of compassion or mercy.[40] Exploiting the widespread belief that those suffering adversity were being punished by God for being sinful (Jn 9:33-34),[41] the Shammaites further distanced the 'impure' from their Jewish roots by quantifying each person's moral and social status,[42] reinforcing an insidious culture of guilt.[43]

This provided a convenient pretext for the Temple's ongoing exploitation of the poor and they contemptuously labelled their peasant victims *am-haaretz* or 'people of the land', a phrase that carried sneering overtones of ignorance and boorishness. As a sly revenue raiser, they would invoke

---

34. Idem. See also Jastrow M and Mendelsohn S, 2002 op cit.

35. Maccabaeus led a prolonged revolt of Jewish religious nationalists against the Hellenistic anti Temple culture imposed by Selucid rulers in the 2nd century BCE.

36. White LM, 2005, p74. See also Finkelstein L, 1989, p249.

37. Jastrow M & Mendelsohn S, 2002 op cit.

38. Borg M, 1995, p53; & Allen C, 1998, p32.

39. Borg M, 1995, p53.

40. Echegaray H, 1980, p52.

41. Grant M, 1977, p51. Also Romer J, 1988, p85; & Vermes G, 2000, p232.

42. Stern M, 1969, p283.

43. Nolan A. 1991, p22-26.

the purity rules to deem non-tithed produce 'impure' and thus effectively unsalable.[44] Combined with Temple tithes and Roman taxes, the purity rules resulted in widespread penury and dispossession.[45] By such means, 'purity' became an "ideology of the dominant elites—religious, political and economic."[46]

Pharisees were particularly active in Galilee, where Hellenistic influences were most pronounced and attitudes towards the Temple ranged from ambivalence to outright hostility.[47] According to Josephus, Pharisees had established a strong presence in Chorazin, Bethsaida and Capernaum,[48] so it is highly significant that those were the three towns that Christ specifically condemned in Matthew's gospels, appalled by their thinly veiled contempt for his compassionate acts of healing (Mt. 11:21-24). Shammaite fanaticism was endorsed by the patrician landowners of that province,[49] many of whom were themselves Temple priests.[50] Though far less zealous than the Shammaites, the Saducean aristocracy no doubt realized how draconian, guilt-laden purity rules assisted dispossession of the hapless *am-haaretz*.

As self-appointed guardians of Judaic purity, the Shammaites shared an uneasy alliance with the materialistic and self-serving Temple aristocracy, both to extend their own power and to insulate Judaism from the Hellenistic inclined Sadducees.[51] While the latter still held most of the political and administrative offices, the hard-line Pharisees became closely associated with them and held the key positions in the Temple hierarchy, effectively dominating its executive functions.[52]

Judaism had traditionally revered the Temple as a fountainhead of compassion, protecting "the alien, the orphan and the widow" (Jer7:4-6). Jesus called it "a house of prayer for all nations"(Mk 11:17) which its exclusivist elites had now turned into a "den of thieves" (Mt 21:13). The

44. Borg M, 1995, p64-5.
45. Borg MJ, 1987, p84-5. Gottwald, N. K, 2008, p128.
46. Borg M, 1995, p53.
47. Freyne S, 1980, p199; Wilson A.N, 1992, p99; & White LM, 2005, p74.
48. Freyne S, 1980, p322.
49. Finkelstein L, 1962, p43-60.
50. Freyne S, 1980, p199.
51. Bryan T.H, 1997, p6-7. See also Freyne S, 1980, p276 and Stern M,1969, p234.
52. Bryan T.H, 1997, p3 and pp15-16. See also Keyser J.D, 1996. *Dead Sea Scrolls Prove Pharisees Controlled Temple Ritual*.

Shammaites were even insisting it was sinful to relieve pain and suffering on the Sabbath—a gross inhumanity that "deeply disturbed" Christ (Mk 3:2–5 & Mt.12:10).[53] Against this greed, corruption, fanaticism and cruelty, Jesus juxtaposed the compassionate ethos of *hesed*; and since the basic prerequisite for *hesed* empathy was a readiness to forgive, Jesus made human forgiveness the center point of his campaign. Thus, the Temple which claimed a monopoly on forgiveness, soon decided Jesus had to be eliminated.

THE UNACKNOWLEDGED CENTRALITY OF *HESED* IN THE GOSPELS

> Jesus entered the temple area and drove out all who were buying and selling there... The blind and the lame came to him at the temple, and he healed them. But when the chief priests and the teachers of the law saw the wonderful things he did... they were indignant.
>
> MATTHEW. 21:12–15

The Holy Spirit of *hesed* that heralded Christ's arrival in Luke's gospel, does likewise in the other three gospels, "descending on him like a dove"(Mk 1:11, Mt 3:16; Jn1:32–4), filling him "with compassion" for suffering humanity (Mk 1:41) and a fierce determination to confront the injustice of Temple dispossession. Christ's opening address, the Beatitudes, is a paean of compassionate empathy with those who suffer and those who devote themselves to relieving that suffering, seeking "righteousness" or justice for the poor, the grieving and the oppressed.[54] In Matthew, the Beatitudes extend over three chapters, clearly establishing the ethical criteria for spiritual prelation. Here the core principles of *hesed* are elucidated—compassionate empathy (Mt 7:12), humility and self-abnegation (Mt 6:1–4) and especially reconciliation and forgiveness (Mt 5:38–42; 7:3–5). In a society that assumed poverty and adversity were marks of sinfulness, Jesus called

---

53. Doering L, 2010, p235–6.
54. Viviano B.T, 2010, p344.

the poor and grieving blessed. The Beatitudes counterpoised *hesed* against the twisted ethos of Temple Judaism (Mt 5:20).[55]

Jesus then immediately put *hesed* into action dedicating himself tirelessly to the distressed multitudes who flock to him. His healing miracles and ethical instructions and parables that compliment them, occupy nearly every chapter of the gospels, up to the last few which are passion narratives. His healing ministries are simple acts of charity and kindness; but they soon acquire a political dimension in attracting the ire of the religious authorities. In the three synoptic gospels, this escalation is first flagged by the same incident: Christ's healing—and forgiving—of a paralytic man (Mt 9:2–13; Mk 2:1–12; Lk5:17–26). This miracle marked the turning point of his mission and prefigured its central purpose: to establish *hesed* as the cornerstone of a New Covenant.

The paralytic healing episode is most extensively described in Matthew 9:2–13. Here for the first time, Jesus incites the hostility of the Pharisees because in curing the paralytic man, he explicitly states he is also forgiving him. These Pharisees, who were undoubtedly Shammaite agents of the Jerusalem Temple,[56] protest that Christ is appropriating a power to forgive that belonged exclusively to God and his priestly representatives in the Temple.[57] Thus they accuse him of blasphemy, the 'crime' they will ultimately use to nail him to the cross. They are further outraged by his consorting with disreputable "sinners" like tax collectors and prostitutes.

Jesus' response to all this is unapologetic. He asserts the power to heal and forgive was vested in him as the "Son of Man" and chides the Pharisees, assuring them that God is not interested in their self-righteous religiosity. Then, referring to Hosea 6:6, he issues them a strict rabbinical instruction: to "go and learn" the meaning of the word *hesed* (Mt 9:13). Much of his audience might have known the popular story that only a few years earlier, Hillel told a disciple to 'go and learn' that the Golden Rule of 'do unto others' was the very essence of the Torah.[58] Now Jesus tells the Pharisees to 'go and learn' that God desires the sacred principle of *hesed*, not the sacrificial rituals of the Temple. Soon after issuing this admonition, Jesus repeats it in

---

55. This verse refers to Pharisees and scribes but the latter would have also represented the Temple, as scribes mainly served the Temple priests as "intellectual retainers." See Horsley R. A, 2007, p10.

56. Falk H, 1990, p347. In subsequent confrontations, the Pharisees are accompanied by Sadducees and later the Sadducean Temple Priests (Mt 21:45).

57. Freyne S, 1980, p276; and Stern M, 1969, pp234.

58. Buxbaum Y.2004, p103–107 & p131.

another confrontation, again citing Hosea 6:6 in chiding the Pharisees for their ignorance of *hesed* (Mt 12:3–13 & Mk 3:5–6).

In Hosea's time, as in Christ's, Judaism had been corrupted by self-seeking religious leaders whose smug entitlement stemmed from a faith lacking the substance of faithfulness (*emunah*). This kind of faith theology in early Judaism, given the title of 'covenantal nomism'[59] by recent scholars, relied on what Paul called "circumcision of the heart" (Rom 2:29). This basically required ritualistic observance and keeping of the Ten Commandments, but anything beyond this was always unquantifiable and purely a matter of personal judgment. Such generalized nomism easily degenerated into the kind of ethical minimalism and displays of virtue signalling that Jesus encountered in Shammaite Pharisees (Mt 23:5–6). John the Baptist threatened the divine axe would fall on such barren elements who were incapable of producing any 'good fruit' (Mt 3:9–10).

It is hard to avoid the impression of bad faith in the way Christian exegetes choose to disregard the singular importance Christ accorded to *hesed* (Lk 3:11) and the blatant theological implications of these Gospel accounts. For example, in the healing of the paralytic man, D Carson perceives Christ's reference to *hesed* in Hosea 6:6 as proclaiming God's covenantal loyalty, the chief manifestation of which is the advent of Christ to forgive Adam's sin.[60] But that observation is utterly baseless. It cannot be overstated that Jesus made no reference to Adam's sin, either here or at any point in his mission, and it is absurdly out of context to suggest he was sending the Pharisees some such cryptic message here.

The obvious point conveyed in Hosea 6:6 and by Christ in his citation of it, was that God expected his compassion to be emulated and replicated in human relationships.[61] That is clearly what the author of Hosea was proclaiming, repeatedly citing *hesed* as form of societal love that God seeks. He attributes Israel's tribulations to its failure to express this love and in particular, he condemns her religious leaders for their unfaithfulness in failing to practice *hesed*. That was the only way to "love" and "know" God and for Hosea, it was the key to Israel rediscovering its spiritual path[62] and building

---

59. Jewish adherents to this faith theology believed they could rely on salvation by virtue of their preordained covenant with God combined with nomism, the observance of ritual and moral obligations of the Jewish Law.

60. Carson D.A, 2010, p265.

61. Edin M.H, 1998, p358–9. Also, Zion N, 2013, p11.

62. Wolff H.P, 1974, p120. See also Bowman J, 2006. *Mercy: Hosea 6:6*.

a strong and harmonious nation. "Burnt offerings" and other such forms of cultic sacrifice and worship, were rejected as inadequate.

The centrality of *hesed* in Christ' teachings and healing miracles is apparent in all the Gospels. Luke and Mark both relate the paralytic healing episode largely as it appears in Matthew; and while they do in a more condensed form and without a direct reference to Hosea 6:6, both frequently cite passages in Isaiah where *hesed*, and its absence among the ruling elites, is a constant refrain.[63] Mark's Jesus invokes Hosea 6:6 when he asserts that his 'New Commandment' of *hesed* reciprocity, to love God and love each other, is superior to "burnt offerings" (Mk 12:29–33). In Luke, Jesus depicts the Holy Spirit as *hesed* and he distils the very essence of *hesed*: "Be compassionate just as your heavenly father is compassionate" (Lk 6:36),[64] again underscoring human forgiveness as the indispensable precondition for *hesed* (Lk 6:27–42). This is reiterated in the parable of the Good Samaritan (Lk 10:25–37), which is quintessentially *hesed* in its intimations of forgiveness and loving kindness. There the close link between *hesed* and human forgiveness is emphatic, with the despised Samaritan representing to Christ's Jewish audience, what a Palestinian might to Israelis today.

Christ's exaltation of *hesed* is also striking in John's Gospel whose prologue describes Jesus as infused with 'grace and truth' (Jn 1:17). That phrase directly invokes the Hebrew term *hesed e'meth*, used throughout the Old Testament to convey God's essential attributes.[65] John relates the paralytic healing miracle in a slightly different setting, with Christ referencing Hosea 6:6 in relation to the Shammaite's Sabbath pedantry (Jn 5:1–18), just as he does when reiterating it in Matthew (Mt 12:2–8). In John, the Shammaites are enraged when Christ heals and 'forgives' a blind man (Jn 9:24–34), just as they are with the paralytic healing in the Synoptics. This miracle, like Christ's later raising of Lazarus, is depicted as bringing great glory to God (Jn 9:3: 11:4), again connecting these compassionate acts to Matthew's *hesed* Beatitudes where God is glorified (and "known" in Hosea 6:6) through the humanity and compassion of *hesed* (Mt 5:13–16). In all four Gospels, these confrontations over the implications of *hesed* intensify and culminate in Christ's crucifixion.

---

63. Beaton R,1999, p22–3.

64. Here the Greek word Luke uses for compassion-*oiktirmones*-is also a synonym for *eleos*, the word mainly used to translate *hesed* in the Gospels. See Wan, Sze-Kar, 2008, p48.

65. Köstenberger A.J, 2005, p43–44.

Apart from the Gospels, *hesed* is also prominent in Acts and the Epistle of James. At the outset of their mission, the 'Spirit of God', of *hesed*, descends on the Apostles, just as it did at the start of Christ's mission. This inspires them to press on with Christ's work[66] and they set about caring for the sick and the poor (Acts 5:12–21) and performing healing miracles while also confronting the Temple cliques on a daily basis. It does not take long before the latter strike with their trademark savagery. First they murder Stephen (Acts 7:59), then James the brother of John (Acts 12:2–3)[67] and later their leader, James the brother of Jesus.[68] The epithet 'Just' or 'Righteous' was given to James in recognition of his dedication to *hesed*.[69] Righteousness is the term so often used to capture the essence of *hesed* in the OT.[70]

James' own epistle is a powerful acclamation of *hesed* justice.[71] He esteems *hesed* as the path to salvation (Jas 2:12–13)[72] and, like Hosea, Isaiah and other prophets, his condemnation of the exploitative rich (Jas 5:1–6) was aimed squarely at the corrupt priestly aristocracy.[73] James would have known that in propagating *hesed*, Jesus was placing himself in the mainstream of the prophetic tradition of social justice. That is exactly where James also stood, having been given the nickname 'Oblias', the legendary protector of the prophets of Israel.[74] The divergent perspectives of James and Paul are stark, Paul's faith in Christ saving death (which James did not share[75]) and James' emphasis on the Mosaic laws and Christ's works of *hesed*, a faithfulness which he seems to have understood to be not so much a product of faith, as its very wellspring.[76]

---

66. Vermes G, 2000, p120.

67. Long P.J, 2013. Though this death—like the Baptist's—was ascribed to the Herod dynasty, it is clear that there was a very close connection between the Herods and the Temple leaders. The Pharisees are often reported as collaborating with the Herodians in the Gospels (Mk 8:15;12:13. Mt 22:16). See also Horsley R.A,2010, p124.

68. Bütz J.J, 2005, p165.

69. Crossan J.D, 1998, p206 & p467.

70. Mckenzie J.L,1995, p566.

71. Johnson L.T, 1998, p194-5. See also Wachob W.H, 2004, p110.

72. Mckenzie J.L,1995, p567.

73. McCartney D.G, 2009, p.236. See also Barnett P, 1999, p318; Ong S.H, 1996, p76; & Johnson L.T, 1998, p194-5

74. Torrey C, 1944, p96.

75. Butz J.J, 2005, p18-19 & p151. See also Wilson AN, 1992, p37. Vermes G, 2000, p114

76. Wachob W.H,2000, p195-6 & Amersfoort J, 2006, p.115

THE WORD WAS *HESED*

HESED E'METH IN MATTHEW AND JOHN

> Society is faceless; *hesed* is a relationship of face to face. The Petaneuch repeatedly emphasises that we cannot see God face to face. It follows that we can only see God in the face of another.[77]
>
> RABBI J SACKS

But we must return to Matthew to fully unpack the centrality of *hesed* in Christ's mission. Immediately after the paralytic healing episode, where Christ first proclaims the singular importance of *hesed*, he also makes his first, albeit tacit reference to a 'new covenant', declaring that 'new wine' requires a 'new wineskin' (Mt 9:16–17). Christian exegesis tends to view this as a secessionist proclamation that his new covenant constitutes a significant departure from the old one.[78] However the exact translation of the Greek word *kainous*, to describe the wineskins, is not 'new' but 'renewed' or 'restored'.[79] Thus the real meaning is that new (*neon*) 'fresh' wine requires a new (*kainous*) 'restored' wineskin. It would have been common knowledge to first century Jews that 'new' wineskins were often recycled old ones that had been soaked in water and treated with oils to make them pliable enough to take the new wine.[80]

With this rich metaphor, Christ's new covenant can be understood not as a replacement of the old Law dominated one, but a reconditioned version of it, wherein the Law was subsumed into *hesed*: 'love God and love each other' (Mt 22:36–40). The 'new' wineskin of Christ's covenant was soft and pliable, just like the hearts Jeremiah predicted it would also be written on (Jer 31:31–34). Jeremiah was strongly influenced by Hosea[81] and his "new covenant" would enable people to "know" God (Jer 31:33–34), just as Hosea 6:6 had declared that *hesed* was the way to "know" God. Thus, knowing God through *hesed* and reciprocating his loving mercy in this world,

---

77. Sacks J, 2005, p54.

78. Wellman J, 2015. *What Is The Difference Between New Wine And Old Wine In The Bible?*

79. Stern D.H, 1992, p37. Also, Pierce C, 2012. *The Process of Restoration*

80. Jenks D.F, 2002, p6. Also Watkins B, 2016. *Renewing the Wineskins*; & Hagin K,1985, p21.

81. Thompson J.A, 1980, p85.

was the essence of the New Covenant that Jesus proclaimed. There was no intimation of any faith in a saving sacrifice which, in citing Hosea 6:6, he assured us God did not want. In short, Christ's New Covenant was simply a revitalized version of the old, in which *hesed*, no longer the exclusive preserve of *hasidim* or even the Jews, was the holy spirit of God, now to be enshrined as the cornerstone of a universalized moral law.[82]

From this point, the Shammaites began to stalk Jesus. He nominated their vicious inhumanity—not his alleged 'blasphemy'—as an unforgivable "sin against the Holy Spirit" (Mt12:31), against *hesed*. Now, Jesus affirmed it was the Holy Spirit that enabled him to heal the sick (Mt 12:28) and he made several other statements linking the tangible "fruits" of *hesed* to the Holy Spirit (Mk 3:30; Mt 7:15-20; 12: 26-33).

Jesus then drew on the story of Jonah (Mt 12:40-41) to illustrate how the religious leaders, like Jonah, had betrayed Judaism, their own people and a wider humanity by shirking their covenantal obligation to practice and propagate *hesed*.[83] But unlike Jonah and the Ninevites, these religious elites had no desire to repent and Jesus warned that their brutality and callous indifference would ultimately be punished by God. He declared this first implicitly in his Parable of the Unmerciful Servant (Mt 18:21-35), and then he bluntly condemned the Pharisees to hell (Mt 23:33-36). In two successive parables, the parable of the Tenants and the Wedding Banquet, he effectively defrocked the Temple leaders and declared that the covenant of *hesed* would now be extended beyond the Jews to embrace all humanity[84] (Mt 21:18-43 & 22:1-14).

Hesed was "the stone rejected by the builders" to now form the "honoured cornerstone" (Mt 21:42). This building metaphor was a Scriptural reference to Isaiah 28:16-17 and Psalm118 where the cornerstone can be readily identified as *hesed*.[85] It may also have been a clever play on words. Shammai himself was a builder by trade and the "builders" here may have been a cryptic reference to Shammaites. Whatever the case, the Gospels strongly support the view of Rabbi Moshe Reiss: "as a Jew and co-religionist

---

82. Spencer F. S, 2010, p373. See also Borg M.J,1998, p13; Askew E & O.Wesley Allen Jr, 2015, p22.

83. Novak R, 2014, p14.

84. This did not imply any supersession of Judaism as some Christians like NT Wright assert, simply an extension of the Judaic covenant to all humanity.

85. Botterweck J.G, et al, 2003, p355; & deClaissé-Walford N, 2015. *Commentary on Psalm 118*.

of Jesus, I am certain he had the word 'Shammai' on his lips as he died."[86] By that time, the Shammaites had taken control of the Sanhedrin,[87] the supreme legal and religious authority of the Jewish nation which instigated and orchestrated Christ's arrest, trial and subsequent crucifixion.

With his arrest and death immanent, Jesus proclaimed his New Covenant of *hesed* forgiveness, would be sealed with his blood (Mt 26:29). Establishing human forgiveness as an indispensable enabler of *hesed*, would become evident as a consequence of his crucifixion, just as forgiveness as a provocation to the Temple would be the cause of it. Forgiveness was the central cause of his life and death, but not Paul's retroactive divine plan for metaphysical forgiveness. It is human forgiveness that Jesus was focused on and he made it abundantly clear that this, not any symbolic sacrifice, was the only way to ultimately obtain divine forgiveness (Mt 6:14–15).

In his last major sermon Jesus set out the purely moral benchmarks for salvation, which would have placed the Temple leaders among the 'goats' who were destined for damnation (Mt 25: 34–46). Just as Hillel had reduced the Torah into the Golden Rule, Jesus compressed the Ten Commandments into two by establishing *hesed* as the cornerstone of his New Covenant.[88] These were to 'love God and love each other' (Mt 22:36–40) and they might be construed more correctly as 'love God by loving each other'. For God's injunction in Hosea and Jeremiah was to know and love him by making *hesed* our life purpose, evincing compassionate love for humanity and seeking justice here on earth. Thus Jesus imparted an epistemic validation to his teachings by insisting that 'true knowledge' of God required *hesed*. That would render *hesed* a core, universal truth and absolute moral value.

John's Gospel strongly reaffirms this. It places great emphasis on 'truth' and on the multiple occasions the word appears, John links it to *hesed* or related matters. It is first used to reference *hesed* itself being the core truth of God's nature (Jn 1:14 &1:17), and then knowledge of this 'truth' is linked to the *hesed* inspired prophets (Jn 6:12–45 &14:17). Next, 'truth' is associated with the "Spirit" which is *hesed* (Jn 4:19–24). 'Truth' is then connected to ethical "works" which for Jesus, all pivot on *hesed* (Jn3:20–21 & 8:44); and finally it is applied negatively to the Pharisees who reject *hesed* truth (Jn 8:31–47). Nowhere is this revealed 'truth' related to 'faith' or any salvific death, either expressed or implied. In fact, as noted previously, Jesus only

---

86. Reiss M. *Christianity: A Jewish Perspective.*
87. Stern M, 1969, p250.
88. Edin M.H, 1998, p359.

uses the word 'faith' once in John and that may have been a redactive insertion. Thus, when Jesus affirms "I am the way, the truth ... no-one can get to the father except through me"(Jn 14:6), the 'I' and 'me' can be read as 'my teachings', i.e., his new condensed commandments of *hesed*, rather than the personalized, metaphysical, supremacist construct that Christians have always imposed on it.

At his trial, Christ said he came to bring truth to the world and Pilate cynically asked him "What is truth?"(Jn 18:37–38). Although Christ did not reply then, he had already given the answer to his Jewish followers a little earlier in John's Gospel: "This is my command: love each other (Jn 15:17) ... hold to my teaching ... and you will know the truth and the truth will set you free" (Jn 8:31–32). To know this truth was to know God (Hos6:6; Jer 22:16–17; 31:33–34; & Isa 58:1–10) and to know God was to know that *hesed* was what God wanted. As Jesus stated with clarion simplicity in John's gospel, only this kind of divine knowledge can secure ultimate salvation (Jn 17:3).

Against this massive Gospel and historical evidence for *hesed* as the crux of Christ's new covenant, we will now turn to an examination of the pitifully frail basis for Paul's metaphysical notion of divine redemption through faith in Christ's sacrificial death. However first there is a hot-button issue that calls for a slight digression. While the overall veracity of the above exegesis and its historical scaffolding may seem secure, many scholars are inclined to demur, balking at the denigration of the Temple establishment which, they believe, feeds into a pernicious and longstanding anti-Semitic narrative. Such concerns however, can be shown as entirely unwarranted.

RACIST RESERVATIONS

> Yet if we admit ... that some Jews were involved [in the death of Jesus], then why blame us all, both then and now? ... Is it not equally unfair to say the Americans killed Lincoln and Kennedy?[89]
>
> SAMUEL SANDMEL

---

89. Sandmel S, 1965, p141.

There is a tendency to downplay the evil excesses of first century Judaism because of its historical associations with vile Christian anti-Semitism that culminated in the horrors of Nazism. It is now accepted that the persecution of Jews throughout European history was largely fuelled by jaundiced interpretations of Gospel accounts of Christ's clashes with the Jewish religious leaders, who were often conflated with the Jewish people. To eliminate even the possibility of such odious associations, some scholars have attempted to argue that the Gospel accounts of these clashes were largely redactive, gross exaggerations or even fabrications. The evidence for this however, simply does not stack up.

The defects of postmodern biblical methodology were canvassed in the last chapter but this particular issue warrants a deeper exploration of those deficiencies. Redaction criticism of the Gospels assumes they were warped by growing hostility between Judaic establishment and Christians in the later first century. Both were then competing for converts and some scholars claim this inevitably shaped an anti-Jewish slant in the Gospel accounts.

But such scholars tend to ignore the solid common ground that would also have existed at that time, at least enough to render such gross distortions highly unlikely. As already noted, *hesed* had become the dominant principle of post Temple rabbinic Judaism.[90] The Gospel writers would have been well aware of that[91] and having focused so much on *hesed* in their accounts, it could be assumed that they might have empathized, as much as argued with, their Jewish adversaries. Once again, it is either ignorance or bad faith that redaction critics studiously ignore the enormous chasm between the pre and post war Jewish leadership and blithely presume the Gospel authors did so as well.[92]

Contrary to the negative thrust of so much current scholarship, the Gospels are not inherently anti-Semitic. Though some insist on labelling them as 'supersessionist'—the view that Christ represented a decisive break with Judaism—that is simply not so.[93] The Gospels were mainly written by Jews. They do not impugn Jews generally and they relate with enthusiasm Christ's Jewishness and his ringing endorsement of Judaic Law, for which *hesed* was both the pinnacle and the wellspring. John's gospel, often cited as

---

90. Freedman D.N & Myers A.C, 2000, p592.
91. Card M, 2013, p70.
92. Hann R.R, 1987, p352.
93. Harrington D.J & Landau Y, 2009, p49–50 & p157.

the most anti-Jewish of the four,[94] quotes Christ declaring: "We Jews know all about him (God), for salvation comes to the world through the Jews" (Jn 4:24). Christ's hostility towards a specific group of Jewish religious leaders was not a swipe at Jews or Judaism in general. As the Gospels clearly indicate, it was entirely directed at the Temple leaders, their exploitation of the poor and their perversion of Judaism in elevating a shallow, dogmatic faith above the faithfulness of *hesed*.

It is abundantly clear that all the Gospels place the burden of guilt for Christ's death squarely on the shoulders of the Temple elites. In Matthew, they had manipulated 'the crowd' baying for Christ's blood (Mt 27:20), a rabble which, in Mark, had been "sent out" by them (Mk14:43). No doubt some Jews were ignorant or deluded or perhaps venal enough to call for Christ's crucifixion; but as the Gospels record, many other Judeans had thronged the streets of Jerusalem to welcome him the week before on Palm Sunday (Mt 21:6–11); and they seem to have been in much greater numbers than the hand-picked rabble lusting for blood before Pilate (Mk 12:12).

Matthew quotes this 'mob' as screaming: "His blood be on us and our children" (Mt. 27:25),which some scholars regard as a venomous curse condemning all future generations of Jews for the murder of Christ.[95] But more discerning exegetes have made the fairly straightforward observation that Matthew, writing shortly after the Great Revolt upheavals of 66–70 CE, was making a well-founded connection between the carnage of that revolt and the religious extremists who inflamed the crucifixion mob.[96] For as noted above, the Shammaites were closely connected with the Zealots, both harbouring violent anti–Roman anger.

This kind of overtly wilful myopia taints scholarly renditions of the historical Jesus, which invariably fail to even register the existence of the Shammaites, even though they feature so dramatically and decisively in the Gospel accounts. Those who do acknowledge their 'zealotry for the law', often suggest it was limited to in-house doctrinal disputes between respectful coreligionists. In his apparent desire to minimize the significance of "intra-Jewish strife,"[97] Professor J.D Crossan calls the Hillelite/Shammaite

---

94. Shorto R, 1997, p187.
95. Crossan J.D ,1995, p158.
96. Kinzer M, 2005, p107. Also Jastrow M & Mendelsohn S, 2002, op cit. These authors point out that the religious fanatics that crucified Christ were also largely responsible for inflaming passions that led to the Roman assault on and destruction of Jerusalem in 70 AD.
97. Crossan J.D, 1998, p583.

disputes 'debates'[98]—even though and on one occasion the 'debate' was apparently concluded by Shammaites murdering their Hillelite rivals.[99] But Crossan seem content to gloss over such events, not because of questionable evidence for "what happened then, but what happened since."[100]

Crossan's loathing of two millennia of Christian anti-Semitism is fully understandable; but that is no excuse for deliberately making politically correct, 'post truth' judgments rather than purely historical ones. This may be quite consistent with his postmodernist approach to history which elevates what he calls, "attainable honesty" above "unattainable objectivity."[101] However the net result of his resolutely post-colonial, anti-Rome slant may be neither truthful nor objective. It tends to associate Jesus more with the anti-imperial grievances of Jewish nationalists like the Shammaites,[102] thereby blurring his steadfast campaign of *hesed* justice against them and their Temple allies.

Geza Vermes likewise detects virulent anti-Semitism in John's gospel where the 'Jews' are accused of harassing and traducing Jesus. However, if John's reference to 'Jews' is placed in its actual context, it invariably refers to Jews in the environs of the Temple and clearly shorthand for 'religious leaders'.[103] Thus John says Jesus went to Galilee to get away from Judea where "the Jews" sought to kill him" (Jn 7:1). But in Jewish Galilee, "the Jews" did not present any kind of threat. A.N Wilson has observed that the term Jews used in the gospels more correctly translates as "Judeans, the men of Jerusalem . . . who had always misunderstood the people of Israel, Samaria and Galilee."[104] In that way, the author of John's Gospel may have tended to stereotype Judeans.

It seems likely that many Judeans would have aligned with the religious elites whose Temple power base was also a source of prosperity for the city and region.[105] Similarly, with reference to Sandmel's observation

---

98. Ibid, p xxxiii.

99. Neusner J, 2005, p266. See also Jastrow M and Mendelsohn S, 2002, op cit.

100. Crossan J.D, 1995, p38.

101. Crossan J.D, 1991, p.xxxiv.

102. In 2013 a book appeared arguing precisely that case, aligning Jesus with the violent Zealots: Aslan R. 2013. *Zealot: The Life and Times of Jesus of Nazareth*.

103. Horsley R & Thatcher T. 2013, p156.

104. Wilson A.N, 1992, p248.

105. Freyne S. 1980, p291. See also Kelly R.H. 1994, p15. As much as 80% of Jerusalem's employment was based on the Temple.

above, many ordinary Southerners in the US would have applauded the assassination of Lincoln. The general public can never be entirely exempted from the guilt of their leaders and Old Testament prophets routinely implicated 'the people of Israel' in the crimes of its elites. What is perhaps more remarkable is that the Gospel writers did not reflexively follow that convention themselves.

In their haste to blame 'the Jews', Crossan further contends that the Gospels authors seek to exonerate the ruthless Pontius Pilate; and he sees the episode of Pilate passing the buck to Christ's Temple accusers, as fabricated for such an ulterior purpose. Pilate was certainly a brutal and capricious overlord,[106] but he would have known he had much more to fear from Christ's fanatical Shammaite enemies than the humble Galilean; and events would soon prove him correct. The Shammaite's were trying to transform the Temple into a nationalistic, anti-Roman stronghold; and this was generating friction between them and their more collaborative priestly allies.[107]

It would be entirely consistent with Pilate's character that he may have seized this opportunity of Christ's trial to hand responsibility for his execution to the Temple leadership, thereby casting himself in a favourable light, while wedging the Caiaphas extremists from the moderate minority (like Nicodemus and Joseph of Arimathea) who were sympathetic to Jesus. Even autocrats are happy to curry populist sentiment and Pilate "knew very well that the Jewish leaders had arrested Jesus . . . because of his popularity with the people" (Mt. 27:18). He was certainly versed in the well-established Roman tactic of divide and rule in Palestine—even Crossan attests to that.[108]

Finally, Crossan argues that past experience had made the Romans acutely concerned about the potential for crowd disturbances at major festivals like Passover. Accordingly, he speculates that local commanders could have acted under standing orders, summarily arresting and executing Jesus after his Temple protest. Crossan even speculates whether any trial, let alone the Gospel's extended one initiated by the high priests, would have actually taken place.[109] Again, his claims carry the strong imputation that the Gospels are a catalogue of falsehoods, if not outright lies.

He bases his position on the Roman response to three other Temple/festival disturbances in the early to middle first century. However only one

---

106. Crossan J.D,1995, p148–50.
107. Regev E, 2010, p152–3.
108. Crossan J.D & Reed J.L,2002, p191.
109. Crossan J.D ,1995, p117.

of these occurred before Christ's time. This was an anti-Herodian protest in 6CE, which would seem to make it more of a 'one off' than a precedent, as far as Pilate and the Romans were concerned. Crossan refers to the "tinderbox atmosphere" of these festival occasions,[110] yet the second incident in 44CE was sparked not by irate agitators but by the Romans themselves. The obscene gesture of a Roman soldier was quickly followed by even more reckless provocations from the Roman procurator himself.[111] That would seem to indicate the Roman authorities were rather less hypersensitive than Crossan suggests. In the last incident, a deranged lone protester was flogged but then released by the Romans; and Crossan regards that as an indication that the Romans tolerated dissent but not when it crossed over into direct action of the kind Christ pursued.[112]

But perhaps the more pertinent factor in this last case is that the Romans might have tolerated dissent, and even some degree of violence, only in so far as it was not directed against them. The lethal force they used in the first two disturbances was in response to actions directed against themselves or their interests. They relented in the third case where the protest was aimed at the Temple. The 6 CE disturbance Rome supressed with force, decades before Christ's Temple disruption, was directed against Herod who was Rome's vassal and widely perceived as such by the Jewish people.[113]

Thus, Crossan's evidence could equally suggest Rome was relatively unconcerned about protest against the Temple per se, especially the disruptive but non-violent and symbolic form it took with Jesus. He may have even welcomed it for deepening divisions amongst the *lēstōn* (Zealots) and their Temple allies. But unlike the Romans, the Ananite priesthood, to which Caiaphas belonged, was ferociously hostile to anything Christian. Crossan himself points out that for a generation after Christ's death, it was this priestly family, not Rome, that was the chief agent of Christian persecution, both in Jerusalem and more distant parts of the region.[114]

To label the fierce confrontations between Christ and the religious leaders in the Gospels as redactive exaggeration, suggests they are incidental or random occurrences, which is absurd. They are central to the Gospel narrative and their general authenticity is widely accepted by biblical

110. Crossan J.D, 1991, p360.
111. Sicker M, 2001, p138–9.
112. Crossan J.D,1995, p54–58.
113. Molnar M.R, p6.
114. Crossan J.D, 1998, p464. Also Chadwick H,1967, p16 & 26.

scholars.¹¹⁵ To dismiss them as political fabrications is to effectively discard the gospels, impugning the writers as frauds for not merely attenuating the truth but grossly and deliberately distorting it. In all four accounts, Christ does not shy away from systematically and deliberately provoking these leaders, at massive personal risk. His purpose was to expose their insidious and deceptive ways and in so doing, reveal the intrinsic nature of institutionalised deceit and criminal injustice. It is clearly these religious authorities—Christ might have called them usurpers— and not the Jewish people as such, that the Gospels blame for Christ's persecution and death. As such they provide no basis for anti-Semitism.

It must be said that the track record of Christian theologians over the centuries has been as hopelessly prejudiced and warped in its view of Jews and Judaism as it has been of Jesus himself. The persecution of the Jewish people throughout history—like the persecution of women, 'heretics' and other minorities, was the product of human ignorance, bigotry, insecurity and often, a despicable envy. But the Christian church bears a large measure of guilt for fostering this vileness. From the late first century, anti-Semitism gathered an increasingly strident tone for many revered Church patriarchs[116] and they took their cue from Paul's supercessionist, gentile Christianity. That made it inevitable that the gospels would be misconstrued, no matter how they had been phrased. Numerous luminaries of Christianity have been complicit in this—and most notably, Martin Luther, who many historians believe must take a significant portion of blame for the holocaust.[117]

Christian authorities should have made it clear long before the Vatican did in the 1960s, that the Gospels can provide no factual basis whatsoever for implicating either the Jewish people, or Judaism per se, with the murder of Christ. But political correctness must also be deprecated. The sinister Temple cliques may have been as culpable then as their extremist counterparts—the militaristic Zionist factions[118]—are in Israel today; and the dangers of guilt-motivated whitewashes for either of these parties should be all too evident.

---

115. Freyne S, 1980, p320.
116. Williams S, 1993. *The Origins of Christian anti-Semitism.*
117. Wallmann J. 1987, p73.
118. Sherwood H, 2012. *Mutiny fear in Israeli army as religious Zionists gain influence.*

3

The Baseless Fabric of Paul's Messianic Visions

> There is nothing (in any of the Gospels) to indicate that Jesus saw his own coming death as a cultic event.[1]
>
> STEPHEN FINLAN

PAUL WAS HIMSELF A ruthless persecutor of the first Christians—a "Temple thug" in the words of one scholar[2]—yet his Epistles studiously ignore the viciousness and corruption of the Temple establishment. Perhaps that was out of shame for earlier doing their dirty work—especially since Paul was a Pharisee and almost certainly, given his propensity for violence against Christians, of the Shammaite persuasion.[3] Paul's subsequent evangelizing studiously avoided any reference to the intense sectarian, political and ethical conflict between Christ and the Shammaites. Instead, he emerged from his epiphany on the road to Damascus, convinced that Christ's mission was overwhelmingly about afterlife redemption, bestowing a universal forgiveness of the original sin of Adam—a sin he deemed so grievous that it necessitated a brutal, atoning, sacrificial crucifixion. The interesting question is where did Paul get such a strange idea? He and his successors maintain it

---

1. Finlan S, 2005, p109.
2. Allen C, 1998, p310.
3. Wright N.T, 1997, p26.

was an epiphany, directly imparted by Jesus. In this chapter, a less edifying, but perhaps more realistic explanation is offered.

Paul had no evidence whatsoever for his claims, beyond his 'voices' and 'visions'. There was little or no basis for them in anything Jesus said, or the context of his life, or the basic theological principles of Judaism on which he operated. Yet Paul was so convinced by his subjective impressions that he sought no further validation, even though that was readily available in the first-hand experience of Jesus' most intimate associates, the Apostles (Gal 1:17).[4]

There is a simple explanation for why Paul did not consult the Apostles: their vision of Jesus was profoundly at odds with his. The Gospels clearly present a very different picture of Jesus from that of Paul, and a far more historically authentic and coherent one. Contrary to the blinkered faith assertions of countless theologians over the centuries, the Gospels are overwhelmingly 'works' oriented, even though they were crafted after Paul's 'faith' perspective had become the dominant theological paradigm of the new Christian movement. The Gospels never mentions Adam or humanity's 'fallen' state. Certainly sin and forgiveness is a major theme, but the forgiveness Jesus offered was a humanized, personalized forgiveness, essential to generating the empathy from which *hesed* arises. It reflected a belief in the human capacity for goodness and carried no trace of Paul's "anthropomorphic pessimism"[5] that an indelible stain of original sin necessitated a slavish dependence on God's grace.

PAUL'S METAPHYSICAL VISIONS AND JUDAIC REALITIES

> It is hardly surprising that the letter of James has always filled theologians with unease ... But we know from Paul that his conflict with the Judaizers ... was all too genuine.[6]
>
> GEZA VERMES

---

4. Vermes G, 2000, p69.

5. This quaint euphemism refers to the conviction that of human beings are incapable of rising above the depravity they inherited from Adam's sin and are totally reliant on God's grace. See Sprinkle P.M, 2013, p237-8.

6. Vermes G, 2000, p114-5. Judaisers were early Jewish Christians who insisted that Gentile converts had to first fully convert to Judaism and observe strict laws like circumcision.

Paul assumed that the grace flowing from belief in Christ's sacrificial death would automatically transmit some degree of God's perfect love—which he expressed by the Greek word, *agape*[7]—transforming human beings into a 'new creation'(Gal 6:15), capable of grace induced virtue. But it did not take long to dispel this illusion as the "good tree" of his new believers began to produce some "bad fruit" (Mt 7:18). Corinthian converts took his justification by faith as a permit for licentiousness and that was not the image Paul needed to attract converts. In desperation, he returned to the Law which was made "for those who are lawless and rebellious" (1 Tim 1:8–11). He even felt constrained to reinstate the Judaic commandments (1Cor. 7:19);[8] and in a one-off *cri de coeur*, Paul, the high priest of faith, even ranked 'love' as a greater virtue than faith (1 Cor13:12).

But Paul's *agape* love was more akin to Plato than Jesus.[9] Supposedly a 'gift' of grace from the Holy Spirit, it was as abstract as his concept of 'faith', over-idealized and essentially confined to Christians. Without first-hand experience of Jesus, Paul, as a Hellenized Jew steeped in Aristotelian ethics that regarded compassion more as a human weakness, may have found the very concept of *hesed* love, its compassion for strangers and even enemies, somewhat strange.[10] It would have seemed even stranger with his erstwhile Judaic beliefs placing him in the truculent Shammaite camp.

Paul seems to have believed that any specific directions about how people might learn to love each other, improve themselves or their societies, was just another imposition of 'Law' and likely to result in shoddy virtue signalling or 'boasting' as he called it (Eph 2:9). If his pessimism was warranted, Christ's intensive teaching—which occupies about eighty percent of the Gospels—would have been a complete waste of time. Though Paul still considered himself a Jew, he had minimal interest in the ethical teachings of Jesus or the prophets or even the Mosaic Law from which interactive human *hesed* evolved into a higher moral law.[11] His main scriptural reference point was not Mosaic Law but Abrahamic faith, a piety that preceded and for Paul, surpassed later obedience to the Laws of Moses.[12] Despite his brief expedient recourse to the Law to curb the debauched Corinthians, he

7. Powell M.A, 2009, p455.
8. Chidester D, 2000, p37.
9. Powel F.F, 2009, p99–100.
10. Carroll V, 2013, p7.
11. Elazar D, 1992. *Deuteronomy as Israel's Ancient Constitution*.
12. Vermes G, 2000, p96. Also McKnight S, 2005, p374.

consistently declared faith in 'Christ crucified' as paramount. He believed that faith would impute grace to believers in the form of personal virtue, despite the evidence of Corinth that it may not. But the overall message was clear. There was ultimately an assurance of redemption through faith in 'Christ crucified'. Little if any human effort was required.

Thus the soteriological primacy of *hesed* in the Gospels and in the life of James and the first Jewish Christians, stands in stark contrast to its omission or cursory attention in the writings of Paul. When Paul uses the language of 'mercy', it is to convey only divine mercy, his assumption, as a compassionately challenged individual, that *hesed* was all about God's unilateral largess towards humanity (Rom 9:15–16; 9:23 ; 11:31–32 ; 15:9). There is no call to emulate Jesus' empathy with the dispossessed *ptochos* or his passion for human justice.

Far from grasping the epistemic truth proclaimed by the prophets and Jesus that *hesed* was the only way to 'know' God, Paul seems to have deemed such knowledge as beyond human capacity (Rom 11: 33–34), given our fallen state. He implored Christians to "be imitators of God . . . as beloved children, and walk in love" (Eph 5:1); but as usual with Paul, this is little more than a platitude. Exactly how we 'walk the walk' and express this love is left unsaid, beyond asserting that it would come as a gift from the Holy Spirit to the faithful. For James, *imitatio dei* was a constant challenge, clearly encapsulated in *hesed* and freely chosen (Jas 3:9–18) For Paul, it was something that could be barely glimpsed at in this world through the prism of unmerited grace,[13] "through a glass, darkly" (1 Cor 13:12 KJV).

This dissonance between Paul and the original, Jewish Christians, is a serious problem for 'Third Quest' Christian theologians and apologists who have largely signed onto the Schweitzer concept of Jesus as an errant Messiah, immersed in his first century Judaic environment. They find themselves now needing to reconcile the main elements of Paul's faith theology with the religious outlook and practices of first century Judaism, or at least the strain of it that Jesus and the Apostles adopted. But that has proven to be a forlorn quest.

Bishop N.T Wright is perhaps the foremost Christian theologian to have grappled with this issue. He has argued that Jesus did see himself as the awaited Messiah, but not a Messiah with the exclusive goal of liberating Israel from foreign domination and restoring its Davidic kingship. Wright

---

13. Hunt M, 2007. *Is "hesed" the same as "agape?"*

claims the Jews were focused on their own salvation[14] but God resolved to use Jesus as a universal Messiah who would achieve general deliverance, not through a victorious battle, but a symbolic, sacrificial death. While far removed from Jewish images of the Messiah, Wright insists the primary, longed for messianic goal of divine atonement was nonetheless accomplished by Jesus, happening "in the middle of time" even though the Jews expected to occur at "the end of time."[15]

However Wright's claims seem to consist of purely tendentious speculation, dubious assumptions, inconsistencies and falsehoods. For a start, Israel's Messiah was not really exclusive—he was always expected to liberate not just Israel but all humanity.[16] Wright's propositions may accord with Paul's version of the meaning and purpose of Christ death, but it is certainly detached from its Judaic moorings and basically at odds with both the Gospel accounts and mainstream Judaism of the first century. Quite apart from being contrary to the Jewish conception of the role and nature of a Messiah, it can also be shown to run counter to Jewish notions of sacrificial atonement, free will, repentance and especially, faithfulness and the limited role of grace in the process of redemption. Such Christian attempts to assimilate these and other related Jewish beliefs, fail dismally to mesh with the realities of first century Judaism and are demonstrably at odds with nearly everything Jesus taught.

GOOD NEWS AND FAKE NEWS

> The Jesus of Paul isn't the Jesus of the gospels.[17]
>
> BOB SEIDENSTICKER

Set against the formidable body of evidence in the Gospels (as well as Acts and the epistle of James), that *hesed* was the resounding message of Jesus, there is really no Gospel basis for Paul's claim that Jesus was the sacrificial

---

14. Dauermann S, 2012. *New Perspectives on Paul and Why They Matter (4)—N. T. Wright*.
15. Wright N.T, 1997, p36.
16. Rich T.R, 2011. *Mashiach: The Messiah*
17. Seidensticker B, 2012. *What Did Paul Know About Jesus? Not Much.*

Messiah. Firstly it can be noted that there is barely even a hint of that idea in Luke's Gospel.[18] There, salvation is linked entirely to *hesed* in the Parable of the Good Samaritan (Lk10: 25–37).[19] The author of John's gospel tends to glorify Jesus as God; but Jesus clearly states there that salvation can only come through knowing God (Jn 17:3) and, as both he and the prophets repeatedly affirmed, that such knowledge is only possible via *hesed*. In John Jesus is described as the Pascal Lamb who 'takes away the sins of the world' (Jn 1:29). But these are the words of John the Baptist, not Jesus; and as Jews often point out, the Pascal lamb was not an atonement offering but was slaughtered to commemorate liberation from Egyptian slavery. That kind of self-sacrifice would certainly cohere with the politically liberationist aims of Jesus but "in no honest way can it be used in conjunction with a typological redemption from sin."[20]

Gospel validation of Christian sacrificial theology relies heavily on two pronouncements, one in Mark and the other in Matthew. In Mark's Gospel, Jesus described himself as a "ransom for many" (Mk 10:45) which is traditionally understood as him acting as a sacrificial substitute for sinful humanity. But again, the word Mark used for 'ransom', *lutron*, had no sacrificial connotations and it carried the very specific meaning of a payment to achieve liberation, typically for slaves. Christians might wish to take that as a metaphor for people being enslaved to sin; but in the context Mark uses it (Mk10:42–45), it clearly implies liberation from the warped values of hierarchical authority and the substitution of an egalitarian alternative, grounded in humility and the *hesed* mentality of loving others as family, without any thought of payback.[21]

Matthew provides the peak statement Christians rely on to support Paul's sacrificial schema, when Jesus announces at the Last Supper that he will shed his blood "for the forgiveness of sins" (Mt 26:28). That may at first seem a fairly clear cut verification of Paul—but the word 'for' can indicate cause as much as effect. Given the huge significance of the issue of forgiveness in Jesus' clash with the Temple, the 'for' can easily be read as causal—ie, Jesus announcing he would have to shed his blood *because* his

---

18. Powell M.A, 2009, p164–5.
19. Danizier D, 2011. *Paul vs. Jesus (and James)*.
20. Sigal G. *Did Jesus fulfill the role of the asham"guilt-offering?"*
21. McKnight S, 2005, p166. See also Robertson B. *Jesus' Death: Ransom or Sacrifice?* Also, Ewart D, 2018. *Holy Textures*.

effective forgiveness of sins had so enraged the Temple's and threatened its credibility.

One Christian biblical linguist denies this, claiming that in the entire New Testament, there are no instances where the Greek word 'for'(*eis*) is unambiguously causal.[22] But that is simply incorrect. There are two instances in Matthew alone where it is clearly causal: 'I baptise you ... for (*eis*) repentance' (Mt 3:11) and 'they repented at (*eis*) the preaching of Jonah' (Mt 12:41). The latter is obviously causal; and in the former, there can be little doubt that for the Baptist, repentance was a prerequisite for baptism rather than a consequence of it.[23] It would not make sense, logically or theologically, to see *eis* as basically telic in either case here.[24]

Thus in Matthew, Jesus can be understood simply as saying that he was being crucified because he had forgiven sins, performing acts of compassionate healing that threatened to supplant Temple authority with the sacred ethos of *hesed*. In accordance with the eighth Beatitude, he was persecuted because of righteousness, the word often used in the bible as a synonym for *hesed*.[25] However, to the extent that 'for' may have been intended to denote a consequence, Jesus could also have been predicting his death would ultimately facilitate awareness of (human) forgiveness as a prerequisite for *hesed*. That was after all the main thrust of his entire hesed mission. How his death may have actually enhanced that outcome, is discussed further in the next chapter.

While Jesus did not present himself as a sacrificial Saviour, he can be regarded as messianic in a more humanist sense. He regarded himself as 'the Son of Man', a title explored further in the next chapter; and he certainly believed God was working through him. He wanted his disciples to realize this but was increasingly frustrated by their paucity of faith in him, even with the solid evidence of his miracles.[26] Initially they saw him as a prophet and eventually they decided he was the anticipated Messiah who, despite his impending death, would later return to complete his liberating task. Peter was the first to defer to him as 'the Christ' and Jesus seemed

22. Harris M.2012, p91.

23. Neither the Baptist nor Jews in general believed repentance could ensue from any ritual but had to precede it. For example, rituals of Temple sacrifice to effect atonement were regarded as meaningless unless repentance had preceded the sacrifice. This will be discussed further below

24. Stedman E, 2009. *Basics of Bible Interpretation*.

25. Mckenzie J.L,1995, p566.

26. Osborne G.R. 2010, p618.

to affirm that in appointing him to lead his new 'church' (Mt 16:18), even though James would actually assume that position.

But Jesus' conception of messiahship seems quite distinct from the prevailing notion of a victorious warrior. Liberation would ultimately need to be achieved by human agency. His life and teachings suggest he had not come to save us but to teach us how to save ourselves. On the two occasions he proactively self-identified as 'the Christ', he specifically limned it in terms of a supreme teacher (*didaskalous*). One was Matthew 23:10 and the other, in John's Gospel in his conversation with a Samaritan woman. In the latter, he also affirmed he was a Messiah but that was in response to her seeking to understand his teaching of *hesed*'emet (Jn 4:21–26).

It is quite consistent with the Judaic Jesus depicted here, that he could regard himself as messianic in that broader, sapiential sense of the word. Jesus constantly refers to himself as 'Rabbi' or 'Teacher' and his disciples repeatedly address him as such, particularly Mary Magdalene when she is reported to witness his resurrection (Jn20:6). Jesus commissions his disciples to represent him not as the Messiah but as a teacher and healer, one who carried the authority of a 'Son of Man' (Mt 10). Even his 'Great Commission', his final statement after his resurrection, makes no specific reference to any salvific achievement but is aimed squarely at gaining converts who would be obedient to his teachings (Mt 28:17–20) of *hesed*.

A messianic *didaskalous* may have sounded less familiar and less appealing to Jewish ears, but at least Jesus signaled the idea. Paul's construct would have been vastly more alien and the basic problem for Christians is that Jesus never gave it any 'oxygen'. If his purpose was to fulfil the role of a Messiah in a very unfamiliar, metaphysical way, imparting forgiveness through faith in his sacrificial death and resurrection, he certainly failed to communicate this to his disciples. The Gospels threw no further light on a sacrificial atonement goal, even though by the time they were written, Paul had garnered wide, if largely non-Jewish, acceptance of Christ's as the sacrificial Messiah. Like the Apostles, the Gospel writers yearned for Jesus to be the promised Messiah. But as a testimony to the honesty of their accounts, they did not attempt to hide the fact that Jesus effectively excluded himself from being Israel's conventional Messiah by refuting the notion of a Messiah having Davidic lineage (Mt 22:41–45; Lk 20:41–21:4;

Mk 12:35–44).²⁷ That was a lineage that both Matthew (1:1–17) and Luke (3:23–37) had earlier gone to great lengths to establish on behalf of Jesus.²⁸

If the Jewish Jesus was out on the same metaphysical limb as Paul, it would seem more than odd that he did not flag it to his disciples. How could the greatest teacher that ever lived, have failed to teach what Christian theologians, starting with Paul, claim was the central purpose of his salvific mission? Nor did he make any strong appeals to unquestioning faith that, despite his very un-messianic death, he was fulfilling what was an unheard of, hitherto inconceivable messianic mission. Instead, in his final major address to his disciples, Jesus appeals not to faith but faithfulness. He proclaims unequivocally, that salvation will not be based on religious faith but on ethical "deeds" (Mt 16:27), the *hesed* compassion shown to, or withheld from,"the least of these my brothers and sisters" (Mt 25:31–46).

ISAIAH'S SUFFERING SERVANT WAS NOT PAUL'S SACRIFICIAL CHRIST

> According to rabbinic thought...the "servant"...refers to the righteous remnant of Israel—the most pious of the nation. The faithful members of Israel who willingly suffer for Heaven's sake...
>
> RABBI T SINGER

Paul claimed his revelation of Jesus as the Christ derived from Jesus himself but it may be that he gleaned it from the book of Isaiah whose 'suffering servant' was 'exalted' (Isa 52:13) and destined to suffer and "bear...the sins of many " (Isa 53:11–12). That certainly seemed to square with Jesus as Paul's 'exalted servant'(Phil 2:6–11); and guided by Paul,²⁹ Christian exegetes have long construed the suffering servant as a prophecy of Jesus

---

27. Finlan S,2005, p103. Also, Keizer L.S. 2010, p29.

28. This disjunction confirms the gospel writers were very faithful in recording what Jesus actually said—in this instance, a pronouncement which ran brutally counter to their messianic expectations.

29. Bauckham R, 2009, p43–44.

the Christ whose salvific death would rescue humanity from the curse of *Adam*'s original sin.[30]

But there are several problems with that rendition. For a start, the servant did not die; and Jew's have always interpreted him simply as a personification of Israel without ever attaching any salvific value to him 'bearing our sins'.[31] Christians also like to ignore the fact that that the 'sins' referred to in Isaiah have nothing to do with Adam or 'fallen humanity', but were mainly acts of gross injustice and brutality, especially perpetrated by avaricious, ruling elites.[32] Placed in that correct context, the Jewish Jesus could indeed have identified himself with Isaiah's servant.

Those who would co-opt Isaiah as a messianic prophesy like to stress the overt similarity between Christ's words at the Last Supper about shedding his blood "for the forgiveness of sins"(Mat 26:28) and Isaiah's 'suffering servant' who was "pierced…for our transgressions" (Is 53:5).[33] But once again, the little preposition 'for' brings them undone. In this passage of Isaiah, the word 'for' definitely denotes cause. Here, it is a translation of the original Hebrew word מִן (*min*) meaning 'from'[34] which indicates Isaiah meant the servant's suffering arose purely from human transgressions, with no telic implications.

A few verses later, the servant's suffering does have telic implications in being said to "justify many" (Is 53:11), the phrase Christians have always used to denote salvation. But that is a Christian translation of the Tanakh. Instead of translating the Hebrew as 'justify many,' Jews prefer to render it as 'cause the masses to be righteous' in a moral sense, indeed, in a specifically *hesed* sense.[35] They do not see it as conveying any kind of metaphysical, forensic atonement.[36] As noted above, Christ's Last Supper statement can be construed in precisely the same way. Christ certainly harboured the same social objective of 'causing the masses to be righteous;' and he almost certainly had Isaiah 53:11 in mind when framing his Last Supper address,

---

30. Bobosh T, 2011. *St. Paul: Christ is the Suffering Servant Exalted.*
31. Beaton R, 2002, p84. Also Routledge R, 2008, p293.
32. Isaiah 1–39. Barton J,1995, p46–47. Also, Souvay C, 1910. *Isaias.*
33. Richards L & Richards L.O, 2004, p590.
34. Hebrew Interlinear Bible. *Isaiah 53:5.*
35. McKenzie J. L, 1995, p566. Jews simply regard the suffering servant as one of the *hasidim* (*hesed* men).
36. Roth M, 2011. *Isaiah 53: The Suffering Servant.* Forensic, in this context, basically means 'legal'.

as Isaiah is Christ's third most frequently cited Old Testament text. Fostering such righteousness—a heightened awareness of *hesed*—is certainly what both he and Isaiah were aiming at. For both, the intention was didactic rather than salvific.

Christians also like to highlight the sacrificial import of God making the servant's "life a guilt offering" (Isa 53:10)—but that cannot be adduced to render the servant as portending a grand substitutionary sacrifice. As explained further below, the 'guilt offering' or *asham* was simply a ritual to complete the process of atonement that hinged on repentance. For the servant, forgiveness of sins would have already been achieved by repentance, forged out of Israel's suffering, or his own suffering as a *hasid*. Through this repentance the sin would have become minor, so that in proposing to make his suffering a retrospective 'guilt offering' (Isa 53:10), God was merely referring to the symbolic *asham* ritual of atonement, not atonement itself.[37]

The Jews have always known the true identity and intention of Isaiah's servant[38] and Jesus would have as well. As the embodiment of Israel, the servant reflected its heroic virtues as well its periodic lapses. He endures perennial suffering for Israel's recurring breach of the covenantal obligation of *hesed*, its infidelity to God primarily manifested in lapses of human compassion and justice.[39] Yet the servant also stands for Israel's righteousness, the embodiment of the *hasidim* whose devotion to *hesed* also made them servants and witnesses of the Lord (Isa42: 1–4 & 49: 1–7).

As the suffering servant, Israel is expected to act as a light to all nations through example and by bringing a knowledge of God to the world (Is 11:9 &58:10). Once more the epistemic issue is paramount. *Hesed* is the font of that knowledge (Hos 6:6) and as the cornerstone of human ethics and morality, *hesed* has the potential to "cause the world to be righteous."[40] At the core of that *hesed* righteousness is a capacity for forgiveness and mercy and Isaiah's servant exemplified this in making an "intersession for the transgressors" (Is 53:12). Jewish historian Josephus records how such hasidic virtue was especially called for at times where Israel was struggling under foreign domination and those intercessions were valued far more than the offerings of priests in the Temple.[41] They inevitably entailed enor-

---

37. Torah 101. *Qorbanot: Sacrifices and Offerings.*
38. Roth M.2011, op cit. CJB is the Complete Jewish Bible.
39. Hanson P.D, 2012, p9–10.
40. Roth M,2011. op cit.
41. Kohler K. *Atonement.*

mous courage, wisdom, generosity and self-sacrifice which would often involve being "pierced for our transgressions" (Isa 53:5).

It can be conceded that the servant did have some messianic associations, as Jews believed that the Messiah would ultimately be selected from the ranks of these *hasidim*.[42] Jesus, himself the epitome of a hasid, could have identified with the servant in this way—as a righteous son of Israel, sharing its tribulations and willing to suffer to implant the seeds of *hesed* justice in this world.[43] As the Son of Man, he believed he was destined to eventually return as the eschatological judge which might also help explain his quasi acceptance of various messianic titles. But that did not make him a victorious Messiah either in his life or death, either literally or symbolically. As B Janowski observes, there is nothing in Isaiah that gives credence to the much grander messianic notion of a sacrificial offering of permanent divine atonement.[44]

PAUL'S FLAWED SACRIFICIAL TYPOLOGY

> "What are your multiplied sacrifices to Me?" Says the LORD. "I have had more than enough of burnt offerings of rams and the fat of fed cattle; I take no pleasure in the blood of bulls, lambs or goats ... who has asked this of you ... ? ... Learn to do good; seek justice, reprove the oppressor, defend the orphan, plead for the widow ..."
>
> ISAIAH 1:11–17

Quite apart from attempting to historicize prophesy in Isaiah, Christian theologians still seek to validate Jesus as their sacrificial Redeemer by linking his death to sacrificial typologies in early Judaism. In accordance with Jewish Law, forgiveness of sin was an issue of critical importance and from the earliest years of Israel's history, animal sacrifice was associated with achieving it. Paul was very mindful of this, declaring "Christ, our Paschal lamb, has been sacrificed" (1Cor 5:7); and "without the shedding of blood there is no remission [of sins]" (Heb 9:22).

42. Singer T. *Who is God's Suffering Servant?*
43. Beaton R, 2002, p22–3.
44. Janowski B, 2004, p67–69.

Taking its cue from Paul, Christianity was always structured around the notion that the ancient Jewish sacrificial system established "the theological principles that apply to our relationship with, and approach to God, through Christ."[45] Thus, Judaic animal sacrifice was superseded by what N.T Wright called the "once and for all"[46] atonement of Christ shedding his own blood. However this theological model is deeply flawed. It flouts God's abomination of human sacrifice, associating Judaism and Jesus with barbaric cultic practice. It also overrates the importance of sacrificial atonement in first century Judaism.

It is one of Christianity's many anomalies that its notion of Christ's atoning death contradicts a "fundamental biblical principle," established in Ezekiel 18, which Jesus no doubt, would have been aware of. This was simply that a righteous person could not die vicariously for the sins of others.[47] That was also confirmed in Jeremiah's assertion that there will be no collective guilt (or innocence) but "instead, everyone will die for his own sin" (Jer 31:30). It is inexcusable that Christians see fit to ignore such clear scriptural directives, just as they gloss over the fact that God is said to have abhorred the very idea of human sacrifice.[48] Their response to the latter might be that Jesus was God and therefore not really a human sacrifice. But it was not until the Council of Nicaea in the fourth century that Christians finally agreed that Jesus was God. Even Paul did not dare make such a forthright claim. Indeed, as G Vermes has observed, it has always been unspeakably blasphemous to Jews that any human being could claim to "share the nature of the Almighty."[49]

If Christianity is seen as a religion steeped in barbaric slaughter, it is because its blood-drenched allusions arose from a warped perspective of Judaism. Some anthropologists believe that all ancient religious sacrifice was a form of institutionalized scapegoating. In projecting human sins onto the sacrificial animal, the ancients encoded and sanctified their own violence. If so, Christ's reputed self-sacrifice could also be taken as a valorisation of savagery.

---

45. Routledge R, 2008, p203–4.
46. Wright T, 2014, p16–17.
47. Singer T. *Sin and Atonement*
48. Federow S, 2012. *G-d hates human sacrifice*. God's disgust with human sacrifice is made evident in Deuteronomy 12:30 & 24:16; Exodus 32:30–35; Psalm 106:37–38; Ezekiel 16:20.
49. Vermes G, 2000, p207.

Christian philosopher Rene Girard tried to get around that problem by arguing Christ's sacrifice was a new departure because Jesus negated the scapegoat trope by being and remaining pure and innocent. However he seems to forget St Paul's contention that "God made the one who knew no sin, to be sin for us" (2 Cor5:21). In taking on our sinful impurities, Jesus would have indeed become the ultimate scapegoat and actually bolstered the myth of "the primitive Sacred who takes part with the group in the killing of the victim."[50]

Girard seems to have based his scapegoat theory of socially sanctioned violence on Freud's belief that people relieved their own guilt by projecting it onto others. But Jesus in fact anticipated Freud by 2000 years in observing this and deploring its social consequences as manifested in the purity law stigmas (Mt 7:3–5; Jn 8:1–11). Such devious shifting of responsibility, inherent in Paul's sacrificial typology, can be seen as the essence of bad faith. It is the very antithesis of the open forgiveness of self and others that Jesus regarded as indispensable to *hesed* empathy.

So now, together with Schweitzer's Jesus as a deluded apocalyptic zealot, we have Girard's image of the Christian godhead as a mainstay of violent projection inversion sociology, in flagrant contradiction of his most basic *hesed* teachings. In this regard, Paul's cult of personality carries the added opprobrium of being a death cult. Yet many Christians still seem quite willing to ignore such odious implications, rather than relinquish their cherished 'penal substitution' theology.[51]

Girard's anthropology was also awry on a more basic level. Long before the advent of Jesus, Jewish cultish practice had moved on from the primitive pagan idea of a propitiatory gift or bribe (*kofer*) to a wrathful God.[52] That notion had been mollified and increasingly spiritualized with the emphasis shifting from fear of God to sorrow and a sense of loss at being separated from him through sin.[53] In the process, the notion of repentance rather than sacrifice, became the real prerequisite for divine mercy; and that became reflected in the more nuanced meaning attached to the sacrificial ceremonies themselves.

There were a variety of Judaic sacrifices. Many were just worship rituals but two, the sin offering (*hattat*) and guilt offering (*asham*), were related

---

50. Hamperton-Kelly R.G, 1992, p94.
51. Finlan S, 2005, p37–8.
52. Kohler K. *Atonement*.
53. Idem.

to sacrificial atonement. However neither provide any theological basis for Christ's supposed self-sacrifice. A *hattat* was designed to achieve cleansing and purification. Its main ritual involved sprinkling blood on the temple altar to purify God's sanctuary of any minor sins, sins of inadvertence, untruthfulness, impious and impure thoughts or sins of omission. That is scarcely a theological antidote model for sin on the scale of Adam's supposed transgression.

The *asham* was designed to atone for more serious sins against a neighbor. However its sacrifice was purely a symbolic completion ritual and could not be enacted until the guilty person had confessed and shown genuine remorse as well as a willingness to compensate his victim or pay the equivalent to a charity. Underscoring the importance of human forgiveness in Judaic tradition, it was also incumbent on the injured party to respond by extending forgiveness. When these primary conditions of repentance and reconciliation were fulfilled, the sin would be downgraded to a status of minor importance and the *asham* would then proceed as a formal confirmation of forgiveness.[54] But it was the preceding repentance and reconciliation, not the sacrifice, that was the pivotal aspect.

Blood was still a symbolic element, especially in the sin offering; but Christian scholar R Routledge is wrong in claiming that "shedding blood signifies death, the death of the animal on behalf of the sinner."[55] On the contrary, blood signified life In Jewish cultic rituals, the life force or soul; and the blood was sprinkled on the altar, not to expiate sin but to purify the altar and symbolize the renewal of the covenant of life.[56] On the Day of Atonement, *Yom Kippur*, sacrificial blood cleansed sin's stain from the altar. The altar symbolized the community and the sacrifice formalized a general atonement between humanity and God. But this was not seen as imparting any blanket forgiveness of sin. *Yom Kippur* was simply a *hattat* ceremony to forgive minor transgressions and one that still required a repentant heart.[57] The animal sacrificed was in no sense taking on serious human sin, which could only be eradicated through repentance.[58] The ceremony was concluded by the transferring of human sin to a scapegoat; but again, that was purely a ritual to expunge residual, minor sin and it did not constitute

54. Singer T. *Sin and Atonement*.
55. Routledge R, 2008, p195.
56. Finlan S, 2005, p13–14 & p37.
57. Kalimi I, *The Historical Uniqueness and Centrality of Yom Kippur*.
58. Singer T. *Sin and Atonement*.

a sacrificial offering. The scapegoat was not slaughtered as a sacrifice but released into the wilderness.

Paul's sacrificial typology may still have reprised a more primitive, bloodletting form of cultic Judaism and the first century Temple priests would no doubt have encouraged people to see it as having intrinsic atoning significance. It has been shown how the Temple sought to exploit guilt to boost its own stocks as a source of forgiveness. Routledge may be partially correct in claiming the 'burnt offering' and the laying of hands on the animal to be slaughtered, had 'substitutionary implications',[59] and the officiating priests would have wished to present it as such.

But it is almost certain that Jesus would have rejected such primitive symbolism, just as he rejected nearly everything about the Temple of his day. How could he have accepted a ritual that implicitly removed personal responsibility by transference of sin to another creature? Surely that was just another example of projection inversion that Jesus sternly reproved (Mt 7:5; Lk 8:7). It was also contrary to his insistence that forgiveness must involve repentance and reconciliation between the wrongdoer and the wronged.

The first century Temple basically ignored the real meaning of the *asham* as purely symbolic. Instead the priests harked back to ancient sacrificial tropes and Paul followed suit. But there is nothing in the Gospels to suggest Jesus understood Temple sacrifices as having any relevance to his mission, either symbolic or otherwise. He had clearly rejected Temple sacrifices in citing Hosea's demand for *hesed* and to the extent that he may have accepted established rituals like the *asham*, he nowhere ever implied that its symbolism could impart real forgiveness, let alone provide a model of atonement for what Paul regarded as, the very deliberate and catastrophic sin of Adam.

---

59. Routledge R, 2008, p194.

THE PRIMACY OF ATONING REPENTANCE OVER THE SACRIFICIAL CULT

> Repentance is a human act, not a mysterious sacrament that works without our efforts ... Repentance is the highest of the virtues in Judaism.[60]
>
> THEODORE LUDWIG

While the Temple still occupied a key place in early first century Judaism, sacrificial offerings themselves were becoming passé in terms of atonement. The Temple was widely and rightly known to be corrupt at this time[61]—not that priestly corruption was anything new. Fuelling the outrage of many ancient prophets[62] was the hypocrisy of priests who engaged in acts of gross cruelty, greed and injustice. Christ of course related strongly to the *tzedakah* (social justice) of the prophets[63] and their exposé of the inveterate wickedness of the religious elites, a recurring theocratic turpitude that had reached its apogee in the first century. For centuries, the prophets had denounced the Temple's sacrificial rites as hollow and self-serving and a strong Judaic consensus had emerged that genuine repentance, not sacrifice, was the only sure means of divine forgiveness.[64]

A host of Old Testament Prophets and Psalmists were expressing God's increasing impatience with cultic sacrifice, not just because heartfelt contrition seemed to be often lacking, but because the ritual itself had become vapid. Some sages regarded sacrificial ceremony as incidental (Prov 21:3 & 1Sam 15:22) but many more subjected it to ridicule. This is perhaps most stridently evident in Isaiah which begins (Is1:10–17) and ends (Is 66:3) with a scathing denunciation of all sacrifice other than grain offerings (Is 66:20). Similar indictments are voiced in Psalms 40:6, 50:12–13 and 51:16–17, Jeremiah 19:4–6 and Hosea 6:6. They are also thinly veiled in Micah 6:6–8, Amos 5:21–24 and Joel 2:13.

---

60. Ludwig T.M, 2016, p123.

61. Evans C, 1989, p342.

62. Hosea, Isaiah, Jerimiah and Ezekiel were particularly scathing about the Temple and its rituals.

63. Borg M.J, 1998, p13 & p24n; Borg M.J &Wright N.T,1999, p72.

64. Mills W.E (ed), 1997, p754. Also Astell A.W & Goodhart S, 2011, p1–38.

Conversely, all of these voices loudly and repeatedly proclaim the virtues of *hesed*—mercy, compassion, humility, forgiveness and justice—above sacrifice.[65] *Hesed* was in fact esteemed as the highest form of repentance.[66] From the very beginning in Genesis, when God received offerings from Able and Cain, he made it clear that their moral behaviour counted far more than their offerings (Gen 4:6-7). Although God purportedly inaugurated his covenant in Exodus with the blood of a bull, there is only one reference in the entire Old Testament (Zechariah 9:11)) to the covenant as being inaugurated with blood. Moses, not God commanded this and the blood was used purely to cleanse the altar and worshippers, not as a form of atonement. Hosea, Jeremiah and Isaiah even contend that God had nothing to do with establishing the sacrificial cult in the first place.[67] For these reasons, as Stephen Finlan concludes that "the whole (Christian) theological claim for the cult is undercut."[68]

As temple sacrifices waned as a means of atonement, the importance of individual repentance waxed. Judaism had long regarded repentance as critically important, multifaceted and very much the responsibility of the individual. It was of an act of free will that did not necessarily involve divine grace; and as we have seen, Jewish repentance required the forgiveness of both parties which again accorded closely with *hesed* mutuality. Conversely for Paul, human repentance was not enough. It had to be "godly" (2Cor: 7:10), initiated by divine grace rather than human volition. Paul viewed repentance as he did works in general—it would inevitably ensue from faith in the saving death of Christ. Thus he saw little point in discussing repentance, beyond suggesting it was not the work of the individual but the Holy Spirit.[69]

But for Jews, repentance was entirely dependent on free will and human contrition. Sacrificial offering at the Temple provided a symbolic convention of repentance but as the Psalmist declared, "You do not delight in sacrifice, or I would bring it; you do not take pleasure in burnt offerings. My sacrifice, O God, is[a] a broken spirit; a broken and contrite heart" (Ps 51:16-17).There were a number of paths to repentance in early Judaism, invariably predicated on the free will of the human agent. Thus 'willful

---

65. Askew E & O. Wesley Allen Jr,2015, p22.
66. Zobel H.J, 1986, p49.
67. Finlan S, 2005, p26.
68. Idem.
69. Ellis P, 2011. *3 Reasons Why I Don't Preach on Repentance.*

defiance' of God had to be corrected with 'willful repentance', expressing a heartfelt contrition and resolving to never repeat the same offence.[70] Most Jews regarded prayer, fasting and *mitzvah* (good deeds), as far more effective means of repentance than any form of blood sacrifice.[71]

Early Judaism recognized many forms of repentance. As is clear from Isaiah's servant, enduring suffering was seen as one of these. Those *ptochos*, those who were 'poor in spirit' that Christ was unable to directly reach, might have derived some solace from the fact that their suffering could also serve as a means of repentance.[72] That it could also lead to positive blessings was Christ's Beatitudes theme. Jewish theologian K Kohler has referred to "the atoning power of suffering experienced by the righteous during the Exile," which, by Christ's time, carried "greater atoning power than all the Temple sacrifices."[73] This is not because their suffering constituted any kind of appeasing sacrifice to God, but because it

> provokes introspection and serves as source of reflection on the sins one has committed, so providing the occasion for repentance, which yields atonement as offerings yielded atonement...through...the sacrifice of one's own will in favor of God's decree. When suffering comes, it brings about submission God.[74]

It would have also of course, aroused divine compassion. Such repentant humility was a keynote of the Beatitudes (Mt 5:1–10). The suffering multitudes were 'blessed' because their suffering, far from manifesting sinfulness as the Temple elites insisted, actually helped with the remission of sins.

But by far the most efficacious repentance came from immersion in the deeper, cleansing streams of *hesed*.[75] Thus, as Proverb 16:6 declared, "by mercy and truth (*hesed e'meth*), iniquity is atoned for;" and in the Book of Daniel, the sinner is urged to "redeem your error with charity, and your sin through kindness to the poor, so that there will be an extension to your tranquility" (Dan 4:24). Isaiah made a strong connection between repentance and *hesed*, so that the "scarlet" sins of Israel "shall become as white as snow" (Isa 1:10–18). Isaiah rated this aspect of *hesed* as the purest form

70. Gruber M.I, 2010, p128.
71. Singer T. *Sin and Atonement*.
72. Gruber M.I, 2010, p68.
73. Kohler K. *Atonement*.
74. Gruber M.I, 2010, p68.
75. Zobel H.J, 1986, p49. Also Gruber M.I, 2010, p128.

of repentance, well above sacrificial offerings (Isa 1:11) and fasting (Isa 58:5–7).

For Jesus and most Jews, the real value of the Jerusalem Temple was its traditional status as a stronghold of justice and compassion (Jer7:4–6; Isa 1:17); and for this reason, Jesus lamented its impending demise (Mt 23:37; 24:2).He had prefigured his prophesy by cursing a fig tree (Mt 21:18–19), an incident which, wedged between his assault on the Temple and his return there to confront the priests, casts the luxuriant but sterile fig tree as a metaphor for the ostentatious but spiritually barren Temple leaders. In Jonah, which may be the final book of the Old Testament,[76] God's final act was to destroy the *kikayon* as a sign to the recalcitrant Jonah (Jon 4:7), the *kikayon* being the leafy (and poisonous) vine/tree sheltering Jonah, which had symbolic associations with the Jerusalem Temple.[77] Jonah clearly preferred the showy, comforting rituals of the Temple (Jon 2:9) to the *hesed* mission God had assigned to him (Jon 4:2); and the book concludes with God destroying the symbolic *kikayon*, Jonah's longed for refuge, leaving him to wallow in pathetic self-pity.

By the first century, the Jerusalem Temple had few defenders and a host of critics in Jewish texts.[78] John the Baptist's movement was just one of many Jewish sects that had abandoned it as the cultic centre of Judaism.[79] John used baptism as an alternative way of imparting symbolic forgiveness[80] and in being baptized by John, Christ was clearly endorsing his anti-Temple protest. In his second citing of Hosea 6:6, when Jesus declared that there was now "something greater than the Temple" (Mt 12: 6), he was probably referring as much to *hesed* as himself. The clear message of Hosea 6:6 was that sacrificial offerings had outlived their usefulness and should be superseded by genuine repentance, forgiveness and reconciliation through *hesed*. Jesus affirmed this in asserting that loving God by loving one's neighbour, was "more important than all burnt offerings and sacrifices."(Mk 12:33)

Like the great social prophets of Israel, Jesus saw the Temple as primarily "a house of prayer for all nations" (Isa 56:7) and a sanctuary for the poor and oppressed (Jer 7:4–6). When he eventually went to the Temple, it was not to offer sacrifices but to protest corruption and injustice and heal

---

76. Ateek N.S, 2008, p73.
77. Lacocque A & P.E, 1981, p88–9.
78. Horsley R & Thatcher T, 2013, p159–160.
79. Romer J, 1988, p179. See also Crossan J.D, 1991, p231.
80. Hägerland T, 2011, p206.

"the blind and the lame who came to him there" (Mt 21:13–14). That was his way of 'worshipping' God (Jn 9:3 &11;4). He obviously regarded the Temple as so corrupted that its cultic functions were now meaningless and he predicted, albeit with some remorse, its impending destruction.

For Jesus, cultic sacrifice long despised by so many of the prophets, had run its course and all that now mattered was *hesed*. His disciples would surely have understood this. Scholars often cite the Apostles continued visits to the Temple after Christ's death, as evidence of their ongoing allegiance to its cultic functions.[81] But this is completely unfounded. Acts makes it clear that these daily Temple incursions were not about worshipping, prayer or sacrifice but healing the sick and protesting against its brutal and oppressive leadership (Acts 2:46–4:21; Mt 21:14)—exactly as Christ had done. The early Christians no doubt still related to the Temple as a "house of prayer for all nations" (Mk 11:17). Interestingly, they continued to observe *Yom Kippur* but by fasting, not by engaging in animal sacrifice. In fact they now referred to the Day of Atonement as 'the Fast' (Acts 27–9).

Early Christian disdain of cultic sacrifice is pronounced in the Clementine Recognitions where Peter reiterates God's disdain for sacrifice in Hosea 6:6.[82] Fourth century bishop Epiphanius claimed the Ebonites opposed sacrifice and he quoted a purported statement of Jesus, preserved by those successors of James and the Apostles: "I came to abolish the sacrifices, and if you do not cease from sacrifice, the wrath will not cease from you."[83] The Ebonites denounced Paul as an apostate from the Law who usurped the leadership of the Christian movement from James.[84] They abhorred the notion of Christ as a vicarious sacrificial offering and regarded Paul's version of the Eucharist as a proposal "to drink the blood of corpses."[85]

Such lurid language may have stemmed from the fact that the Ebonites were also vegetarians, continuing a strong tradition that reached back to the first Jerusalem Christians and very possibly, to Christ himself.[86] In that respect, a recent archaeological discovery is particularly interesting. Digs under the site of the Jerusalem Temple have revealed that it was a

---

81. Just a few examples are Dunn D.G, 2009, p231; Wilson A.N,1992, p186; & Bütz J.J, 2005, p68.

82. Akers K. 2000, p113.

83. Freyne S, 1980, p276.

84. Powel F.F, 2009, p8.

85. Finlan S, 2005, p27.

86. Akers K, 2001.*Was Jesus a Vegetarian?*

veritable slaughterhouse in the first century, the scale indicating animal supply and butchery was a major commercial activity there.[87] Given all the preceding arguments, as well as the claim that God's kindness was not just limited to humanity but extended to animals—cattle (Jon 4:11) and sparrows (Lk 12:6)—at least one Christian theologian asserts "a compassionate God is ... incompatible with all (sacrificial) atonement theories."[88] It would seem that by the time Christ arrived, many Jews were coming to a similar conclusion. Not however, Saul of Tarsus who remained closely wedded to the more primitive cultic traditions and myths of the Jerusalem Temple.

PAUL'S GRACE NEGATES FREE WILL AND ALIGNS HIM WITH CHRIST'S MORTAL ENEMIES

> The concepts of grace and faith were invented by Paul. Neither exists in the Hebrew Bible.[89]
>
> RABBI ISRAEL DRAZIN

For centuries, the big issue seen to divide Judaism and Pauline Christianity was the relative importance of faith and works in attaining salvation. Particularly since the Reformation, this has been a yawning chasm between the two faiths; but in recent decades, Jesus scholars have attempted to bridge it by crafting a 'new perspective on Paul' (NP or NPP). E.P Sanders has argued that Second Temple Judaism was characterized by 'covenantal nomism'—faith that the covenant ensured all Jews were under God's grace and could ultimately rely on that for salvation. This meant that the works they assiduously performed, were actuated by that grace or intended as 'markers' to signify their elect status, not as a means of meriting salvation in themselves. This they claim, brings Paul more into harmony with a Judaism that was aligned with his faith/grace paradigm, for all he really did was to substitute faith in Jesus for faith in covenantal election.

However closer investigation suggests that while covenantal nomism may aptly represent some elements of Judaism, especially those associated

---

87. Ghose T, 2013, op cit.
88. Finlan S,2005, p101.
89. Drazin I.2013. *Philosophers reject the concept of grace.*

with the Jerusalem Temple, most Jews did not place such strong reliance in God's grace and certainly not to the extent that this overrode independent human agency, especially for moral initiatives.[90] For Paul, humanity was so compromised by Adam's sin that it was incapable of doing anything to merit its own salvation (Rom 5:18–19). Without divine grace, which was now only available through faith in Jesus Christ, God's judgment would ultimately consign people to damnation.[91] Such an uncompromising theological position is referred to as "strong predestination" where salvation and damnation are entirely beyond human control.

But such a bleak scenario was quite abhorrent to the mainstream Judaism of the first century.[92] As Judaic theologian K Kohler declared,

> Judaism has ever emphasized the freedom of the will as one of its chief doctrines. The dignity and greatness of man depends largely upon his freedom, his power of self-determination . . . This certainly indicates that the moral freedom of man is not impaired by hereditary sin, or by any evil power outside of man himself"[93]

If reliance on divine grace was a major strand of Judaism at the time as NP scholars claim, it would surely have bred at least some degree of complacency or at least, equanimity. That may have manifested in the attitude of the smug high priests and their Shammaite cronies; but as the previous chapter reveals, ordinary Jews were obsessed with their sinfulness and longed for forgiveness. This of course, suited the purposes of the Temple establishment whose covenantal nomism assumed an exclusive right to forgive sins through sacrificial offerings. These were presented as a quick, unmerited way to secure atonement and return to the covenantal fold; and judging by the volume of butchered animals, there were still plenty of Jews gullible enough to believe it.[94] But the dominant first century Judaic perspective was that repentance and meritorious works were indispensable to forgiveness.[95]

Long before the NPP, Christian theologians attempted to downplay the dissonance between Paul and James, claiming they both would have

90. Eskola ,1997, p396–412.
91. Baugh S.M. 1998. *God's Purpose According To Election: Paul's Argument in Romans 9*
92. Eskola T.1997, p403–4 & p412
93. Jacobs J & Broydé I, 1918. *Free Will.*
94. Ghose T, 2013, op cit.
95. Eskola T, 1997, p396 & p404

agreed that "faith without works is dead" (Jas 2:14–26).Their argument is simply that both expected good works to arise from faith. But as G Vermes is not alone in deciding such attempts at convergence are "hopeless."[96] Given the overriding importance Paul attached to faith, it is hard to imagine him endorsing such a strong affirmation of works; and it begs the question as to why James felt the need to endorse works so emphatically, if he and Paul did were both on the same page in believing that works naturally flowed from grace.

In fact, both men use the same scriptural verse (Genesis 15:6) to advance their contrary views about justification—Paul in Romans 4:1–3 (faith alone) and James 2:21–24 (faith and works—faithfulness).[97] Paul was repeatedly dismissive of 'works-righteousness', but that is the resounding theme of James' letter. For James, the initiative for *hesed* stemmed not from divinely bestowed grace, but human volition and especially a desire to obey the law of God and the ethical injunctions of Jesus. His entire Epistle is a plea for people to rise above their lower instincts and in doing so, it is they that must take the initiative in repenting and not rely on God doing it for them (Jas 4:7–10).

Thus, the key difference between Paul and James was that the latter sustained a deep Jewish attachment to free will, befitting free human beings made in God's likeness (Jas 3:9). For James, justification relied basically on *emunah* faithfulness[98] and in particular, our ethical choices in relation to *hesed* (Jas 2:13). Paul's subjective faith epiphany, with its relatively scant interest in ethical behaviour and its predestination implications, was completely at odds with the works theology of James, Jesus himself and Judaism in general. This basic divergence over free will and reliance on grace, was where Paul and most of his Jewish contemporaries parted company.[99]

Nonetheless NP scholars have laboured to validate their new perspective by claiming some of the Jewish prophets had themselves expressed an 'anthropomorphic pessimism' that led them to a similar faith/grace dependency.[100] Preston Sprinkle cites Deutero-Isaiah, Ezekiel and Jeremiah

---

96. Vermes G, 2000, p114. See also Foster P, 2011, p86; &Wilson A.N, 1992, p37.

97. Danizier D, 2011. *Paul vs. Jesus (and James)*.

98. Keenan J.P, 2005, p213.

99. Jacobs J & Broydé I, 1918. *Free Will*. Although a faction of the Essenes embraced predestination, the great majority of Jewish opinion in the first century and subsequent Rabbinic Judaism upheld the notion of free will.

100. Sprinkle P.M, 2013, p237–8.

arguing that they had come to largely despair of the depravity of the world. Sprinkle even maintains these prophets had abandoned the Deuteronomic code of repentance and believed divine agency (grace) now overshadowed human agency (free will repentance, law observance and *hesed*), so that everything now hinged on faith in God's unconditional forgiveness of Israel.[101] Sprinkle particularly highlights Ezekiel in proclaiming that Israel's condition was "beyond hope" and it must in future rely totally on God's unilateral mercy.[102]

However this assessment is completely at odds with Jewish interpretations of these texts which maintains they establish that "forgiveness is always and only consequent on repentance—the idea of an arbitrary grace (being) almost totally absent."[103] Judaic exegesis sees these prophets very differently to Sprinkle. Far from promoting abject dependence on divine mercy, Jews regard the book of Ezekiel as an assertion of individual responsibility;[104] and chapter 18 of Ezekiel certainly attests to that. As one Jewish commentary points out, Ezekiel, far from giving up on his fellow Jews, even saw it "as his prophetic mission to strive to reach his brethren and compatriots individually, to follow them, and to win them back to God."[105]

Perhaps Sprinkle's misconception arises from the fact that the Jewish prophets tended to relate to the collective nation rather than individuals. Thus, pronouncements of unmerited divine largesse may be taken as applying to Israel as a nation under the Abrahamic covenant, rather than to individuals. Ezekiel in particular tended to see the covenant as similar to a treaty between nations.[106] It was the sins of the nation (and especially its ruling casts), that the prophets often despaired of—and for good reason, given the many self-inflicted calamities that befell Israel over the centuries. Beneath that gloom however, was a confidence that *YHWH* would always ultimately adhere to the original Abrahamic covenant of divine mercy to his 'chosen people'. But that mercy did not extend to individuals who failed to repent. Here the Mosaic covenant was quite emphatic. It demanded individual repentance for sin, initiated not by any 'sacrifice' or the gratuitous dispensation of divine forgiveness, but by free will.

101. ibid, p38–67.
102. Sprinkle P.M, 2013, p61.
103. Unterman A. *Forgiveness*. 2008.
104. West J. K, 1981, p338 .
105. Hirsch E..G, Cornill K.H, Schechter S & Ginzberg L. *Ezekiel*.
106. Hayes J.H, 2013, p277.

Sprinkle also seems to forget that a characteristic of prophetic writing was its stridently polemic quality, driven by a passion to impart an urgent message. This invariably resulted in hyperbole and dramatic rhetoric that was designed to shock its readers into changing their ways, a correction that would presumably be redundant if the prophets believed divine judgment had already been effected. It is extraordinary that Sprinkle seems not to realize that God in fact commissions Ezekiel to exhort the people to repent and warns that He will hold him at least partly accountable if they do not (Ezek 3:16–27). Then God himself calls on Israel to repent (18:31–32) and predicts dire consequences if it does not.

This kind of dramatic overreach also utilized a philosophical convention known as 'conditional futurism.' What was stated as a divine *fait accompli* had conditional strings attached. Jews of course accepted that God was omnipotent and interventionist, but they also believed that his ordained human destiny was not set in stone and human beings could alter the course God had set for them. In Ezekiel, God spelt it out precisely:

> if I say to the wicked man, 'You will surely die,' but he then turns away from his sin and does what is just and right—if he gives back what he took in pledge for a loan, returns what he has stolen, follows the decrees that give life, and does no evil, he will surely live; he will not die. (Ezek 33:14–15)[107]

If Ezekiel rarely exhorted his people to repent, that was probably because it was the obvious point of his warnings and would have been taken for granted. Moreover, Ezekiel would have known that repentance naturally attended suffering, and he envisages a world of suffering to be endured by Israel before the final restoration.

Similar objections can also be levelled at Sprinkle's detection of unilateral divine agency in Isaiah and Jeremiah, which he describes as "evident" in the former and "prevalent" in the latter.[108] Again, Sprinkle flaunts the usual Christian disregard of the Jewish conviction that Isaiah's servant is in fact the nation of Israel, or the embodiment of its *hasidim*, not a prophesied Messiah. Clearly, the servant is deemed to have merited forgiveness through suffering induced repentance.[109] Sprinkle also dismisses explicit calls for repentance in Jeremiah as perfunctory, "only hypothetical,"[110] which would

---

107. Goetz J, 2013, p 1 & p54.
108. Sprinkle P, 2013, p38–67.
109. Shulman M, 2003. *The Zohar on Isaiah 53*.
110. Sprinkle P, 2013, p59n.

make it somewhat comical that such calls for repentance are made more than 100 times in Jeremiah. Again Sprinkle seems unaware of the destiny altering implications of 'conditional futurism'.

Like Hosea, Jeremiah declared *hesed* as the way to know God (Jer 31:31–34)[111] and that knowledge was not some kind of enlightenment, bestowed on a helpless humanity by a divine dominator.[112] The prophets envisage it being forged through harsh experience and heartfelt repentance, as well as through their inspired teachings. Grace may assist the practice of *hesed* but it did not spontaneously generate it, otherwise Christ might not have needed to devote almost his entire mission to elucidating and demonstrating it.

Turning to Jewish texts around the time of Jesus, the links between Paul and Judaism become even more tenuous. Sprinkle actually concedes that almost all of these texts, to varying degrees, assumed human agency as the essential element of repentance and salvation. There were some quarters that upheld the primacy of divine grace but even the most radical of these never quite abandoned the need for at least semi-autonomous human agency in the form of repentance. In fact Sprinkle is forced to conclude that there is a basic 'discontinuity' between Paul's strict faith/grace doctrine and the prevailing first century Judaic presumption of human agency in repentance and forgiveness.[113] Contrary to the hopes of Sprinkle and most Christian NPP scholars, Paul's notion of human depravity and total dependence on God's grace (Rom 5:18–19; 8:7–8) has been found to be diametrically at odds with mainstream Judaism of the first century.

This is not to deny some strands of Paul's pessimistic soteriology were present in early Judaism. But unfortunately for Pauline apologists, they are found in the Judaic fundamentalism espoused by fanatics like the Shammaites; and their locus was the Jerusalem Temple. In their perverted form of Judaism, an inflated sense of covenantal entitlement is laid bare, along with a Jonah like preference for ritualized faith over ethical faithfulness, and cultic sacrifice over *hesed*. For the Shammaites, 'covenantal nomism' consisted of faith in Abrahamic election combined with a 'zeal for the law' in which works were perfunctory markers of that elect status.[114] This theological mindset constituted a "pattern of religion," evident in Paul's

---

111. Berkovits E &Hazony D,2003, p139.
112. Rosenberg B.H, 1992, p57.
113. Sprinkle P, 2013, p237-249.
114. Wright N. T, 1997. *What Saint Paul Really Said*, p26-9.

doctrines which likewise upheld the primacy of faith and regarded works as purely a manifestation of God's grace.[115] The conclusion is as stark as it is obvious: Paul was very closely aligned with the 'covenantal nomism' of the Temple establishment.[116] Both he and the Shammaites believed in the primacy of 'justification by faith'; for the latter it was faith in Israel's election and for Paul, faith in Christ.[117]

It is at this point that Sprinkle's case—and indeed Christian theology itself—really comes undone and Paul is revealed in his true colours. While Paul professed to have belonged to the Hillel school in his pre-Christian life, it is obvious that his brutality and bigotry would have placed him in the Shammaite camp. Even the renowned N.T Wright now concedes this;[118] and though Paul recanted, his altered purview did not extend to his basic Shammaite theological assumptions. Sprinkle nominates the Quamran *Hodayot* as the text that most closely corresponds to Paul's 'pessimism' and even his notion of irretrievable original sin is canvassed there.[119] The *Hodayot* were hymns of thanksgiving composed by an extremist faction of the Essenes who were aligned with the violent Zealots;[120] and, as revealed in Chapter Two, the Zealots were closely associated with Shammaite Pharisees.[121] Shammaites even modelled their prayers on the hymns of the *Hodayot*.[122]

It may be concluded therefore that the rigorous faith/grace doctrines of Paul, while largely foreign to mainstream Judaism, found their closest antecedents in the *Hodayot*; and that consequently, Pauline Christianity most closely resembles the fringe theological purview of the Shammaite fanatics who conspired to murder Christ.

Jesus, on the other hand, like most Jews, identified with the Hillelites[123] who believed atonement would be effected more effectively through *hesed* than animal sacrifice, aspiring to "perfection of way as a delectable free

115. Collins J.J and Harlow D.C. 2012, p404.
116. Maston J, 2010, p4
117. Collins J.J and Harlow D.C. 2012, p404
118. Wright N.T, 1997, p26
119. Sprinkle P.2013, p202 & p248.
120. Gruber E.R & Kersten H,1995, p208. These scholars suggest that the extremists were not Essenes but belonged to a radical group within the Qumran community which some Essenes were a part of.
121. Wright N.T.1997, p27-8. See also Jastrow M & Mendelsohn S, 2002 op cit; & Ilan T, 1999, p74
122. Auvinen V 2003, p226-228.
123. Beckstrom E.A. 2013, p175.

will offering."[124] In fact it was not faith and ritual but charity, justice and other *hesed* related principles that were prominent in Second Temple texts and rabbinic sources and by the first century, these were even being codified into sacred law.[125] Accordingly *hesed* became the dominant ethos after 70 CE with the emergence of Rabinnic Judaism under the leadership of Yohanan ben Zakkai.[126]

Hillel himself was strongly influenced by the Book of Sirach where his cherished Golden Rule, underpinning *hesed*, was first expounded.[127] Sirach epitomized the polar opposite of the *Hodayot* in regarding 'works righteousness', and specifically *hesed* reciprocity, as the only sure means of salvation.[128] The Gospel record of Christ's teachings are replete with allusions to the Book of Sirach. They feature in Beatitudes and Sermon on the Mount, the Magnificat (Lk1:52) and various other statements of Christ (Mt 7:16–20 &11:28; Mk 4:5 & 16–17).[129] Renowned scholar Henry Chadwick is convinced that Jesus directly paraphrased Sirach in his ancillary statement to the Lord's Prayer (Mt 6:11),[130] where he affirmed the crucial soteriological role of human forgiveness, human agency, as prerequisite for *hesed*.

Sirach strongly upheld the basic principle of free will as did (and still do) the vast majority of Jews.[131] The key point that many Christians seem determined to gloss over, is that Judaism has never had any real concept of the 'bondage' of the will due to Adam's sin, a bondage that is in fact contradicted by Genesis itself. Soon after Adam's sin supposedly enslaved humanity, God orders Cain to "master" his base instincts (Gen 4:6–7); and in Deuteronomy 30:14, Moses affirms the abundant capacity of humans to obey God's commandments. Amazingly, Paul deliberately distorted the latter. In an "unparalleled" attempt at biblical manipulation, he totally erased Moses' ringing endorsement of free will and inserted his own version

---

124. Murphy F.J. 2010, p194–5. Also Buxbaum Y, 2004, p142; & Falk, H, 1990, p347.

125. Garcia J. 2015, p20–22.

126. Nunnally W.E. 2012, p299.

127. Olar J.L. 2001. *Ecclesiasticus: the Wisdom of Ben Sirach*. Sirach may have first expounded the Golden Rule in Judaism, though it can be found in other ancient traditions like Buddhism and Confucianiam.

128. Birmingham M. 2000, p510.

129. Olar J.L.2001, op cit.; & Marshall T. 2010. *Sirach: About a Biblical Book Rejected by the Reformation*.

130. Chadwick H.2000, p28. Also Falk 1990, p347.

131. Eskola T.1997, p404.

(Rom10:8)—which has Moses advocating reliance on faith.[132] Paul was indeed the progenitor of Christian bad faith in more ways than one.

Predestination was the logical extension of all faith/grace doctrines and Paul seems to have clearly understood that (Eph 1:3–6,11. Rom 8:28–30 & 9:18–22). Augustine, Calvin and others forged Paul's original sin doctrines into full blown predestination,[133] a pernicious doctrine that trashes the 'dignity of man', made in the image of God. Humanity is reduced to a 'walking shadow', the mere plaything of a deity that we could only honestly relate to as capricious and sadistic. Though Paul and even Augustine may have accepted the theoretical possibility of free will, their insistence that every human being was at the mercy of God's grace, effectively negated it. Christian diehards regard this contradiction, this nihilism, yet another 'mystery', the default switch they constantly throw to paper over the myriad anomalies embedded in their shoddy theology of faith.

The case against Pauline Christianity is really quite overwhelming. The humanism latent in Judaic tradition and patent in the teachings of Jesus, is completely at variance with Wright's grand scheme of Israel longing to be liberated from its "enslavement to evil."[134] Indeed, the small minority of Jews who inclined to such a view, were none other than Christ's mortal enemies. The intensely positive and life affirming mission of Jesus is not the stamp of one who had despaired of human nature and become resigned to placing all hope in divine grace. Jesus affirmed the basic goodness of people as manifest in the humility and innocence of children (Mt 18:10,19:14), to whom the Kingdom of Heaven belonged (Mt 19:4). He challenged us to aspire to perfection through *hesed* (Mt 5:48 &Lk 6:36), hardly the sentiments of an 'anthropomorphic pessimist'.

Pauline faith is simply bad faith, backed up with two thousand years of convoluted theology and intellectual posturing on which Christian stakeholders continue to rely to prop up their faltering credibility. Common sense reality and historical reality is ignored. As repeatedly stressed, if Christ's purpose was to instil faith in his sacrificial persona as the sine qua non of salvation, he would have surely expatiated on that point in a similar way to which Paul did. Yet he said nothing that can be clearly construed

---

132. Singer T. *Does Judaism believe in original sin?*

133. This is referred to as 'strong predestination' meaning that people are preordained not just for heaven but also for damnation.

134. Borg M.J &Wright N.T.1997, p104.

as such and instead, constantly pointed away from himself to God.[135] The stark reality that Christians need to accept is that the Jesus of the Gospels, the Jesus that instructed James and the Apostles, is a very different entity to Paul's protagonist. As P Ingram observes, the Gospels contain no passages that "explicitly assert the ontological necessity of faith in Jesus as the Christ, for salvation."[136] They do however proclaim with fidelity and repetitive consistency, the ontological necessity of *hesed*.

So Jesus can easily be perceived as a humanist—yet some may still object to that label. Humanism cannot readily assimilate belief in an interventionist God who was "Lord of heaven and earth" as Jesus did (Mt 11:25). Therefore Christ's assurance that God will respond to our supplications, when he so often does not, needs to be explained. That will be undertaken in Chapter Five; but first there is an even bigger problem for any prospective Christian humanist: how can Christ's devotion to an omnipotent and loving God be reconciled with his tarnished creation, a world so afflicted with appalling suffering and evil? As beautiful as the idea of *hesed* may be, it begs the question as to why the presence of this suffering made *hesed* so necessary in the first place.

Such matters tend to move beyond historical and biblical analysis and into the realm of philosophical theorizing. However, working within the same scriptural parameters of Jesus, it is very possible to construct a humanist version of Genesis that is at least as plausible as the traditional understanding yet infinitely more congruent with the mission of Jesus presented here. What follows is a novel proposition, one of an omnipotent God who, by both choice and necessity, opted to play a very limited role in our affairs. It is a hypothesis that could go some way towards resolving the problem of theodicy, of reconciling a good God with evil in his creation. At the same time it may also provide a plausible explanation of just exactly who the humanist Jesus was—and the ultimate purpose of our existence.

---

135. Borg M, 1995, p29.
136. Ingram P.O, 2006, p 44.

4

Jesus Reveals the Purpose of Human Existence: Spiritual Evolution

> The problem of evil is the central point where philosophy begins, and threatens to stop. The experience of inexplicable suffering and basest injustice, forces us to ask whether our lives have meaning, or whether human existence may be deeply incomprehensible.[1]
>
> SUSAN NEIMAN

THE ENTIRE HISTORY OF humanity has been a struggle of survival against hostile and malign forces, both natural and man-made. For most people, most of this time, life has been "solitary, poor, nasty, brutish and short."[2] Despite great improvements in the past few centuries, this continues to be the case for countless millions of people. The need to respond to this calamity with compassion would fully account for Christ nominating *hesed* as the central purpose of our lives. But if *hesed* were to become the 'gold standard' of humanism then the torment it aims to mollify must be reconciled with the loving Creator who Christ claimed to represent.

This theodicy dilemma has been recognized as "the underlying problem in all theology"[3] and Christians have long struggled, in vain, to provide

---

1. Neiman S, 2016. *The Rationality of the World: A Philosophical Reading of the Book of Job.*
2. Hobbes T. *The Leviathan,* ch 13.
3. *The Catholic Encyclopedia,* Volume XIV.

Jesus Reveals the Purpose of Human Existence

any satisfactory answer. St Paul interpreted the Old Testament Book of Genesis as placing the blame on Adam's original sin of disobedience and the temptations of 'the devil', without ever addressing the basic question as to why God would have created a world in which evil and sin could possibly exist in the first place. The Book of Job grappled with the issue and suggested that God as the imperious *YHWH*, was prepared to expose humanity to horrendous suffering by making a rather reckless bet with Satan that even in the face of dire evil and suffering, humanity would remain faithful to Him and preserve its basic goodness (Job 1:6–12). Elsewhere in the Old Testament *YHWH* is implicated in monstrous acts of genocide (1 Sam 15:2–3)[4] which, even read figuratively, can scarcely be reconciled with an all loving God and a book that purports to be 'holy'. In fact, it is amazing that profanities like these were not excised from the bible long ago as the rantings of a crackpot. Taken on face value—as Christian fundamentalists do—such episodes render much of the bible as obscene and blasphemous.

This *YHWH* is often quite distinct from the merciful, just and loving God of Jesus, the God who affirmed the priority of *hesed* in Hosea 6:6, the stern, but absolutely just (Jn 5:30) God of the Jewish prophets, whose abundant love could surely not create a world with such torment and grief. It is hardly surprising that gnostic Jews and Christians concluded *YHWH* was not the supreme God Jesus called *Abba* (papa). But if not God, then who was *YHWH* and how did so much hate and anguish enter the world? Conventional Christians are content to shrug off these enigmas as yet another 'mystery'. But the humanist version of Christianity presented here demands some kind of plausible explanation. What now follows is an attempt to provide one. It proceeds from the very opening lines of the Bible, the first chapters of the book of Genesis, where *Elohim* not *YHWH*, is the Creator of our universe.

---

4. YHWH in the scriptures is frequently implicated with heinous crimes—see for example Genesis 19, Numbers 31 and Judges19: 23–28.

BAD FAITH

GOD IS ELOHIM, ADAM IS YHWH—AND JESUS

> The story of the banishment from Eden is in truth, the story of how the human race gained its freedom.[5]
>
> FOURTH CENTURY BRITISH MONK, PELAGIUS.

The Christian humanism advanced in this book of course grounds itself in evolutionary science and rejects 'creationist' scenarios as infantile. It accepts the scientific evidence that the universe emerged some 12–14 billion years ago and regards the Genesis story in the bible as purely allegorical. However if that allegory is to have any significance beyond a fairy-tale and if it is assumed to have had a divine source, it would have to contain some revelations about the nature and purpose of creation. On those assumptions, the following hypothesis may be considered.

The creation story occupies the first four chapters of Genesis, but scholars agree it was actually written as two separate accounts, representing the divinations of two distinct authors.[6] The first of these wrote the opening chapter and the first three verses of Chapter two. There God appears as *Elohim* and while he creates the world and humanity, he does so from afar, a mystical 'hovering' light, shaping the world with his measured logos, yet detached from it like a craftsman reviewing his handiwork.[7] The world he creates is said to be entirely 'good', which in biblical terminology, is usually taken to mean 'perfect', totally free of evil.[8] From Genesis 2:4, however, a different storyteller takes over. God becomes *YHWH—Elohim* or simply *YHWH*, and the change is dramatic. Now the deity is decidedly anthropomorphic, male, heavily involved in his creation, very much 'hands on' in moulding Adam from the dust and immediately intervening in human history, making threats and demanding his instructions be obeyed.[9]

This *YHWH* soon emerges as distinctly fallible and injudicious, almost as if learning 'on the job'. As an early Christian Gnosticbishop put it, he is "inconsistent...lacking in foresight...as if he either censured

---

5. Boyce J, 2014, p15.
6. Good E.M, 2011, p31.
7. Armstrong K, 2011, p.12.
8. Sarfati J.D, 2013. *Was God's finished creation perfect?*
9. Hamilton V.P, 1990, p153.

Jesus Reveals the Purpose of Human Existence

his own past judgements, or could not forecast his future ones."[10] *Elohim's* androgynous *adam* (human) now becomes a male Adam and *YHWH* tries to match him up with a partner from the animal world. Discovering Adam is not into bestiality, *YHWH* finally casts Eve from Adam's rib, implying her subordination to him.[11] *YHWH* then issues an overtly ludicrous instruction to these first humans that they must not seek wisdom by eating from the 'tree of knowledge', or they will suffer death. When they disobey him and opt for knowledge and wisdom, he angrily evicts them from their earthly paradise into a world of mortality, travail and tribulation. For that rebellious 'sin of disobedience', Christian doctrine, starting with Paul, holds all humanity responsible and worthy of perdition.

Atheists and humanists have a field day here, ridiculing Judaism and Christianity for embracing a god that is manifestly inadequate, prizes ignorance and is prone to petulance. But a more lucid reading of Genesis would draw a distinction between *Elohim* and *YHWH* and have the first human freely making the choice for mortal life.

In Chapter 1, God (*Elohim*) created man and woman simultaneously, both combined in the androgynous *adam* (Gen 1:27). This *adam* was created in the image of God, as a prototype of humanity and placed in Eden, the prototype of a perfect world (Gen 1:27–31). The Kabbalah refers to *adam* as *Adam Kadmon* (the Supreme Man), the human endowed with the *sefirot* or ten divine attributes, the most dominant of which was *hesed*.[12]

In Chapter 2, despite the different *YHWH* scenario, two salient factors remain constant: firstly, *adam* had been given the ability to act independently of the Creator by virtue of free will; and secondly, *adam* is told that dire consequences will ensue if he/she chooses to 'eat the forbidden fruit'. This is generally understood as God testing *adam's* obedience, threatening punishment for non-compliance. But perhaps this should be read not a threat from *YHWH* but a warning from *Elohim*—that eating this fruit from the Tree of Life, seeking full "knowledge of good and evil" (Gen 2:9), would necessitate opting for mortality and the profound suffering that went with it.

---

10. Marcion. Gospel of the Lord.

11. Armstrong K, 2011, p.13–19.

12. The ten *sefirot* are broadly categorized into three cognitive attributes and seven (including *hesed*) that are emotive. *Hesed* was ranked highest as it was seen as the impulse for life itself. See Leiberman S, 2000. *Kabbala #10: Chesed—The World is Built on Kindness*.

Thus *adam* would have confronted a massive existential dilemma: humanity could either continue in the paradisiacal garden of Eden as scions of God, or opt for total freedom which would involve making moral decisions (Gen 2:17).[13] Freedom was indivisible from mortality and its attendant suffering and by choosing this path, *adam* would acquire knowledge of suffering, how to respond to it with compassionate empathy and the sense of liberation arising from that.[14]

These were the bittersweet fruits of the 'tree of knowledge'. The essence of knowledge, of gnosis, was personified as Sophia in ancient Judaism, the Greek goddess of wisdom who Jews tended to conceptualize as the feminine aspect of God;[15] and the essence of Sophia's wisdom was her compassion.[16] But compassion cannot be actualized without suffering—which in turn requires mortality in an imperfect natural world. *Adam*'s choice therefore, was to suspend his/her own celestial existence, opting for mortality and the freedom and purest experience of love (Jn 15:13)[17] that went with it.

So, it may have been that *adam*, driven by a longing to emulate God and experience this compassionate love, freely and bravely took up the challenge. As Pelagius observed, *adam* was foregoing paradise to experience real freedom, individual responsibility and full knowledge of transcendent love. God presumably anticipated *adam*'s decision and the world of suffering that it would unleash. God's warning about the 'forbidden fruit' can be taken as an attempt to dissuade *adam* from that course. But God could hardly have compelled *adam* not to take it, not to seek ultimate wisdom and freedom. Having given *adam* free will, such an intervention would have immediately nullified it. It could be argued that foreseeing the horrific evils that were unleashed by *adam*'s choice, God should not have created *adam* in the first place. But such a decision would have been simply life negating. Most people who bring children into this world, do so in full knowledge of the horror of death and worse. It would be fatuous to suggest that God, in whose image we are made, should have acted any differently.

This may still beg the question of natural evil. But once Paradise was lost and mortal life begun, so also was finite, material existence, unleashing

---

13. This free will theodicy was developed by American philosopher Alvin Plantinga, See Plantinga A,1977, Ch 4.
14. Sherwin B.L,2006, p64.
15. Reid L, 2005, p10.
16. Borg M,1995, p.103 &106.
17. Lewis H, 2017. Lenten Refeflections 5: *Compassion as integrative love-force.*

Jesus Reveals the Purpose of Human Existence

titanic natural forces that were bound to collide and compete in accordance with the law of natural selection. The suffering inherent in mortal life could hardly transpire in a perfect natural environment and would need to reflect a parallel instability and unpredictability in nature.

Perhaps the primal decision for mortal life was also inexorable. God's gift of free will can be seen as a validation of liberty as a core universal human principle. There may have also been a kind of cosmic imperative for God's love to find expression through the creation of human children. Mortality may have been the only way to express the plenitude of divine love, a fullness that could only be realized in contrast to its opposite. Like the necessity of darkness for the existence of light, compassion would require a backdrop of suffering. The creation of life in all its forms, including mortal, may have been be a primal, existential necessity; and in a monist universe, God would be inseparable from that natural order. Thus, the theodicy problem could also be approached in terms of primal necessity, inexorability.

Jesus seems to have shed further light on these Genesis issues in his intriguing Parable of the Tares (Mt 13:24-43). Conventional Christianity has interpreted the parable as a trite allegory of how there are faithful and faithless people who cannot be differentiated until God makes his final judgment. Augustine used the parable to justify his morally invisible church in which the saved and the damned were indistinguishable.[18] In this he completely ignored Christ's demand that his followers should be "the world's light ... (for) ... all to see" (Mt 5:14 LBE). Similarly Augstine, and subsequent generations of Christians, glibly ignored Matthew's portentous claim that the parable actually reveals "mysteries hidden since the creation of the world" (Mt 13:35)—and that would link it directly to Genesis.

In the parable, Jesus declares that he, as the 'Son of Man' (*ben-adam*),[19] propagated the human race by sowing 'good seed'. However the goodness soon became tainted by evil while 'men' were "asleep" and evil ('the devil') entered the world. This account would be consistent with *adam*, not God, initiating mortal life and carry the strong implication that Jesus and *adam* were one and the same. In being 'asleep', it may be surmised that *adam* was not fully aware of the ramifications of his/her decision and perhaps, of the diabolical levels evil could reach. For evil would not be just the pain of death itself, but the product of a more insidious ego assertion unleashed

---

18. McGrath A.E, 2011, p412-413.
19. Tverberg L, 2001. *Why did Jesus Call Himself the "Son of Man?*

by the primal impulse of self-preservation. The parable then seems to infer that life is essentially a process of spiritual evolution, either towards God as the 'wheat' (ego transcendence) or away from him as the 'tares' (ego gratification).

The titles given to Jesus now begin to make more sense. Just as *adam* was created by God as "the son of God," so also Jesus, as an incarnation of *adam*, would be the 'the son of *adam*'—and thus, both the son of Man and the son of God. Scripture provides solid support for this proposition. Many scholars and indeed, most Christians, believe Jesus regarded himself as the mystical 'Son of Man' figure that appears in the book of Daniel, the 'One like a Son of Man' to whom God assigned dominion over the entire world (Dan 7:12–14) as well as making him the eschatological judge.[20] Since God (as *Elohim*) had also assigned "dominion over . . . every living thing on earth" to *adam* (Gen 1:29–30), it is logical to conclude that adam and Jesus are one and the same. The books of Sirach and the Wisdom of Solomon[21] both link the phrase 'Son of Man' with Adam[22] and both these apocryphal sources are repeatedly cited by Jesus in the Gospels.[23] Furthermore, Luke's Gospel establishes Christ's origins as both the 'Son of Adam' and the Son of God (Lk 3:38).

It is also significant that apart from Jesus, only two other individuals in the bible are referred to as the Son of God. One was Melchizedek, a mystical priest in Genesis who is generally regarded as a Jesus-like figure. The other is Adam himself.[24] There are in fact multiple biblical assertions that Melchizedek, Jesus and Adam were incarnations of each other.[25] Melchizedek is a melding of the Hebrew words *melek* (king) and *chesed*, which makes Melchizedek, like Jesus, the sovereign embodiment of *hesed*.[26] Moreover, the Ebonites, heirs to James and the original Apostles directly

---

20. Henceforth, the masculine pronoun will generally be applied to the androgynous adam, but purely for convenience sake. Jesus was constrained by the sexist attitudes of his time to use 'Son' language of the Scriptures and it would be unnecessarily confusing to not follow suit here.

21. These are two of seven 'wisdom books' the Hebrew Bible, written as late as the second and first centuries BCE.

22. Freeman C.A, 2009, p257.

23. Ruscillo L, 2007. *The Primacy of Christ and Wisdom Literature.*

24. Williams K, 2014. *Jesus as the Reincarnation of Adam*; & Zavada J. *Melchizedek— Priest of God Most High.*

25. Millett M.G, 2015. *Reincarnation and Christianity.*

26. Jett D, 2015, p5.

instructed by Jesus,[27] also perceived Jesus as Adam.[28] St Paul called Jesus the 'new Adam'(1 Cor 15:45) but he may have been more accurate in identifying him as the original *adam*, or if he had Kabbalistic knowledge, *Adam Kadmon*.

Thus, Jesus as *adam* emerges as both 'the son of Man' and 'the Son of God' and it is possible to complete the triangle by also identifying him closely with the Holy Spirit, who Jesus reified as *hesed* (Lk 4:18–19).[29] The Holy Spirit was also referred to as Sophia who Jews related to as the divine 'womb of the universe' as well as the insightful, creative, compassionate and nurturing life source.[30] Since Jesus identified himself as a child of Sophia (Lk 7:35), he can be regarded as the Son of God, conceived by the Holy Spirit (Sophia) and incarnated as the Son of Man (*ben adam*). That spiritual triad may still be highly speculative but at least it is more logical and comprehendible than the mystifying abstraction of the Trinity. An early Gnostic expressed it thus:

> This is the first thought, his image; she became the womb of everything, for it is she who is prior to them all, the Mother-Father, the first man, the holy Spirit, the thrice-male, the thrice-powerful, the thrice-named androgynous one.[31]

Coming back to earth, it is quite possible to harmonize these divine origins with evolutionary theory. Once *adam* chooses mortality, the 'big bang' occurs and according to the Kabbalah, the *sefirot* (divine attributes) are shattered (*shevira*) in the creation of a physical universe. Adam becomes overseer of the new universe, God is effectively sidelined by deference to free will and evolution takes its course. Following the Kabbalah guidelines, at some point after the emergence of primates, 'sparks'[32] of *adam*'s *sefirot* create the 'missing link', infusing a particular species of primate which becomes *homo sapiens*. Thus, primitive men and women appear, derived from the same 'dust' as the animals, entering the world "clothed … in the skins of animals" (Gen 3:21), but unlike the other animals, possessing a

---

27. Butz J.J, 2005, p16–17.

28. Buck C, 2012, p4.

29. Durland W, 2010, p66.See also Hilton Danan J, 2010. *Do Jews believe in the Holy Spirit?*

30. Borg M, 1995, p103–108.

31. *The Apocryphon of John*.

32. In the Kabbalah, sparks are elements of the *sefirot* that remain enmeshed in earthly matter after the *shevira*.

vague awareness of God, self-conscious, embarrassed by nakedness and fearful of their mortal vulnerability (Gen 3:7). *Adam* as a demiurge, must now oversee this new humanity, acutely aware of a sacred responsibility to guide humans towards their spiritual destiny, without impinging on their autonomous free will.

But beginning with Cain, some of his human creatures degenerate into savagery and this called for a limited intervention in their affairs. Initially, according to the bible, *YHWH* did so frequently and quite overtly, threatening and rewarding and ultimately choosing the Jews as a vehicle for his reformist project. The Jews naturally related to him as God, gave him the name *YHWH* and worshiped him in sacrificial rituals. With the moral state of humanity remaining precarious, he eventually incarnated as Jesus (and perhaps as earlier luminaries like Melchizedek and the Buddha); but because the ancient world was intensely patriarchal, the androgynous *adam* was always obliged to incarnate as a man to have any credibility in promulgating his higher ethical system based on *hesed*.

Thus it is proposed that *adam*, *YHWH* and Jesus were one and the same. The name 'Jesus' itself means '*YHWH* saves' or '*YHWH* helps'.[33] In Exodus where *YHWH* first introduces himself to the Jews, he tells them that this name translates as "I am" (Ex 3:14); and in John's gospel, Jesus seems to directly identify himself as *YHWH*, stating "before Abraham was, I am" (Jn.8:58).[34] It is thus no great leap to conclude that Jesus was presenting himself as *YHWH*, the primordial *adam*. As the Son of Man he equated himself not with God but with the semi divine entity in the book of Daniel. However given his human limitations, Jesus may have had only an imprecise understanding of this identity.[35]

The need for *adam*/*YHWH* (*a*/*Y*) to incarnate as Jesus was very real. Evil had become palpable after Cain murdered his brother Able in a jealous rage, sparked by the maladroit *a*/*Y* himself who favoured Abel's sacrificial offering. Firstly *a*/*Y* tried punishment, even attempting to start over with the legendary flood. Eventually he selected the Jews to become a moral exemplar for all humanity and he formed a covenantal relationship with them, based on the principle of *hesed*—that God's steadfast, merciful empathy must be reflected in the social interactions of humanity. But the Jews

---

33. Boxall I, 2014, p19.

34. Hamblin W, 2011, p9.

35. Reincarnation is often understood as preceded by the soul passing through a 'sea of forgetfulness'. See Grof S, 1998, p162; also Davidson J, 1995, p440–442.

JESUS REVEALS THE PURPOSE OF HUMAN EXISTENCE

naturally assume *a/Y* is dictatorial like all the traditional gods and thus they both worship and fear him, ascribing all their actions, from loving kindness to violent retribution, to fulfilment of his will. Such misconceptions probably explain the biblical accounts of *YHWH*'s genocidal brutality. If so, they might be read as a projection of the atrocities of mere mortals onto their god. *a/Y* may have been on a steep learning curve, but hopefully not that steep otherwise all his moral and spiritual credibility would be shredded.

Thus it may be assumed that *adam* needed some time to digest the fruit from the tree of knowledge because as *YHWH*, he was certainly far short of being an omnipotent demiurge.[36] Perhaps by the time he incarnated as Jesus, he had attained a more mature wisdom, a view held by at least one noted theologian.[37] The early moral inconsistency of *YHWH* may also explain why Jews in antiquity so often strayed from their avowed monotheism.[38] Indeed, the Hebrew word for Israel can be translated as "one who struggles with God."[39] Ultimately, this gave rise to the Christian gnostic observation that *YHWH* was a lesser god, an inferior demiurge who actually created this flawed world while the supreme God was "enthroned in unapproachable distance."[40] That tends to accord with both the schema presented here as well as the Kabbalah.[41]

But Gnosticism went in another direction. It did not see any divine 'sparks' in the physical world, only corruption and degradation. Such anthropomorphic pessimism made Paul a Gnostic icon[42] and in Gnostic contempt for the Jewish god *YHWH*, can be found some of the earliest seeds of Christian anti-Semitism.

Jesus was probably familiar with the Jewish mysticism of the Kabbalah.[43] In fact some recent studies provide strong evidence that he was well versed in its ancient wisdom.[44] A detailed investigation of that is beyond the scope of this work, but it is interesting to note that of the Kabbalah's

---

36. Armstrong K, 2011, p.13.Also Pagels 1979, p78–9.
37. Nolan A, 1991, p137.
38. Good E.M, 2011, p44; & Armstrong K, 2011, p10–11.
39. Armstrong K, 2011, p4.
40. Jacobs J & Blau L. *Gnosticism*.
41. Theosopedia: *Jehova*.
42. Pagels E, 1992, p1ff.
43. Simmans G, 2007, p164–167. Also Keizer L, 2010, op cit, p9–11.
44. Westerman P.A, 2017. *Jesus & Kabbalah: The Hidden Treasure*. See also Keizer L,2010, op cit.

seven *sefirot*, the greatest was *hesed* because its loving kindness was regarded as the divine impulse that initiated all life[45] and enshrined its basic purpose.[46] For Jesus, *hesed* also sustained life and had the potential to realize its plenitude (Jn 10:10). It was the key to having life in abundance and, as the Parable of the Tares indicated, growing to spiritual fruition by the time of the 'final harvest'.

But a/Y had only faltering success in implanting *hesed* and the prophets constantly lamented human deficiency. Thus, a/Y may have decided to make one last, dramatic attempt to instil *hesed* by becoming its living exemplar, a *hasid* par excellence, in the person of Jesus. Yet evidently it would not suffice to simply teach and exemplify *hesed* as the prophets and *hasidim* had done—he would have to lay down his life in the process of doing so. There are several reasons why he may have resolved on that course.

Firstly, it would be natural that a/Y felt constrained to undergo the worst of human suffering himself. Having initiated a world where suffering was so intense and pervasive, he may have felt it was incumbent on him as the Son of Man, to partake of it; and the agony of his crucifixion would affirm his (and God's) solidarity with our mortal predicament.

Secondly, he might have realized a dramatic act was needed to capture the essence of *hesed*, 'writing it on the heart' (Jer 31:33) and imprinting it on the human psyche. A purely didactic campaign had had only limited impact as the ancient prophets discovered. Since *hesed* was an inherently spiritual disposition, it had to be properly absorbed over a longer term and within a soteriological framework. Christ's life amply demonstrated the sublime beauty of *hesed*; but that, and even the miracles associated with practicing it, were barely enough to convince his disciples 'of little faith' and thus per se, would be unlikely to impregnate and illuminate the human soul. A more dramatic illustration would be necessary.

Thirdly, Jesus' mode of teaching was basically to contrast a virtue with its antithesis. Thus he taught the full ramifications of *hesed* by juxtaposing it with its antithesis, the Temple ethos; and since he presented his life as a lesson in *hesed* mercy, a merciless death would serve to illustrate its opposite and drive the point home. Moreover, the social justice imperative of *hesed* also required that he expose those who were the source of the injustice; and that would have accelerated his collision course with the Temple elites which could only have had one outcome: heroic martyrdom. In these

---

45. Leiberman S, 2000. *Kabbala #10: Chesed—The World is Built on Kindness.*
46. Miller M, 2012. *Chesed, Gevurah, & Tiferet.*

respects, his twisted body on the cross would be an enduring testament of *hesed*, the ultimate expression of divine love, justice and solidarity.

But his death would not be in vain. He had repeatedly urged his disciples to adopt a constructive attitude to suffering, taking it as an opportunity to produce "bountiful harvests" of compassion and justice and thereby "demonstrate the glory of God" (Jn 15:8 & 11:4). His resurrection would soon affirm this as the ultimate vindication of his suffering, sealing the inevitable triumph of compassionate love and the indomitable human spirit, in the midst of abject horror and despair.

All this may be conjectural but it surely carries more moral cogency, rationality and positivity than the traditional Christian ontology. It provides a sound philosophical underpinning for Christian humanism because it makes us the masters of our own destiny. It implies that while humanity has no 'original sin' that needs atoning, our thrusting egos give us dangerous propensity to ignore or disengage from the suffering of our brothers and sisters. The crucified Christ serves as a constant reminder of our responsibility as empathetic human beings, made in the image of God. From the murder of Able, the whole sweep of human history demonstrates how easily evil can spiral out of control and take us to the depths of depravity. Christianity itself has too often been caught up in that spiral, perpetrating a multitude of crimes that would scarcely be conceivable had it been attuned to the sublime humanism of Jesus that is unpackaged here.

ONE LIFE IS NOT ENOUGH: JESUS AND REINCARNATION

> But when you see your images that came into being before you and that neither die nor become visible, how much you will have to bear!
>
> JESUS IN GOSPEL OF THOMAS: 84

The Parable of the Tares makes it very clear—as do the repeated warnings of Jesus throughout his mission—that failure to exercise the responsibilities of *hesed* could result in spiritual regression and even perdition. The Tares Parable clearly envisages the human spiritual journey as a protracted process, one that can go in either direction, and one that will continue to the 'final harvest' at the end of time. But few if any complete such a journey in a single lifetime. Clearly more than one lifetime would be needed for any final judgment to be "absolutely fair and just" (Jn 5:30 LBE) because so many people have been born into life situations where genuine free will requiring informed, rational discernment, would be scarcely possible.

Human reincarnation thus becomes essential for imparting any basic justice, rationality, and purpose to our existence, past, present and future. Yet there is an inordinate resistance to the notion of reincarnation—and Christ's evident endorsement of it—from traditional Christian theologians and Jesus scholars in general. Both, however, may need to reconsider their positions.

In their book The Original Jesus, German scholars E Gruber and H Kersten present a strong case that reincarnation was just one of a number of Buddhist ideas that had seeped into the Eastern Mediterranean world and become well entrenched by the first century. They reveal how the parallels between the life and teachings of Jesus and the Buddha are quite extraordinary. Like Jesus in his Judaic context, the Buddha struggled against a religious elite of Brahmin priests who exploited sacrificial ritual and the stigmas of the Hindu caste system to enhance their own status.[47] Just as Jesus initially followed the ascetic John the Baptist, the Buddha adopted as his mentor Rudraka, also an ascetic penitent. Both spiritual masters eventually moved away from these lesser lights though not before co-opting some of their followers. Both then meditated in solitude, rejecting temptations of the devil—their ego desires—before starting their missions. Both multiplied the loaves and fed the multitudes, walked on water and had to rescue disciples who tried to copy them.[48] The parallels are striking and do not end there.

These concurrences between Christ and the Buddha have been known for some time and de facto suppression of them might be added to Christianity's bulging catalogue of bad faith. They go well beyond coincidence or Jungian archetypes[49] and there are really only two possible explanations: either these stories were plagiarized[50] or Jesus and the Buddha were incar-

---

47. Gruber E.R & Kersten H, 1995, p10 &20.

48. ibid, p121–167.

49. Psychologist Carl Jung identified several basic archetypes or social and cultural patterns of human belief that are universal in place and time.

50. Although Buddha predated Jesus by about 500 years, many of the records of Buddha's life were written during the Common Era, so any copying could have worked either way.

Jesus Reveals the Purpose of Human Existence

nations of the same demiurge, be that *adam/YHWH* or Krishna. The latter would be a tantalizing way of explaining the close alignment of their teachings[51]—which also included a shared awareness of reincarnation.

Buddhist missionaries from India had established a strong influence in the Eastern Mediterranean from around 250 BCE and their core doctrine of reincarnation had been absorbed into orthodox Jewish faith well before the advent of Jesus. Jewish historian Josephus attests that by the first century, reincarnation was largely embraced by the Pharisees[52] and that is certainly evident in the Gospels (Jn 9:34; Mt 11:14). A growing body of scholars now believe that Jesus and James were actually Hillelite Pharisees themselves.[53] Contemporaries of Jesus like Philo of Alexandria and Josephus both endorsed reincarnation.[54] They also affirm that the Essenes, with a faction of whom both John the Baptist and Jesus had close connections,[55] were also devotees of Pythagoras who was a strong believer in reincarnation. Many of the Essenes seem to have been influenced by the Therapeutae, a Jewish monastic sect based in Alexandria which had developed a syncretic fusion of Judaism and eastern spirituality.[56] It may be an indication of these powerful mystic influences that James and the early disciples called themselves 'the Way', the same title used by the Therapeutae.

As befitting their extremist version of Judaism, the Shammaite Pharisees harboured a warped view of reincarnation. Probably like the Brahmins of Buddha's time, they exploited its karmic elements to underpin their self-serving culture of guilt. Christ's disciples were undoubtedly mindful of this when they asked him if a man who was born blind, was being punished for his sins (Jn 9:1–3), obviously in a previous life. The same karmic assumptions were also evident in the Pharisee's accusation that the man's blindness was the result of him being "born in sin" (Jn 9:32–34). Jesus of course promptly dismissed that vindictive notion and proceeded to cure the man. But he did not challenge the underlying presumption of reincarnation. Given the unavoidable presence of afflictions like blindness in the world, he

---

51. Gruber E.R & Kersten H, 1995, pp.79-167. There is also a good summary by Williams K, 2014. *Jesus as a Reincarnation of* Adam.

52. *Josephus Antiquties*. 15.371-378. See also Davidson J. 1995, p416.

53. Butz, J.J, 2005, p145.

54. Burke A.G, 2018. *May a Christian Believe in Reincarnation?*

55. McNamer E, 2009.*The First One Hundred Years of Christianity in Jerusalem*. Also Prophet E.C & Prophet E.L, 1997, p83.

56. Gruber E.R & Kersten H, 1995, p191-193.

simply advised his disciples to adopt a positive attitude and, in the spirit of *hesed*, to regard such adversity as an opportunity to respond with compassion and thereby reveal the 'glory' of God's intrinsic nature—his holy spirit of compassion.

Linguistic evidence in the Gospels also supports reincarnation. German scholar Günther Schwarz has extracted much of Christ's native Aramaic dialect from the original Greek language of the Gospels, and concludes that the actual words of Jesus in John 3:3 were: "unless a man is born again and again, he cannot be readmitted into the Kingdom of God."[57] Born again is usually understood in biblical idiom as a metaphor for spiritual awakening. But an epiphany is expected to occur just once. The repetition of 'again' suggests a rather more literal meaning. Similarly in the gospels as well as various apocryphal and Gnostic texts, Jesus uses the metaphor of the human body as a 'prison'. His warning that we will remain in "prison ... until the last penny is paid" (Mt. 5:26) seems to have been borrowed directly from Plato, who described reincarnation in terms of the body being "a prison in which the psyche is incarcerated, kept safe until the price is paid."[58] The Gnostic gospels of course are replete with Jesus references to reincarnation, such as the above heading quote from the Gospel of Thomas. It is also a major teaching of the Kabbalah.[59]

Factoring in reincarnation also helps to rationalize otherwise nullifying Gospel passages. EP Sanders for example, cites Jesus' statement that some of his followers would still be alive to witness his second coming (Mt 16:28) as proof that he was a deluded apocalyptic prophet.[60] Yet in the context of reincarnation, the reference to 'being alive' may be readily construed as the last of many reincarnated lives that could extend millennia into the future, right up to the 'final harvest'.

That Christ was not more explicit about reincarnation may also be attributed to him being reluctant to challenge the prevailing mania about the immanent end days and arrival of a Messiah. But reincarnation was a widely embraced tenet of both early Judaism and Christianity and remained so for hundreds of years.[61] Early Church proponents of reincarnation include Justin Martyr, Clement of Alexandria, St Gregory of Nyssa and even

---

57. ibid, p90–91.
58. Freke T & Gandy P, 2002, p164.
59. Dubov N.D, 2009. *Reincarnation*.
60. Sanders E.P, 1993, p178.
61. Burke G, 2016. *May a Christian Believe in Reincarnation?*

Jesus Reveals the Purpose of Human Existence

Augustine.[62] Origen of Alexandria, the 3rd century theologian described as "the greatest teacher of the early Church after the Apostles,"[63] almost certainly believed in reincarnation and that was the first charge (anathema) laid against him in his heresy trial.[64] This took place a few centuries after his death at the instigation of Emperor Justinian and took the form of a star-chamber tribunal. It was stacked with Eastern bishops with the aim of branding Origen and his doctrines heretical,[65] no doubt reflecting their concern that reincarnation might impinge on the self-ordained authority of the church to broker the eternal fate of its followers.

Just as the message of Jesus was predicated on reincarnation, his ultimate goal was also similar to that of the Buddha. Everyone must achieve redemption through their own efforts by targeting higher levels of spiritual enlightenment.[66] As the Parable of the Tares implies, evil will remain an inexorable part of life for that spiritual growth to proceed over aeons until the 'final harvest' takes place at "the appointed time" (Mt 8:29). Each lifetime is vital to either advancing or retarding that process and must not be wasted (Mt 24:45–51). For both the Buddha and Jesus, it meant becoming constantly mindful of human suffering and responding with compassion. In John's Gospel, there are echoes of Buddha's 'unitary consciousness'.[67] There Jesus speaks of the ultimate goal for humanity to grow to spiritual maturity in a virtually organic relationship with each other and God,[68] "the glorious unity of being one" (Jn 17:22), like the branches of a productive vine that bear the abundant fruits of God's compassionate love. The essence of that unity was 'knowing' God through *hesed*, as Jesus commanded in endorsing Hosea 6:6.

It is about time Christians took a closer look at reincarnation; and while doing so, they might also like to consider the numerous, well-documented accounts of memories of previous lives recovered through clinical

---

62. Dubay E,2017. *The Truth About Reincarnation.*
63. Oderberg I. 1973. *Reincarnation as Taught by Early Christians.*
64. Davidson J, 1995, p421–424.
65. Semkiw W. *Reincarnation, Jesus, the Bible, New Testament & Christian Doctrine.*
66. Gruber E.R and Kersten H, 1995, p 126.
67. Pagels E, 2003, p49–53 & p74–5.
68. Buddha did not factor any divinity into this though some Buddhists believe a unitary consciousness implies the existence of a godhead. See Hick J, 2006, p98.

hypnosis.[69] The late Dr Elisabeth Kübler-Ross, a noted psychiatrist who specialised in counselling terminally ill patients, became convinced of reincarnation through myriad accounts of near death experiences. Common to all these was the notion of human advancement, an acute realisation of "what could have been ... that all your life on earth was nothing but a school that you had to go through in order to pass certain tests and learn special lessons."[70]

Despite the strong evidence for reincarnation as integral to Christ's teachings, there is a stubborn resistance to it in Western theological discourse, an unwarranted presumption that it is somehow more fanciful than Christian eschatology. Though scenarios vary between sects, the preferred Christian schema seems to be that we hang around in some kind of limbo for millennia awaiting the final judgment day. Then we are reclad in our old, restored bodies prior to judgment, like a man who dons a suit for a court appearance. Is that more or less sensible and rational than reincarnation?

Reincarnation and spiritual evolution are key pieces in the jigsaw of Christ's humanist message. The Gnostic gospels, the Kabbalah and even the gospel of John are steeped in the kind of mysticism and references to the deeper and obviously longer term spiritual refinement that Christ now projected for humanity.[71] Not just his closest followers, not just Christians, but "every man and woman in all the earth" would eventually have to target the higher ethical and spiritual principles of *hesed*[72] (Jn 17:2–24 LBE). In the process, they will need to bear their own 'crosses' (Mk 8:34) and ingest the substance and the spirit, the 'flesh and blood' (Jn 6:53) of Christ's compassionate wisdom, in order to steadily progress to a higher form of consciousness. If, and when, that point is reached by many or most of humanity, presumably the 'final harvest' would be at hand. Conversely, if such spiritual growth does not occur, we might expect that harvest to arrive prematurely, possibly in the form of a catastrophic war.

Instead of being daunted by the magnitude of this challenge, we can take a longer term view provided by reincarnation and find solace in Christ's assurance that God generally imposes only 'light burdens' (Mt

---

69. See for example Tucker J, 2005. *Life Before Life*. This is just one of many works that provide strong evidence for reincarnation.

70. Kubler-Ross E, 1991. *On Life After Death*.

71. Pagels E, 2003, p49 & p74.

72. Here Jesus says spiritual redemption is achieved by seeking to 'know' God and as Hosea and the other prophets clearly stated, such knowledge was attained through *hesed*.

11:30) commensurate with our abilities (Lk 12:48). Few will be expected to reach sublime pinnacles of *hesed* virtue and enlightenment, especially in one lifetime. Christ insisted that we all have "tasks assigned to us by [God]" (LBE Jn 9:4). What else could these be other than 'tests' and 'lessons' as Kubler-Ross's patients called them, designed to achieve spiritual enlightenment over a series of reincarnated lifetimes—as Jesus inferred in the Tares Parable.

Human spiritual evolution is clearly in its infancy, if indeed the process has even yet begun. We probably have far to go, but there is no room for complacency. Christ cautions that our cycles of reincarnation require embracing the Holy Spirit of *hesed* (Jn 3:5-8). Presumably, the more we follow this course, the more stimulating and spiritually enriched will be those successive lives as we progress towards ultimate salvation. Conversely, if we prevaricate and remain self-absorbed, stubbornly disinterested in—or worse, hostile to—the vital needs of others, we may even regress towards spiritual darkness.

That may or may not manifest in our temporal situation (Mt 24:42-51). As Christ inferred when asked about the 'sins' of the blind man, our spiritual status may not be reflected in the actual circumstances of our lives. There is no karmic inevitability. He re-affirmed a disturbing message of the Old Testament book of Job that, "rain ... (can fall) on the just and the unjust" (Mt. 5:45), such is the randomness and precariousness inherent in all mortal existence. Our terrestrial lives will always remain a difficult and sometimes agonising 'prison sentence'. Christ's spiritual humanism may give us the best chance of shortening that sentence and taking larger strides towards a higher wisdom and enlightenment; but there are no guarantees of an easy passage.

CHRISTIANS CAN GO TO HELL

> Not all who talk like godly people are godly. At the Judgment many will tell me, 'Lord, Lord, we told others about you ... ' But I will reply ... go away, for your deeds are evil.
>
> MATTHEW 7:21-23(LBE)

Bad Faith

In their desperate quest to staunch a haemorrhaging membership, many Churches have opted for a 'feel good' approach, discounting the possibility of hell and pushing the whole concept of divine justice into the background. But there is no avoiding the fact that Jesus warned of divine retribution and even eternal punishment. As much as he emphasised forgiveness, mercy and the ultimate prospect of being reunited with God, there are stern warnings that even the most ardent biblical revisionists and sanguine optimists, would be unwise to ignore. As the Son of Man, Jesus clearly stated that he would return at 'the end of time' to judge "the sheep and the goats" (Mt 25:32). This may sound harsh and vindictive—and so it would be if Christian theology was correct with divine judgment hinging on religious belief rather than basic decency, and ensuing after just one lifetime.

It is surely one of the most egregious examples of human folly to imagine that God would punish on the basis of religious affiliation or adherence to some abstruse, metaphysical notion or religious dogma. Yet that is what many Christians still believe, even though it would seem contrary to all our instincts of basic justice. It is nonsensical to assume divine justice could be at odds with human justice or life would be played out with a stacked deck. God's judgments, like ours, would necessarily relate to moral behaviour with no guaranteed salvation for serious transgressors—and that includes smug, evangelical Christians (Mt 7:21–23).

Yet the 'free gift' of divine forgiveness is what many Christians now seem to be banking on, having deemed the prospect of hell to be a jarring note in their happy hymn book. As a result, Christianity has become less Voltaire's "bridle to the wicked"[73] and more like a spur to 'prick the side' of wicked intent. Recent sociological research has found a strong correlation between little or no belief in divine punishment and rising crime rates in a wide range of nations and cultures across the globe.[74]

Jesus was very explicit: we will be judged, rewarded or punished (Mt 13:40–43); and that judgement will not on be based on faith beliefs but "deeds" (Mt 16:27)—specifically, those deeds relating to moral actions and particularly *hesed*, the degree of empathy for, or withheld from, "the least of these brothers and sisters of mine" (Mt 25:34–48). Yet Christians still insist on the primacy of faith, believing 'good works' flow from the grace that faith provides and that the divine judge will rely on those works as

---

73. Voltaire, 1768. *Epistle to the Author of the Book, The Three Impostors.*
74. Shariff A.F & Rhemtulla M, 2012. *Divergent Effects of Beliefs in Heaven and Hell on National Crime Rates.*

Jesus Reveals the Purpose of Human Existence

evidence of authentic faith.[75] But not knowing (or particularly caring) that *hesed* must animate and shape those good works, inevitably brings them back to reliance on faith to curry favour with their Creator through 'good deeds'. That diminishes God as a petty moralist while also ensuring a minimal commitment to the wellbeing of others. Neither augers well for our precarious world.

'Faith alone' traditionalists are largely disinterested in transformative social initiatives and even try to obfuscate the clear meaning of Christ's last major statement in Matthew 25. Bible commentator D.A Carson, evidently oblivious to the centrality of *hesed* and the *ptochos* in Christ's mission, blithely construes 'the least of these my brothers' as Christ's evangelical emissaries and the 'sheep' and 'goats' as those who will embrace or reject his 'free gift' of sacrificial redemption.[76] But again, if that were so, why did Christ not simply say that, instead of focusing so much on human compassion? In fact Carson's evangelical slant is really quite perverse. It would exalt the ranks of doorknocking 'god-botherers' and imply certain damnation for millions of Jews and others who have turned away these tiresome proselytizers, leaving in limbo even more millions who might otherwise count themselves lucky for never having encountered them.

It is surely less risible and more ethically sound to take these Matthew verses on face value where the 'brothers' are simply and obviously the *ptochos*, the desperate hordes of impoverished and oppressed humanity. James was condensing Matthew 25 when he said "there will be no mercy for those who have not shown mercy to others. But if you have been merciful, God will be merciful when he judges you" (Jas 2:13). He was also clearly paraphrasing his brother's Lord's Prayer strictures on *hesed* forgiveness (Mt 6:14–15) and underscoring Christ's stern warning in various parables like the unmerciful servants (Mt 18:21–35) and the treacherous Tenants (Mt21:33–44).

However the human tendency to be judgmental can often override mercy and forgiveness, breeding a callousness capable of transitioning anyone into becoming an agent of suffering and evil themselves.[77] Nazi Germany presents a case study in how vindictiveness (in the wake of defeat after World War 1) can set individuals and an entire nation on a slippery slope to perdition. Germans are of course no morally different to anyone

---

75. Wright N. T, 2003. *New Perspectives on Paul.*
76. Carson D.A, 2010, p586; & Osborne G.R. 2010, p934–940.
77. Baron-Cohen S, 2011.*The Science of Evil.*

else and that is why human forgiveness and hesed is so important and faith is so dangerous. When human evil flourishes, it is so often facilitated by the deceptions of ungrounded faith, be it faith in ideology or theology. Take away the smokescreen of faith with its dogmas, 'softly spoken magic spells' and other sundry claptrap, and the clear ethical accountability and human empathy that Jesus demanded, gives the wicked nowhere to hide.

As the creator of our mortal predicament, it could be assumed that Jesus, as *adam/YHWH*, was intensely sympathetic to our plight. He clearly stated his desire that no one "should be lost" (Mt 18:14) and affirmed "every sin . . . will be forgiven men" (Mt 12:31). However there was one sin he assured would never be forgiven, a "sin against the Holy Spirit" of *hesed* (Mk 3:29). Heartless cruelty and cynical contempt for the basic rights of others, will not escape divine justice. 'Feel-good' Christian preference for focusing on Christ's forgiveness, blithely ignores his zero tolerance for this category of sin; and this wilful denial of ugly realities—combined with smug expectations of afterlife rewards—is conducive to the kind of complacency and moral equivalence that has permitted some of the most shameful episodes in Christian history. The amoral complacency of many Christians in the face of clerical child abuse and their persistent lack of empathy for its victims, may well be a consequence of this over indulgent sense of forgiveness.

The vicious religious elites that orchestrated Christ's crucifixion, dwelled in this pit of smug faith entitlement and, having sinned against the Holy Spirit, were destined for damnation (Mt 12:31 & 23:33). Probably they were not inherently evil—it is more likely their faith fixations had allowed them to drift in that direction until their lack of compassion finally caught up with them, opening the floodgates of callousness and ego excess. Christ often used the language of 'Satan' and 'the devil' because that was how most of his followers understood evil. But he probably shared Buddha's perception that evil is not a dualistic externality. As suggested earlier, it arises mainly from the inherent condition of our mortality, what Zen Master Kido Inoue observed as

> the instinct of self-preservation (which) . . . is the life-force that holds the self as absolute and negates others. The horrible will to fight and compete for survival . . . to preserve the self by denying the existence of others, takes charge . . . the basic root of the problem lies within the human mind.[78]

---

78. Kido Inoue. *The Spirit of Buddha*.

This foundational ego drive incites desire, which may be readily seen as the root cause of suffering. The craving to satisfy sensory and illusory appetites—which the Buddha called *dukkha* and *anatta* is ultimately futile as these appetites are insatiable and the pleasures ephemeral. Both Jesus (Mt 18:7–9) and his brother James (Jas 1:14) made similar observations. Jesus equated the self-serving impulses of the human ego with 'Satan' (Mt 12:25–29) and warned that before making judgments or attempting to right wrongs, it was necessary to 'bind' this 'strong man' (Mk 3:27) so that 'Satan' can no longer break back into our private or social domains. The only way to do this was through forgiveness—recognizing the dark impulses within oneself that needed forgiveness and then transferring the same forgiveness to others, thereby evoking *hesed* empathy and facilitating the transmission of God's grace (Mt 18:2–5).

Thus in the Tares Parable, "the devil" is made responsible for human sin and suffering; and like the demon Mara in Buddhist tradition, it can be taken as a metaphor for the constant cravings of the human ego, self-assertion prompted by the basic instinct for self-preservation. It was the prospect of ego gratification that the devil used to tempt Jesus away from his mission (Mt 4:1–11). *YHWH* told Cain that he, as a human being, must use his free will to "master" his dark ego desires (Gen 4:7). The Buddha called for transcendent 'detachment' and Christ expressed the same idea as a paradox: "anyone who holds on to his life shall lose it" (Mt 16:25–26).[79] The psychological and social imbalances generated by ego desire tend to fuel a cycle of destruction and suffering that can ultimately consume both the individual and society, physically and morally if not constantly brought to heel through the humbling process of forgiveness. It is easy to understand the parlous state of our world in this light. The corrective Christ offered was not his sacrificial death. It was the cultivation of *hesed*.

Jesus also foresaw the risk of *hesed* itself becoming corrupted by the ego and degenerating into self-righteous virtue signalling, or 'boasting' as Paul called it (Eph 2:9). Thus, he constantly emphasised the need for child-like humility (Mt 18:2–4), an attitude of serving rather than being served (Mt 20:27–28) and of self-forgetfulness, seeking anonymity and non-recognition in helping others, not letting your "left hand know what your right hand is doing"(Mt 6:1–4).

---

79. In this passage, 'holding on' to life is immediately equated with pursuit of material, sensory pleasure.

Similarly, he was aware of the pitfall of overweened compassion. Throughout the OT, divine justice oscillated between *hesed* and severe judgment and this led to a Kabbalistic understanding of *YHWH* who drew people to him with his right hand (*hesed*) and pushed them away with his left (*geruvah*).[80] Jesus was certainly attuned to that dialectic. His *hesed* urged people to forgive enemies and 'turn the other cheek', but his *geruvah* tempered any forgiveness of the religious leaders who had wilfully and repeatedly sinned 'against the holy spirit'. He especially warned that abuse of children also fell into this category, issuing a threat that should chill the spine of pedophiles and those churchmen who have attempted to shield them (Mk 9:42, Mt18:6, Lk17:2).

Yet it is not for humans to make any ultimate moral judgments and thus Jesus urges us to 'love our enemies' (Mt5:44). For him, love equated to compassion and he asked us to extend compassion even to wrongdoers. That is a constructive approach and often warranted. It is quite natural to feel compassion for those whose lives have spiralled out of control into depravity and are in desperate need of rescue and rehabilitation. It would even be natural to have some pity for child abusers if, as in so many cases, they were themselves abuse victims in their childhood.

But *geruvah* must create a balance and 'turning the other cheek' is not always practical. Christ's pacifism was abundant at the outset of his mission in an atmosphere of trust and goodwill, when, as he put it, "anyone not against us is for us" (Lk 9:50). But as his own deadly enemies circled, there was a distinct shift. Now he would declare that "anyone not helping me is harming me" (Luke 11:23). Initially he sent out his disciples with a staff—later he urged them to carry a sword. The culmination of this tension was his own physical assault on the corrupted Jerusalem Temple.

Jesus did set the bar extremely high in asking us to love our enemies (Mt 5:44), to be prepared to give up all our belongings (Mt 19:21) and "be perfect as your heavenly Father is perfect" (Mt 5: 38-48). But it should be noted that his pedagogic technique often involved overstating a position before qualifying it to allow for the frailties of human nature. In these instances he was projecting ultimate ideals which very few might be capable of realizing, at least at this stage of our evolution. In the interim, we can take solace from Luke's parallel verse to Matthew 5:48, that *hesed* compassion can be an adequate substitute for perfection (Lk 6:36).

---

80. Leiberman S, 2000. *Kabbala #12*.

But Christ's repeated plea for detached forgiveness and enhanced compassion was, and is, largely achievable. It was clarion call of liberation and enlightenment in his time and its necessity can scarcely be overstated today in a world plagued with vindictive and violent hatreds. As the core prerequisite for *hesed*, human forgiveness should have always formed the bedrock of Christian education. But such insightful, wisdom was constantly overshadowed by a theology of metaphysical forgiveness with its attendant dogmatism, ritualistic pedantry, afterlife obsessions and Easter delusions. These doctrinal follies blinded Paul and his successors to a stark reality: that Christ's emphasis on forgiveness stemmed entirely from his abhorrence of an insidious culture of honour and shame that pervaded first century Judaism and the entire Mediterranean world,[81] negating human empathy, fuelling violence and ultimately nailing him to a cross.

The sad irony is that in failing to perceive Christ's enlightened teachings on *hesed* forgiveness, the early church patriarchs contrived a theology of faux forgiveness structured around the sacrificial cross, one that actually established new benchmarks for stigmatizing guilt. It was an illusory guilt based not on human conscience but on human gullibility: self-reproach for our confected 'original sin' and angst about an insufficient faith in the absurd idea of God, in flagrant disregard of his own strictures (Jer 31:30; Deut 24:16), making a blood sacrifice of himself to atone for it.

The simple reality is that Jesus was not offering easy rides to heaven for devout believers, 'cheap grace', as Deitrich Bonhoeffer once called it.[82] He had only 'crosses to bear' (Mt 16:24; Mk 8:34; Lk 9:23) and salvation would ultimately have to be earned, entirely by our own efforts, by keeping our egos in check. It is clear that he was not just assigning this ethical responsibility—these crosses—to his close disciples but to all humanity, as here he was addressing both them "and the crowds" (Mk 8:34).

However the 'crosses' would not necessarily involve extreme levels of suffering and self-sacrifice that he and the early church martyrs had to endure. Salvation would only be achieved by advancing our spiritual evolution through self-denying humility, forgiveness and human empathy. But the key point that Christ constantly stressed was that much will hinge on individual capacity. For the less advantaged and those more heavily afflicted with suffering, he envisaged only 'light burdens' (Mt 11:28–30). A simple

---

81. Crossan J.D,1994,p70.

82. Bonhoeffer was a German theologian who was murdered by the Nazis for opposing Hitler.

act of mercy or kindness may suffice—even merely giving a cup of water to someone who is thirsty (Mk 9:41), or in the case of the crucified thief on Calvary, a mere expression of remorse and empathetic contrition (Lk 23:43). But for those endowed with education, talents, resources and awareness, more will be needed. Christ was quite explicit: "Much is required from those to whom much is given, for their responsibility is greater" (Lk 12:48).

However Jesus was not moralistic. Heaven would not be just a repository for the virtuous—it would make room for sinners as well. The whole point of striving for hesed perfection was not to actually become perfect (or even worthy of God) as much as to reduce the risk of falling captive to the ego and sliding backwards into callous indifference. For 'that way madness lies', threatening our future both here on earth and in the world to come. In that respect, Christ's main purpose in propagating *hesed* was negative, avoiding the insidious tendencies of the human ego.

Nonetheless, Jesus preferred to accentuate the positive, particularly in terms of enhancing our spiritual evolution here on earth. His new moral order was based not on negatives—'thou shalt not'—but positives: love God by loving each other (Mk 12:30–31). This condensed commandment of *hesed*, like a vine pruned for maximum fruit yield (Jn 15:2), was intended to produce positive action, elevate human civilization and forge a new, more humanistic and rational faith that might find some empirical verification in terms of social improvements (Jn 15:5–8). We now turn to how this might transpire in today's world.

5

Christian Humanist Theopraxis

> If enough people lived … in nonviolent protest against systemic evil, against the normalcies of this world's discrimination, exploitation and oppression—the result would be a new world order we could hardly imagine.[1]
>
> J.D CROSSAN.

IT IS THE CENTRAL contention of this book that the only way J.D Crossan's ideal could ever be translated into reality is to jettison the bankrupt theological system on which Christian religion rests and recast it into one based on the spiritual humanism of Jesus. With our world in turmoil and secular humanism in tatters, it is perhaps the only conceivable option for anyone serious about securing a more stable future. So how realistic is such an expectation and what steps can be taken towards realizing it?

Christ's *hesed* strictures do not call for saintly rectitude but nor are they such as to be simply noted and adopted like some lifestyle choice. They would require a steadfast commitment involving spiritual exercises focused on expanding compassionate empathy, disciplines to be practiced on a daily basis. They would need to be embedded in schools and constantly refined with regular communal gatherings to resolve how they should be translated into action.

The prophet Hosea nailed the challenge when he described God lamenting the ephemeral nature of human compassion, "like the morning

---

1. Crossan J.D, 1998, p279.

mist... that disappears" (Hos 6:4-6). Jesus was undoubtedly well aware of this lack of steadfast resolve but he nonetheless insisted that "whoever wants to be my disciple must deny themselves and take up their cross daily and follow me" (Lk 9:23). That command extended to all his followers—get empathetically involved, make deliberate decisions to raise the level of human happiness and act on them to the best of your ability. Evil triumphs when good people do nothing. It is not that the evils are too overwhelming, complex and intractable; the real problem is human emotional transience, a lack of steadfast moral energy.

Genuine empathy, especially if it involves engaging with human suffering, is often daunting and emotionally draining. Many recoil, prevaricate, resort to tokenism, turn to less confronting causes or just fall back on slogans, platitudes, charity and 'band aid' solutions. Those who do embrace the big challenges often experience 'compassion fatigue' or rarely make a significant impact as they do not command enough public support.

Human diffidence and lethargy may explain why Paul's less demanding, 'cheap grace' Christianity became ascendant. Indeed, it is almost possible to imagine Jesus imparting that faith centred alternative to Paul on the road to Damascus, as a desperate attempt to ensure the very survival of his new movement. But today, with so much awareness of and capacity to respond to human suffering, Christians should be more confident and realize that much of it could be ended swiftly if churches shook off their torpid faith, got off their knees and accepted their Christ ordained role of moral leadership.

In formulating a Christian humanist theopraxis, a new set of spiritual exercises would need to be devised to complement and strengthen social and political activism. At the same time, decisions would need to be made about what was no longer relevant; and it is clear that many longstanding practices and assumptions would need some radical overhauling.

CHRIST'S HUMANIZED APPROACH TO WORSHIP, FAITH AND PRAYER

> I loathe, I spurn your festivals, I am not appeased by your solemn assemblies. If you offer Me burnt offering... I will not accept them... Spare Me the sound of your hymns, and let Me not hear

the music of your lutes. But let justice well up like water, righteousness like an unfailing stream . . . says God.

Amos 5:21–27

Jesus was staunchly egalitarian. "You have only one teacher," he declared, "and all of you are equal as brothers." (Mt 23:8 LBE). He authorized Peter, the 'rock', to lead his 'church' after his death (Mt 16:17–20);[2] but this leadership was not set in stone and Christ's brother James actually took over. Jesus may have regarded institutionalized leadership as just another necessary expedient rather than a permanent fixture. His concern was for human empathy and social ethics, not controlling hierarchies.[3] His entire mission was a struggle against those forces, which during his time, as so often before and since, had become corrupted by their own power.

But alas, it did not take long for the Christian churches to become entrenched power structures with hierarchies of clerics, jostling to broker our eternal fate. It is now time to sweep away what remains of these decaying anachronisms along with the religious 'festivals' and 'solemn assemblies' and to focus on fulfilling the priorities of Jesus. He rarely, if ever, engaged in public ritual and there is nothing he ever said or did that could justify the obsession with worship that has always been the hallmark of organized Christianity and religion in general.

Church worship practiced by Christians is a throwback to the Temple sacrifices and primitive concerns about currying the favour of a wrathful God, evincing an obsequious piety that today comes across as both tedious and phoney. From the time of Constantine, the church has appropriated a dogmatic, omniscient God-ordained authority that identified Christ and Christianity with the state and the authoritarian values that go with it. Christians, like their fellow 'people of the Book', have maintained a dogged attachment to an omnipotent, meddling deity who craves our adulation, even though it lumbers them with the theodicy albatross and all its noxious spinoffs.

---

2. Bible.org, 2001.*What did Jesus mean when he said, "Upon this rock I will build my church"?* Despite this appointment. it was Christ's brother James not Peter, who would lead the early church.

3. Crossan J.D, 1994, p100–101.

In a society where messianic expectation was rife, Jesus disappointed many by not fulfilling the traditional role of a Messiah. Though his disciples were convinced he was the Messiah and wanted to worship him, Jesus disparaged this. Instead he washed their feet (Jn 13:1–17) and insisted that "the Son of Man did not come to be served, but to serve"(Mt 20:28). He did not go to the synagogues or the Temple to pray or sacrifice or worship but to teach *hesed* and illustrate it by healing people there (Mt 21:14). It is more than possible that the humanist Jesus regarded worship rituals, like the Temple sacrifices on which they were largely based, as having outlived their relevance. That is certainly the gist of Hosea 6:6. Indeed, he may have even seen sacrificial worship as a form of blasphemy in that it treated God as a kind of pagan deity whose capricious cruelties invited fear and whose inflated ego demanded grovelling adulation and rivers of blood.

Christ was actually quite explicit about how God should be worshipped. The purpose of worship was to glorify God's goodness through faithfulness, 'good deeds' actuated by the hasidic virtues outlined in the Beatitudes (Mt 5:16).[4] He affirmed that this *emunah* would bring "great glory to my Father" (Jn 15:8). In a definitive statement on worship, Jesus told the Samaritan woman: "Yet a time is coming and has now come when the true worshipers will worship the Father in the Spirit and in truth, for they are the kind of worshipers the Father seeks" (Jn 4:23). As previously noted, the 'the phrase "grace and truth" (*hesed e'meth*) is used frequently in the Old Testament to denote the compassionate nature of God;[5] and it was employed by John in his opening chapter to capture the essence of Jesus (Jn 1:17). Now Jesus uses the phrase in talking about worshipping in "the Spirit and truth," having already identified 'the Spirit' as *hesed*. (Mk 3:30; Mt 12:18; 7:15–20 & 12: 26–33; Lk 4:18–19). Worship for Jesus was not ritualistic but humanistic. It meant giving human *hesed* practical expression.

Christ related to God as a child would to its parent, using the intimate term *Abba* (papa), which hardly fits the image of an imperious, jealous god. He never engaged in the repetitive rituals that were performed in his day and still continue in ours. He asked his disciples to commemorate his Last Supper, and again, practicalities of establishing his church would have called for such formalized re-enactments in the tumultuous years following his death. But once his legacy became entrenched, is far less clear that he

---

4. Lúcás Chan Y.S, 2012, p194.
5. Köstenberger A.J, 2005, p43-44.

wanted the Last Supper commemoration sacralised into the 'Eucharist' and repeated as the centrepiece of ceremonial worship for centuries.[6]

Similar pragmatism can also be detected in his pronouncements on those other pillars of conventional religion, faith and prayer. To the extent that Jesus asked people to believe in him personally, he did not appeal to faith as much as the clear empirical evidence off his faithfulness– namely, his compassionate miracles. Thus in John's Gospel, he entreats the disciples to "believe them, even though you don't believe me" (Jn 10:38). Later in the same gospel, he seems to contradict this in a unique call for 'blind' faith, reprimanding the so called 'doubting' Apostle Thomas and blessing those "who have not seen and yet have believed" (Jn 20:29). But here the author of John's Gospel may have had a covert agenda. According to scholars G Ridley and E Pagels, it is likely that this episode is a Johannine insertion designed to counter the influence the Gospel of Thomas and the gnostic inclined 'Thomasine Christians' who believed in their capacity to achieve salvation through personal efforts, independent of faith in Christ's saving death.[7]

In Chapter one it was suggested that the words and actions of Jesus recorded in the Gospels can be regarded as generally authentic records. But the doubting Thomas story does appear to be a solitary exception, a fairly likely instance of Gospel redaction to suit a later Christian agenda, particularly Bishop Irenaeus' determination to inaugurate a 'patristic tradition' based on Paul's metaphysical faith.[8] Even so, the word 'faith' appears only once in John's Gospel—and only in its negative form as 'faithless'.

However if it was the authentic voice of Jesus, it could still be explained in terms of pragmatism, an acceptance of the need for his persecuted, fledgling church to rely on a degree of unquestioning faith. Jesus guaranteed his disciples that faith would enable them to 'move mountains' (Mt 17:20) and given their ability to perform healing miracles, perhaps that metaphor was not overstated. But as emphasised earlier, when Jesus spoke of faith, like most Jews of his time, he usually meant faithfulness (*emunah*), faith expressed as *hesed e'meth*.[9] If so, he can be construed as saying *emunah* could move metaphorical mountains, at least in terms of improving the world.

---

6. In the recently discovered Gospel of Judas, Christ openly mocks the Apostles practice of the Eucharist. See Journeaux T,2012. *The Gnostic paradox in the Gospel of Judas.*

7. Pagels E, 2003, p58 & p69–72.

8. idem.

9. Shapiro R.M,2013, p89–90. Also Andrews D,2008, p45–46.

Similarly, Christ is on record strongly endorsing the efficacy of prayer (Mk 11:24); but this time, he seems to be directing his sermon specifically at his close followers, 'the Twelve', rather than humanity at large (Mk 11:11 & 22-24). Like his endorsement of 'faith', his advocacy of prayer was usually in the context of enabling his Apostles to perform miraculous acts (Mark 11:22-25). He seems to have regarded prayer and faith as the conduit for receiving the grace of the Holy Spirit which was also the source of miraculous powers.

It would, of course, be simpler and more comforting to just accept Christ's ostensible guarantee that prayer works, except for the fact that it so often does not. That is understandable because if prayer was answered regularly, where would the line be drawn between God's benevolence and human autonomy? Millions of prayers went unanswered when devout Jews desperately reached out for deliverance in the Nazi death camps. If there was ever a final refutation of the utility of prayer, that was surely it. It only invites contempt to shrug off such horror as another inscrutable mystery or, worse, adopt the despicable position that God is uninterested in the plight of non-Christians in general and Jews in particular. For centuries, Christians harboured these vicious subtexts and to the extent that they still do, atheism would be a better option.

Christ's strictures on prayer are not straightforward. He even seems to contradict himself, saying that it is important to pray and then asserting that prayer is unnecessary as God already knows what we need (Mt. 6:31-33). Yet his main point was clear enough: he linked prayer with *hesed*. While he assured his disciples that 'God' would respond to prayer, he characterized that response as sending the "Holy Spirit' to those who ask him" (Lk 11:5-13). It is certainly consistent with his *hesed* priority that Jesus would commend prayer directed at transmitting divine compassion, the Holy Spirit, as grace. He also understood prayer as a contemplative spiritual exercise, best done in solitude rather than in group gatherings (Mt 6:6); and instead of being a parroted, repetitive incantation it should take the form of an intimate, confiding in God (Mt 6:5-14). "Don't recite the same prayer over and over" (Mt 6:7-8 LBE) Jesus cautioned, yet Catholics regularly engages in group prayer sessions like the Rosary where the 'Hail Mary' is repeated up to fifty times.

Jesus also proposes that prayer should not be self-orientated but detached and focused on the needs of others and be undertaken in the *hesed* spirit of steadfast resolve. He gives the example of a man who persistently asks for bread, not for himself but for "a friend on a journey" (Luke 11:6). The request is ultimately granted because of the supplicant's persistence and altruism which are of course, two of the principal qualities of *hesed*. Similarly Jesus uses a parable about a woman constantly imploring 'a judge' to grant her 'justice against an adversary' until the judge relents (Lk 18:1–8). That parable appears to condone self-interested prayer but her perseverance in the cause of 'justice' also carries more detached, higher *hesed* overtones. That is not to assume that prayer will necessarily be answered through *hesed*.

If a renewed humanist Christianity were to develop alternate forms of spiritual practice, it would need to take these considerations into account. It would then regard prayer as more of a solitary, meditative exercise in pursuit of spiritual growth and empathetic discernment. The pivotal Lord's Prayer that Jesus provided (Mt 6:9–15) as a guideline for praying can be read as replete with humanist, *hesed* overtones. In this light, it enjoins us to work together to bring the Kingdom of Heaven into this world, particularly by striving to remove hunger and extreme poverty. It seeks a greater level of human empathy, reciprocating God's merciful forgiveness by forgiving others, relying on compassionate love to avoid serious sin and make inroads against evil in our world. Read in this light, the Lord's Prayer enshrines the formidable challenge Christ presents to us. But finding this compassionate resolve may be less daunting now, thanks to a recent scientific breakthrough.

NEW SOCIAL/SPIRITUAL FRONTIERS OF COMPASSION

> Our fundamental question was, 'Can compassion be trained and learned in adults? . . . Our evidence points to yes . . . It's kind of like weight training . . . we found that people can actually build up their compassion 'muscle' and respond to others' suffering with care and a desire to help.'[10]
>
> HELEN WENG, RESEARCH PSYCHOLOGIST AT THE UNIVERSITY OF WISCONSIN-MADISON.

---

10. Ladwig J, 2013. *Brain can be trained in compassion.*

In 2013, research psychologists in the US announced they had discovered a process of teaching and learning compassion. Blending ancient Buddhist meditation with auto-suggestion techniques, the test case participants eventually developed a significant increase in empathetic attitudes and behaviour. This was not just a 'morning mist' phenomena. MRI scanning showed it resulted in changes to the subjects' associated neural systems, indicating the new sensibility could become embedded in the psyche. The report stated that those who undertook this training course became more sensitive to other people's suffering; and while they found this challenging emotionally, they were able to regulate their emotions so as to persevere with caring and wanting to help, rather than turning away.[11]

Hopefully, this will be the start of a major social breakthrough; but even if it is, Christianity will still have a vital leadership role to play. Even after five years, the focus of these secular compassion courses has remained quite narrow, a means of personal life enhancement for those fortunate enough to access them; and while this might have some benefits, any larger world transformations will necessitate compassion becoming the central focus of our lives. That would involve new awareness derived from a spiritual movement focused on reducing suffering, lived out every day, sustained by divine grace and spurred by a new ethics based soteriology.

Hesed is frequently translated as 'grace' which suggests it cannot become fully actualized in a secular context. *Hesed e'meth* must be brought into the equation. Jesus was quite *adam*ant about this: "no branch can bear fruit by itself . . . I am the vine, you are the branches . . . apart from me you can do nothing" (Jn 15:5). Similarly, he suggested that "humanely speaking" people can achieve little—but "with God, anything is possible" (Mt 19:26). He insisted that compassion should be exercised 'in my name' and using the spiritual guidelines of *hesed*. (Mt 10:40–42 &19:26; Mk 9:38–41). Having identified himself and God with the most vulnerable and distressed, he promised that wherever people are compassionately engaged 'on his behalf', he would also "be there amongst them" (Mt. 18:20 & Mt 25:40) He even assured us of divine grace and "bountiful harvests" in these activities (Jn 15:8).[12] But grace is amorphous and Jesus was not making himself a crutch.

---

11. idem

12. Conventional Christianity might interpret 'bountiful harvests' as referring to evangelizing. But the ensuing phrase that these bring "great glory to my Father" links it to *hesed* compassion, as shown by the context of that phrase in John 9:2–4 & Matthew 5:16. In both these instances, Christ implies suffering should be regarded as an opportunity to exercise compassion.

We must still do the heavy lifting and carry our own crosses. Perhaps the only substantial help we can expect from him has already been given 2000 years ago in his enlightened teachings.

'Love is the answer' John Lennon intoned, and who could disagree? But unlike the rock star, Jesus went beyond the platitude and showed us how to tap the wellsprings of love in a meaningful way. Plato had believed Utopia could be engineered through proper education and social planning. St Paul thought perfect love would arise spontaneously through grace from faith in the mythical Easter sacrifice. More recently Marxists expected altruism and fraternity to gush forth in abundance once the 'relations of production' were changed and social and political conditions were favourable; and when that did not happen, they resortes to dangerous authoritarianism and social engineering. Meanwhile, hippies thought transcendent love was latent in their countercultural beliefs and lifestyles and made more accessible by drugs. But these rosy vistas all too often ended in disillusionment, brutality and depravity. That was perhaps inevitable given the impossible contradiction between pure spiritual love, unconditional and universal, and these artificially contrived substitutes in their sensory, political and ideological guises.

Unlike its secular counterpart, Christ's humanism imposed a spiritual regime of humility that subordinated the ego to a vastly bigger principle. In deprecating thoughts of personal recognition (Mt 6:3),[13] Jesus affirmed that selfless detachment could override faux compassion. He recognized this variant of bad faith in the Pharisees flouting their holiness in the marketplace (Mt 23:7) or what might today be called 'virtue signalling'. He cautioned against secular idealism, equating it to cleaning out a dirty house only to make extra space for even more nastiness to re-enter. The cleared space became a vacuum that must filled by something far greater than human aspirations—the compassionate, Holy Spirit of God (Mt. 12:43–45). It was a sagacious metaphor, verified by some of the bitter lessons of the past.

History is littered with the wrecks of lofty humanist ideals, revolutions and wars of liberation that have foundered on the jagged rocks of human pride and dogma. In the modern era, a recurring pattern was established in the French Revolution when secular humanism spawned Jacobin terror. This nearly strangled the revolution's glorious offspring—liberal democracy—at its inception. Fortunately, freedom ultimately prevailed; but so many other secular upheavals since then have been a disaster, replacing

---

13. Hooper R (ed), 2007, p126–7.

one odious status quo with an even worse one. Human ego is the 'strong man' that needs to be reined in (Mk 3:27). It generates indifference to others, often manifesting as narcissism and hubris. It is the stumbling block on which secular humanism constantly falters. It is the reason why the West must now embrace Christian humanism and its latent ethos of *hesed*.

NEW SOCIAL AND POLITICAL PRIORITIES

> The Jewish God has no preferential option for the poor; rather, the Jewish God has a preferential option for justice.[14]
>
> J.D CROSSAN

Christians have been content to sign on to secular agendas instead of formulating their own unique, *hesed* based perspective. Global warming especially has become the *cause célèbre*; and important as that issue may be, Christians take their cue largely from 'green' activists whose one eyed agendas have been criticized for being both environmentally ineffective and worsening poverty.[15] Global warming is well down the list of priorities for today's Third World *ptochos* and it has been argued that the billions allocated achieve insignificant outcomes for the environment could save millions of lives (and also reduce global warming) if was targeted more wisely.[16]

Climate change strategies have become mired in ideology and should be shaped by detached, expert analysis, not 'groupthink' conformists who might have vested interests in either fossil fuels or government handouts and regulatory red-tape. There is so much political hype and spin involved that all sides seem uninterested in seeking any objective truth. In fact the whole Left/Right spectrum has basically lost its credibility.

The Left, used to be a seedbed of creative ideas and humanism, but no longer. It's solution to most problems invariably involves high spending and a relentless expansion of the bureaucratic, consultancy and legal complex, to which many amongst its ranks belong. Traditionally a champion of social justice and human rights, the Left has developed marked regressive

---

14. Crossan J.D, 1988, p 322.
15. Lomborg B, 2011. *Does Helping the Planet Hurt the Poor?"*
16. Lomborg B. 2017. *Climate change: Paris Agreement makes too little difference.*

tendencies. Increasingly steered by a radical fringe, it has devolved into being the champion of single issue, micro causes rather than seeking the transformation of society as a whole. There is even a strong tendency to curtail free speech through political correctness and even intimidation.[17] Bereft of any coherent vision of radical social reform, the Left's mindset is relentlessly negative. The sins of the West have become its default position and there is a Europhobic disdain for the spectacular achievements of Western civilization and its still unfulfilled potential. So much time and energy is devoted to 'first world problems' and exclusive rights campaigns while real monstrosities like sweatshops, slavery, child marriage or female genital mutilation, tend to be downplayed or ignored.

Misplaced priorities are not peculiar to Leftist thinking. In a world where countless millions are starving and traumatised by violence and deprivation, conservative Christians prefer to direct their attention to the 'pro-life' rights of the unborn and the terminally ill. They base their ethics on the sanctity of human life which is a fine principle—but also for them, a rather malleable one when it comes to waging unjustifiable wars like the Iraq campaign. Too often they have found themselves being hoodwinked by professed high-minded ideals that mask more ignoble, misogynistic and imperialistic ambitions.[18]

Vested interests are even more thinly veiled on the Right where glib rationalizations are trotted out about free markets and private gain for public benefit, that so often fail to materialize. Global corporate capitalism with a 'too big to fail' mentality, has relied on bail outs and rigged, undeserved bonuses that accord more with the worst aspects of socialism than traditional liberal values of individual initiative, productivity and merit. Populist deceptions like protectionism, xenophobia and tax cuts for the rich are often substituted for sound economic policies.

Perhaps these shallow Left/Right allegiances can be transcended by drawing on Kabbalah wisdom which was evident in Christ's own political pragmatism. *Hesed* and *geruvah* can actually be seen as analogous to political tendencies with *hesed* broadly representing the Left's impulse to altruism and generosity and *geruvah*, the Right's inclination to caution and austerity.[19] Both common sense and life experience should confirm the

---

17. Steyn M, 2014. *The slow death of free speech*. Also Strassel K, 2016. *The Liberal Hypocrisy of Free Speech*.

18. Hossein-Zadeh I, 2006, p101 and p111.

19. Miller M, 2012. *Chesed, Gevurah, & Tiferet*.

Kabbalah insight that a balance between these tendencies—*tefiret*—is more conducive to wisdom. Rigid adherence to trite ideology is little different to the dangerous theological delusions of faith. Surely it is time for us to move on from clichéd 'left' and 'right' stereotypes and think within a (not so) new Judeo-Christian framework.

Jesus certainly did this. While he could be called a social revolutionary humanist, he does not really fit into such neat categories. Those who have sought to pigeonhole him forget that he was variously, pacifist and belligerent (Mt 5:39 & Mt 10:34), both egalitarian and competitively individualistic (Mt20:1–16 & 25:14–26), a fervent champion of children and marriage yet ferociously hostile to the patriarchal family unit. (Mt 19:9–14 &Mt10:34–35).[20] Christ's humanism was distinctly pragmatic, assessing each situation on its own particular merits (Lk 14: 28–32). While *hesed* certainly entailed the strong helping the weak, it also deprecated paternalism. *Hesed* compassion would always seek to enhance human dignity and equality, emphasising self-help rather than dependency.[21]

In prioritizing the *ptochos*, Jesus strongly empathized with the two groups that have borne the brunt of cruelty and injustice through the centuries: women and children. His endorsement of female equality was entirely to be expected given his (and humanity's) androgynous origins in Genesis1; and this found expression in his egalitarian attitude to women and the prominent role they played in his mission. Christ's feminism was revolutionary for its time,[22] even to the extent of revising the old Mosaic divorce laws to enable women to initiate a divorce (Mk: 10:12).[23] Interestingly, Jesus was strongly against divorce—except in cases of abuse and infidelity (Mt 19:9)[24]—because it gave some legal protection to vulnerable women

---

20. Crossan J.D, 1994, p58-60. See also Schussler Fiorenza E,1985, p264. Jesus effectively waived the Fifth Commandment in denying respect and 'honour' to misogynistic patriarchs.

21. Jacobson S, 2017. *Daily Omer Meditation*.

22. Swidler L, 2007, p..ix.Also Borg M, 1987, p133-4; Pagels E,1990, p84-5: & Chadwick H, 1967, p58.

23. Myers C, 1988, p266.

24. Though Jesus did not explicitly mention abuse, he probably understood infidelity as including marital violence. Apart from that being a reasonable assumption given his abhorrence of violence, it can also be given a scriptural basis. Jesus would have known that both Hosea and Jeremiah depicted *YHWH*'s covenant with Israel as a marriage in which Israel has been unfaithful. But that infidelity was manifest largely as internecine violence between northern Israel and southern Judea. In Jeremiah, *YHWH* specifically deplores this metaphorical spousal abuse—both on a human and divine level (Jer 3:1–10 & 5:4ff)—and promises to rectify it with a "new covenant" (Jer 31:31). Jesus knew this, having linked his own new covenant of *hesed* to Jeremiah (see Ham C.2000, p64).

and children.[25] His attitude to the latter was equally radical. Regarded as insignificant nobodies,[26] Jesus exalted children as the paragons of humanity, its most sublime and spiritually advanced constituents (Mt 18:10 & 19:14). He declared that the Kingdom of Heaven belonged to children (Mt 19:14) and he privileged them with a unique relationship to God (Mt 18:10). In fact, his elevation of the rights of these long-oppressed stratas of humanity, which has become largely realized in the modern era, may be one of the few sure signs of some progress in our spiritual evolution.

These principles would provide the starting point for a new spiritual humanist world order aimed at regenerating Western democracies, making them exemplars for the entire world and entrenching human freedom. The immediate aim would be to stem the growing threat to democracy so that more advanced Western countries can extend the blessings of prosperity, liberty, security and dignity to the rest of the world. So what policies could this new Christian humanism bring to the table, initiatives that are not presently canvassed in the global market place of ideas? Here are, perhaps, a few examples.

Family renewal

The importance of a loving family cannot be overstated and the ongoing decline of family life is a cancer at the heart of Western civilization. Countless research projects have established that children predictably do best when they are born and raised by their two natural parents,[27] a fact described by one sociologist as possibly "the most unassailable truth in all social science."[28] Such realities cut against the social grain today so it is significant that Christ bucked the same trend in his time by strongly opposing divorce, evidently with the welfare of children in mind. It would be no coincidence that his general prohibition of divorce is quickly followed

---

25. Ironically divorce prohibition was one area in which Jesus tended to side with the Shammaite school against the Hillelites. But the Shammaite position would probably have been based on Genesis 2 literalism—Eve fashioned from Adam's rib and thus subordinate to him—and aimed at tightening patriarchal control. Jesus however was interested in the rights of women and children and the basic legal protection marriage afforded them. See Myers C, 1988, p266.

26. Crossan J.D, 1994, p62–64; & Crossan J.D, 1991, p269.

27. Sammut J,2014. *Interventionist child protection policies are right.*

28. Carlson A, 2010. *Why we need a renewed culture of natural marriage.*

by his sanctification of children in all three synoptic gospels (Mt 19:3–12; Mk 10:2–12; Lk 18:16).[29]

The first biblical expressions of human *hesed* were mainly directed at family members and that is still the best place for it to be nurtured. In fact a 26 year longitudinal study showed a strong link between compassionate adults and loving fathers who spent regular quality time with them as children.[30] Conversely there is little doubt that family breakdown is a root cause of the catastrophic explosion of violent, drug infested ghettos in most US cities where over two thirds of African American youth are now a product of single parent, overwhelmingly fatherless households.[31] Today, throughout the entire Western world, 40% of children live in fatherless homes and this has been a major contributor to escalating crime, youth suicide, mental disorders, drug and alcohol abuse and educational regression.[32] It may also be the root cause of the endemic nihilism that has infected our schools and universities and left them with a cynical disdain for the most glorious achievements of Western civilization.

Several urgent steps are called for. Schools must educate children about the pitfalls of single parenting and welfare policies should discourage it. The divorce process for people with children should be made less straightforward unless, of course, violence or abuse is involved. In that instance, a woman and her children must be able to exit the partnership swiftly and safely. But now easy divorce has now become a mantra of secular faith and marriage has been devalued. That makes conservative Christian opposition to Gay marriage somewhat ironic, as Gays, in wanting to sign on to marriage, are effectively endorsing and buttressing it. But family law should

---

29. In Luke Christ's eulogy to children occurs a few chapters after his divorce prohibition but in Matthew and Mark, it follows it immediately. Jesus is of course on record as launching a virtual declaration of war on families. But as J.D Crossan has pointed out, this was specifically, an attack on intergenerational family relationships which, at that time, had become corrupted by a patriarchal ethos that underpinned the broader social and political network of oppression. See Crossan J.D, 1994, p58–60. Also Schussler Fiorenza E.1985, p264. Thus Christ characterized marriage in terms of abandoning the (patriarchal) family to form a new, equal and indivisible union . Schussler Fiorenza E,1985, p143.

30. Koestner R, Franz C & Weinberger J, 1990. *The Family Origins of Empathic Concern*.

31. Child Trends Databank. (2015). *Family structure*.

32. Thurston J, 2015. *The 9 Devastating Effects Of The Absent Father*. The damage caused by divorce stems from a child's emotionally gutting realization that the parent did not love him or her enough to stick around. Divorce also means that children only get half the supervision and guidance they require.

cover all couples who have children, including Gays and de facto couples, and establish clear liability, both financial and custodial, if one partner is responsible for breaking the family contract.

Heedless of Christ's attitude to children and divorce, Christian leaders have been mute in the midst of an epidemic of broken homes and parental betrayal that is ravaging western societies at their most basic level. Pope Francis has recognized that it has "brought spiritual and material devastation to countless human beings, especially the poorest and most vulnerable."[33] But as usual, neither he nor any likeminded churchmen seem prepared to follow up their lamentations with action. Indeed, the Churches are increasingly accommodating easy divorce instead of working to reduce it and protect its child victims.[34]

New social responsibilities.

If the ethic of enhanced responsibility starts with parenting, it must then be extended to the wider society. The Global Financial Collapse (GFC) in 2008 was a reckless dereliction of duty, caused by capitalism failing to do what it claims it is best at: producing wealth. Instead, it had reverted to the 1920s mania of dodgy, speculative investment, the creation and manipulation of sub-prime mortgages to flood the market with bad debt. So depleted is Western society of any sense of civic responsibility that its capitalist system seems poised to repeat the same greedy dereliction.[35]

A major driver of this dishonesty was inflated salaries and bonuses paid to CEOs. Too often, they were rewarded for simply improving the bottom line through outright fraud, reducing incomes of middle executives, predatory destruction of small business, asset stripping and mass sackings. There must be a heightened emphasis on productive growth, based on investment in capital equipment and larger, well paid workforces. Taxation rates could be linked to this kind of productivity. So also could executive salaries with bonuses only paid as escrowed share issues linked to the long term growth of the enterprise.

The high unemployment rates are also a blight on capitalism and Western societies with massive numbers (particularly of youth) feeling worthless and alienated. Employment should be stimulated with public spending.

33. Severance M, 2014. *The Vatican's Colloquium on Marriage.*
34. Burke K, 2002. *Anglican church doors open for divorcees to remarry.*
35. Baker P, 2017. *Get ready for the next financial crisis.*

But rather than relying on increased taxation to pay for this, it would be more sensible to crack down on tax evasion. The Panama/Paradise papers exposé in 2016–17 revealed tax rorts deprived the world of hundreds of billions of dollars annually.[36] If the capitalist system expects to survive, it cannot continue to operate at this level of deceit and greed. It must temper the lust for accumulating individual fortunes with a new ethos that seeks to reduce vast inequalities and distribute wealth more equitably.

That ethos might also help to generate a new social contract whereby employers took responsibility for ensuring full employment. For example, all unemployed could be obliged to work and all businesses, both public and private, also obliged to employ scaled quotas of them. The demeaning, dead-end 'dole' could then be abolished and replaced with at least 2–3 day's work with payment roughly equating to the dole,[37] now redirected through the employer. Employers would be getting free labour but would have a responsibility to train these people. They could only keep the worker for a limited time on this basis before he/she would have to move to another workplace. The initiative and timing in choosing a workplace would lie entirely with the employee and that should eliminate employer rorting or relying on this (largely) free labour as an alternative to filling natural job vacancies. Workers who posed a problem for employers could be dismissed and obliged to do more menial work in government run work teams. Local authorities would also run literacy classes and sheltered workshops for those who are unable to engage in the wider economy through lack of education or disability.

The benefits of such a scheme would be manifold. The unemployed would gain regular, ongoing work experience, training and an invaluable opportunity to showcase their talents to the employer in a work avenue of their own choosing. Productivity increases would boost the economy while also inculcating a new ethic of mutual obligation and social solidarity. In a looming future of robotics, this renewed social ethic could become even more critical. Robotics carries the potential to boost productivity and wealth as well as free people for more creative and satisfying pursuits. But left entirely to free market forces, a roboticized economy could lead to mass impoverishment and inequality on an almost feudal scale. All those directly replaced by robots would have to receive an income commensurate with their prior remuneration; and education would need to become attuned to

---

36. Poppick S, 2015. *Corporations Dodge $200 Billion in Taxes Each Year.*
37. 'dole' is the term often used to denote unemployment benefits.

these new marketplace realities so that all are equipped to continue making worthwhile contributions to their community.

Major social reforms of this kind do not necessarily require vast amounts of money. So often money is wasted on bloated bureaucracies, that many secular activists seem to find irresistible when supporting NGO's engaged in preventative work, could be vastly more effective and cheaper. There are countless instances of this world wide but by way of example, two in Australia can be singled out, both involving groups that have produced stellar results for disadvantaged minorities they assist. One is the Australian Indigenous Education Foundation (AIEF) which is funded by both government and corporates on a dollar for dollar basis, yielding outcomes that are at least twice as effective as other projects in that sector.[38] The other is called Youth Insearch and it has had stunning success in helping victims of child abuse turn their traumatized lives around.[39] Yet governments seem incapable of grasping that billions of dollars per year could be saved in giving even minimal levels of support to these vital life-saving and life changing preventative programs.

Stability, security and the application of Western power

If a wake-up call was needed to jolt our complacency, it should have been the tragedy of the Democratic Republic of the Congo (DRC). There, it has been estimated that at least 5 million died as the direct result of a civil war that raged during the first decade of this century, making this the deadliest conflict since World War Two.[40] Nearly half of the fatalities were among children under the age of five, even though they make up only 19 per cent of the total population.[41] Over the same period, 1.8 million women were raped.[42] The UN named a hundred or so major corporations as profiteering from and fuelling the horrendous carnage and devastation of the Congo. But no action was taken and Western governments even attempted to shield these companies.[43]

---

38. Mcleod D, 2013. *Indigenous PM for Australia.*
39. *Youth Insearch Annual Report, 2016–17*, p16–19
40. McGreal C, 2008. *War in Congo kills 45,000 people each month.*
41. CBC News, 2008. *Crisis Caused 5.4 Million Deaths in Congo.*
42. Adetunji J, 2011. *Forty-eight women raped every hour in Congo.*
43. Hari J, 2008. *How we fuel Africa's bloodiest war.*

So many atrocities like this tend to be either ignored or treated with despairing resignation. But if Christianity is to ever live up to its founder's expectations, it will need to get off its knees and out into the real world and take the lead in tackling these horrific crimes directing the all its energies and resources to that end. The alternative is to continue to drift until these horrors accumulate—as they surely will—to the point of global conflict.

Yet in the many of the countries where Christian humanist activism is most urgently needed, Christianity has made itself a major part of the problem. The Russian Orthodox Church is particularly culpable, supporting Vladimir Putin, not only a blood drenched tyrant but perhaps the greatest kleptocrat in history.[44] In Central America, millions of people are fleeing horrific violence and cruelty of uncontrolled gangs who prey on them.[45] But the burgeoning Christian sects there, charismatic evangelists and Pentecostals,[46] mostly promote political passivity.[47] They enjoin the desperate masses to turn inward to the 'Spirit'—not the holy spirit of *hesed* but their shamanistic 'charismatic' Spirit with its bogus miracles of healing.[48] Thus they trade on human misery like charlatans selling fake remedies to the terminally ill.

In the same vein, Pentecostalism preaches a 'feel good prosperity gospel' that concocts false hopes of wealth as a manifestation of faith, touting a 'theology lite' that emphasises divine rewards and downplays the fear of divine punishment,[49] traditionally a deterrent to criminal behaviour. In fact recent research has found a strong correlation between violent, sociopathic behaviour and religions that emphasise divine benevolence rather than divine retribution.[50] The removal of Voltaire's 'bridle to the wicked' is prov-

---

44. Pearson N, 2017. *Drone footage shows Putin's 'secret island mansion*. Putin may have become one of the richest man in the world by thieving from the Russian people.

45. Taylor G & Dinan S, 2016. *Violence surges in Central America, threatening new refugee flood.*

46. Catholicism has declined and Pentecostal Protestantism has increased dramatically in Latin America generally. While Catholics are still a majority, some 25% of them have become charismatics which means regressive fundamentalism now attracts about half the Christian population of the region.

47. The Economist, 2017. *Luther's Reformation.*

48. Olson R.E, 2016. *The Dark Side of Pentecostalism*. See also Pew Research Center— Religion & Public Life, 2014. *Pentecostalism.*

49. Kaufmann E.P, 2010, p81.

50. Adams T.M, 2011, p39. Also Shariff A.F & Rhemtulla M, 2012, op cit.

ing disastrous for regions like Central America where Pentecostalism and violence have both grown exponentially in recent decades. Once more, the sordid underbelly of bad faith is revealed in all its ugliness.

While the West has a shameful imperialist legacy and any future interventions must avoid imposing Eurocentric solutions, its advanced standards of human rights as well as its economic and military strength, obligate it to play a dynamic role in bringing the rest of humanity towards the standard of living it enjoys and others (mostly) aspire to. *Noblesse oblige*, the responsibility that comes with power and privilege, was a key component of *hesed* Christ taught (Lk 12:48) and he illustrated it in his parable of Lazarus and the rich man (Lk 16:19–31).

Taking resolute action against murderous regimes is clearly more daunting than giving 'scraps from the rich man's table' to the beggar, Lazarus. However the Lazarus story can be taken metaphorically. When the West finally found the courage to make limited interventions in places like Bosnia and Kosovo in the 1990s, Sierra Leone in 2000, Afghanistan in 2001(the first campaign), and more recently against ISIS in Iraq and Syria, it managed to reign in protracted brutality with minimal effort and 'scraps' of force. Western military intervention should always be carefully weighed and proportionate; but there will be an ongoing need for it in a world where evil often runs rampant.

However many are denying the possibility of the West playing such a constructive role, preferring to flaunt a permanent black armband and wallow in self-flagellating guilt. The 'post-colonial' intellectual elites—like some of the Jesus scholars referred to in Chapter Two—have managed to instil a politically correct mentality that tends to blame the problems of poverty and oppression mainly on ex-colonial masters, often affording 'home grown' oppressors a smokescreen for their crimes. This kind of befuddlement has clouded the West's rational judgment, its compassionate sensibility and capacity for moral leadership. Such was particularly evident in the European response to the refugee flood from 2015.

Many Christians praised Chancellor Angela Merkel who opened the floodgates to refugees from Syria and Iraq. But this was less compassion than misguided altruism. It was a prime example of *hesed* without *geruvah*, possibly also induced by an overweened guilt neurosis for Germany's Nazi past. Compassion should never be counterproductive but this open door policy was just that. Triggered by the tragic image of a drowned child, it encouraged a mass flight across the Mediterranean, with thousands more drowning in the process. The influx of refugees has seriously amplified the risk of terrorism within Europe and imposed massive financial strains on economies teetering on the brink of recession.

The responsibility for assisting these refugees should have fallen heavily on oil rich countries of the region like Russia, Iran and Saudi Arabia who are largely responsible for escalating the civil war in Syria. Certainly a vastly better option for Europe would have been to turn back the boats and pour money into transforming squalid camps on Syria's borders into more habitable, medium term settlements, providing education, training, security and hope as well as a base from where a more orderly and generous processing of migrant applications could proceed

To some extent, Europe has belatedly done this; but it has repeated its folly with refugees from Africa, by using its navies to pick up victims of people smugglers and bring them to Europe. Enough are plucked from the sea to spur others to follow. But only a small percentage are lucky, the others drown or become prey, in their millions, to slave traders. Most would undoubtedly just return home if they could to escape the hellholes they are now trapped in. But instead of providing the means for their safe repatriation, Europe refuses to grasp the nettle of this human catastrophe and instead, like Pope Francis,[51] bask in a warm inner glow of deluded do-goodism.

Campaigning against slavery should be one of the world's top priorities, but it is virtually ignored. There is still revulsion at the centuries of African slavery; but today's slave trade is vastly greater with some 35 million estimated victims.[52] Once again, it is women and children who bear the brunt of this horror. Sex slavery in places like India and Thailand is especially pernicious in the way it preys upon children. Sex tourists indulging in this depravity should be especially targeted with decoy police and hidden cameras used to trap them. Specialist Interpol forces need to be integrated with local authorities to target pedophiles in the same way they monitor and destroy terrorist cells, particularly in places where the trafficking problems are acute

Terrorism has been the overriding preoccupation but one its propellants has been the failure to provide Palestinians with their own state, one of the world's incendiary injustices. Both sides are to blame. Israel has repeatedly obstructed moves towards this statehood by expanding its

---

51. Dearden L, 2016. *Pope Francis 'to take 12 refugees on his plane back to Italy' after visit to Greek island where thousands trapped.*

52. Elliott L, 2014. *Modern slavery affects more than 35 million people.*

settlements on the West bank. Palestinians, especially Hamas, indoctrinate children with hatred of Jews and refuse to acknowledge Israel's right to exist. This reflects the dominance of ultra-nationalist religious extremists in both camps.

If Israel fostered the emergence of an economically viable Palestinian state on the West Bank, it could be a powerful stabilizing force to isolate Hamas terrorists in Gaza and galvanize support from moderates across the region. This would especially be so if it was backed up with cessation of Israeli settlements along with enhanced trade, investment and employment opportunities for the new West Bank state. This would be much wiser than taking Palestinian land and storing up more hatred for the future. Jews as much as Christians need to become as attuned to the spiritual humanism of their tradition and fully imbibe the wisdom of their *hesed* legacy. Then they might be able to wrest back control from militant, Zionist extremists before they plunge Israel into a catastrophic war, just as their Shammaite/Zealot counterparts did 2000 years ago.

World Development

World poverty has reduced dramatically in recent decades and proponents of free trade claim much of the credit for this.[53] But In 2015, nearly 800 million people were still malnourished. Millennium Development Goals set in the early 1990s for realization by 2015, were not met. In Sub-Saharan Africa, extreme poverty has been actually increasing[54] and typically associated with horrific levels of violence, disease, fear and repression.

In response to world economic development, Christians tend to support well-meaning but ultimately inadequate campaigns like 'Make Poverty History'.[55] This kind of beneficence too often plays into the hands of corrupt regimes who happily thieve and waste so much of the money thrown at them. In the context of Africa, billions of dollars in aid and debt write downs have fallen far short of commensurate poverty reductions. Moreover, grandiose goals like abolishing poverty in a generation have also been criticised as unrealistic. The NGOs who set the lofty targets are not

---

53. The Economist, 2013.*The world's next great leap forward: Towards the end of poverty*.
54. Hunger Notes, 2015. *World Hunger and Poverty Facts and Statistics*.
55. Howker E, 2009. *All in a good cause?*

monitored and seldom held accountable for underperformance. The net result can be paralysing despondency.[56]

One of the keys to ending poverty is to reduce corruption and this will involve empowering the poor to recognize it as a major cause of their problems. This kind of public vigilance has taken off in Brazil where politicians are now required to fully disclose their personal incomes and assets. Some have been given gaol sentences and while the short term consequences have been disruptive, a more educated populace is now starting to give anti-corruption measures the priority they deserve.[57] Another suggestion has been to oblige publicly listed resource companies to disclose detailed information about payments to governments, as a condition of stock exchange listing. As well as a stick, there should also be a carrot. Perhaps bonuses or an economic version of the Nobel Peace Prize could be given to political leaders who expose and punish corruption and achieve significant economic development, poverty reduction and improved health and education outcomes.

Robust trade and investment should take precedence over 'dead aid' and activists might do better to direct their energies towards redressing the basic inequity of impoverished states, excluded from the main channels of world trade. A growing number of sceptics believe that financial aid has in fact been counterproductive, feeding corruption and breeding an attitude of mendicant dependence.[58] A better option might be to confine charity to the desperately needy and divert aid funds to the delivery of emergency relief. Corruption is so endemic that development aid should only be delivered 'in kind', in the form of building schools, hospitals, roads etc, and training and using local labour. Rather than cancelling debt altogether, repayments should be diverted into such infrastructure projects and perhaps the contracts for these could be awarded to companies from creditor states by way of compensation.

The same approach should be taken to resource development projects where royalty payments, to the tune of billions of dollars annually, are largely devoured by corrupt politicians and their retinue of parasitic hacks.[59] A typical example of this is Shell Oil's operation in the Niger Delta

---

56. Easterly W, 2006. *The White Man's Burden.*

57. Ramkumar V, 2016. *The Good News in Brazil's Two-Headed Crisis.*

58. For a good general discussion of this and other problems associated with development assistance, see Moyo D, 2009. *Dead Aid.*

59. Lawder D, 2016. *IMF: Global corruption costs trillions in bribes, lost growth.*

which has brought little development but major environmental and social dislocation, rampant crime and violence. It has also been suggested that an Oil Revenue Distribution Fund be set up to direct all money directly to the populace as dividends. There is growing evidence that these kind of direct cash handouts to poor people to spend as they think fit, can be more effective that channelling aid through corrupt bureaucracies.[60]

All this is idealistic but it is also rational and by no means wildly utopian. Yet there seems little prospect of anything like it materializing in our secular world where self-aggrandizing elites, political opportunism, identity politics and ideology are the order of the day. Neither left nor right-wing policies show any sign of arresting the decline of the West, let alone making significant inroads against world poverty, violence and oppression. This will surely continue unless tribal allegiances to Left and Right are themselves rendered meaningless in a new spiritual humanist setting.

The greatest triumph of the West was its ultimate propagation of liberal democracy and basic human rights and it is disturbing that these freedoms are still withheld in so many countries and even being threatened in the West itself.[61] It is vital that this trend is reversed and the radiant blessings of *hesed* humanism are unveiled to light up the Judeo-Christian world as a beacon of hope. Ultimately the entire world will need a spiritual renewal based on this kind of compassionate awareness. Most cultures and religious traditions have their own rich spiritual humanist veins and our future may hinge on whether enough people have the wisdom to tap into them, replacing bad faith religion with a new, rational faith in the spiritual potential of humanity to shape a better future.

---

60. Palley T.I, 2003. *Lifting the Natural Resource Curse.*

61. Many Western universities have now become vanguards in the suppression of free speech: Tickle L, 2015. *Free speech? Not at four in five UK universities.*

Conclusion

> Everyone here will ultimately be judged, will ultimately judge himself, on the effort he has contributed to building a new world society.[1]
>
> ROBERT KENNEDY

JUDAIC *HESED* THAT CHRIST made the cornerstone of his humanist teachings, required people to proactively "merge with the other person, to identify with his pain, to feel responsible for his fate."[2] If human spiritual evolution is to gather momentum—indeed, if we are to even survive—developing this capacity is the critical first step. Only if Western societies are prepared to take it can we expect to mollify political conflicts and reach some consensus on real priorities.

Jesus tried to steer us in this direction two thousand years ago but Paul took Christianity down a blind alley; and there seems little doubt that many of the atrocities committed by Christianity through the centuries, would not have been possible if Christ's *hesed* had become the guiding, spiritual humanist principle of Christian life. Christian anti-Semitism and probably even the holocaust itself,[3] might have been avoided. But *hesed* was shackled from the outset of the Christian era when elites and hierarchies called the shots and ignorance prevailed at all levels. It can only be hoped that today, in more humane, informed and democratic societies, its time may have finally arrived.

The humanist Christ presented here commands new political and spiritual heights, one that radiates a grandeur that can light up the deepest

---

1. Kennedy R.F, 1966. *Day of Affirmation Speech*.
2. Zion N, 2013, p44.
3. Michael R, 2006. pp. 105–151. See also Wallmann J, 1987, p73; & Shirer W.L,1960, pp91–2.

Conclusion

recesses of our dark and dangerous world. Here is a Christ who, as *adam*, the human, can serve as an ultimate role model for humanity. His perfection may be elusive to us mere mortals, but not his humanism. He stands as a paragon of humility and selfless compassion, an authentic and sublime expression of divinity in human form. In this revitalized Christianity, we can find clear life purpose as well as a template for the best of humanity, a 'Son of Man', a pure human spirit cast in the image of a compassionate God, reaching out for something greater than itself and finely attuned to the pressing needs of this world.

This figure is a polar opposite to the hackneyed, creedal Messiah who, as God incarnate, supposedly sacrificed himself to redeem us depraved, helpless sinners. It is time to ditch this bad faith once and for all, with its negative intimations of human inadequacy, quietism, victimhood and entitlement. It props up a theological edifice that is primitive, life negating and riddled with contradictions. But the hierarchies that jealously guard this tottering ruin will resist change as they have too much invested in it. Even though they may be holding back a spiritual revolution that could take Christianity and the world to new 'sunlit uplands', they will strive to cling on to their threadbare theology, poised to administer the last rites to Christianity and perhaps Western civilization as well.

The problems of this world are made intractable, not by their complexity as much as the lack of genuine resolve to grapple with them. In short, not enough people care enough. Some Christians believe they can reconcile a Christlike compassion with their notions of faith based salvation, and no doubt a few have succeeded. But they will remain isolated from the wider congregations. All experience suggests that given the choice, people will default to 'faith' minimalism rather than seek the more demanding humanist frontiers Jesus traversed. Largely unaware of the *hesed* teachings of Jesus, Christian activists co-opt secular agendas that promise little and deliver even less. Locked into to their ideological battle lines and comfort zones, those secularists remain largely deaf to the anguished cries of a tormented world. Self-interest and political point-scoring trump urgent human needs while politicians and activist leaders chant their outworn ideological mantras. Well intentioned Christians who stand behind these limp banners, have achieved little more than rancorous discord within their own confused congregations.

Ineffective and cruelly counterproductive refugee policies and the generally passive response to horrors like slavery are clear indications of a creeping moral atrophy. Germans have been condemned for allowing Nazism to persist but what choice did they have in a terrorist police state? The West today has no excuses for its inaction. We cannot claim to be deceived by propaganda or intimidated into silence by a Gestapo. In a real sense we are all complicit in the criminal atrocities that keep recurring, carelessly purchasing iPhones that originated in the Congo blood pits and remaining passive, like the Russian Orthodox Church, in the face of Putin/Assad war crimes in Syria. We surely can and must be better than this.

Advocates for the *ptochos* and their dark, tortured lives, are in short supply. Jesus observed that "the harvest is so great and the workers so few" (Mt. 9:35-38) and it seems likely that only a humanized Christianity can bring a critical mass of people 'into the field'. Such revitalized Christianity would show clear leadership and make its own distinctive and vital contribution, winning new found respect and admiration. The world is crying out for this kind of leadership and Christians, based in the privileged Western world, have a vital responsibility to take action. But burdened with a theology that is inane, obtuse and obstructive, and a track record that has constantly reflected that, Christianity may never rise to this challenge. In its dogged denial of the spiritual humanist stamp of its founder, Christianity may be sowing the seeds of its own destruction and dragging the West down with it.

For those who would concede the logic of this book, the implications are stark. In rejecting the humanist Jesus, Christians may be effectively choosing to continue dwelling in the darkness of an archaic theology. Like the ancient Israelites who clung onto their false gods, this would be the ultimate expression of bad faith, a betrayal of God and humanity and perhaps, ultimately, a 'sin against the Holy Spirit'. But quite apart from any afterlife chastizement, we might seal our own temporal fate. By persisting in its current aimless trajectory, the world will continue its drift into dangerous orbits; and it is surely only a matter of time before we all luck out catastrophically.

Unlike conventional Christianity, Christian Humanism provides a far more rational, consistent and positive view of Jesus, as one who came not to save us but to show us how to save ourselves. As the Son of Man, he is both a humanist teacher and semi-divine beacon of justice, calling on us to seek a higher level of *hesed* awareness that might enable us to improve this world and take control of our own destiny. Responsibility for this is placed squarely where it belongs, with us. This Jesus is not a progressive liberal or

CONCLUSION

doctrinaire liberationist but a true social/spiritual revolutionary; and the kind of Christianity he envisaged was not a hierarchical religion centred on worship but a dynamic, grass roots spiritual and political movement.

The historical Jesus was heavily involved in challenging the evils of his time, confronting systemic brutality and oppression of the Temple by trashing its shallow, faith based 'covenantal nomism' and elevating the covenantal imperatives of compassion and justice enshrined in *hesed*. He translated *hesed* into action by championing the *ptochos* in their struggles against the vicious elites. Because their oppressive power relied so heavily on inculcating guilt, Jesus offered merciful forgiveness of *hesed* as the natural antidote. That was the essence of his humanist mission of forgiveness and it was squarely centred on this world, not some mystical faith-based forgiveness in the next. His purpose was to expose the scope of human evil and the power structures, relationships and belief systems through which it is typically transmitted to spread so much grief and misery. As vicious as they were, the corrupt Temple cliques of the first century were not unique either then or since then. It was central to Christ's mission to reveal them for what they were: paradigms of oppression and fanaticism that have tortured, exploited and enslaved humanity in all societies and cultures throughout history.

Jesus was not offering any easy solutions, although the crosses he called on us to bear would be far less onerous than his. Luther was overwhelmed by the stress of meeting arduous 'requirements' for salvation. But his perception was narrow because his own compassionate sensibility was patently miniscule. Like the medieval monks who bickered over how many angles could fit on a pinhead, Luther fretted over how many trivial good deeds it would take to appease a wrathful God. For Christ however, the quality of *hesed* was not strained. It was based on the principle 'from each according to his abilities' (Lk 12:48) and it factored in more than one lifetime.

Spiritual humanism was reprised by the 16th century Kabbalist Isaac Luria who coined the phrase *tikkun olam* (repair the world) by repairing the shattered *sefirot* or emanations of God of which *hesed* was the most prized.[4] Such a challenge will require bold leadership, intellectual skill and self-sacrifice for some. For most, it should impose no great demands beyond a desire to expanded compassionate awareness, fulfil the duties of democratic citizenship, perhaps some regular charity or volunteer work or even simply, and most importantly, devoted parenting. What really matters

---

4. Leiberman S, 2000. *Kabbala #10: Chesed—The World is Built on Kindness.*

is that Christ's *hesed/geruvah/tiferet* model of compassion becomes the inspiration and guiding principle of our lives.

This kind of love is far removed from the feel good, self-gratifying altruism that so often passes for compassion. It will need to be taught, explored, absorbed and enacted as a life-long spiritual experience; and hopefully research teams like those at Wisconsin-Madison university will help to refine these processes and make them accessible to the broad populace. Promoting that learning, infusing it with spiritual depth and giving it practical expression, would become the chief function of a Christian Humanist 'church'. Its other task would be to set up think tanks and workshops to develop policies through analysis and rigorous debate of diverse viewpoints; and, once a consensus was reached, mobilize Christians to seek change. This of course would run parallel to the enhancement of ongoing Christian health, education and welfare services.

But there would also need to be some radical changes in personnel. Church hierarchies may have been necessary to help the fledgling church survive and grow but they were basically at odds with Christ's democratic egalitarianism. Christian Humanism would dispense with the platitudes of pompous old men and tend to be a ritual free zone. Sunday gatherings would abandon traditional worship and hollow incantations which were never part of Christ's agenda. There would be scope for spiritual exercises and those who could develop and teach them. The focus would now shift to loving God and humanity, in spirit and truth, *hesed e'meth,* while focussing on critical human needs.

It is thus likely that the strongest opposition would come from the clerical standard bearers of bad faith, doggedly clinging to the power and privileges they derive from a corrupted theology. However any defectors from the Christian flock might find inspiration in the example of Christ himself who operated outside institutional boundaries of Judaism, founding a movement to displace the supernumeraries who had interposed themselves between humanity and God. They might also fruitfully reflect on the proposition that just as time was running out for the debased 'covenantal nomism' of Christ's day, so also has Pauline, Augustinian and Lutheran orthodoxy run its doleful course.

As a ginger group, Christian Humanists would attempt to seize the moral high ground, keep the spotlight fixed on the darkest recesses of human suffering and peak the conscience of humanity. From that 'mustard seed' a giant, life-sustaining tree could grow. It is time for Christianity to

CONCLUSION

lead, to acquire the bold vision and purpose of its founder. It must jettison the puerile 'mysteries' of ungrounded faith and the moral bankruptcy implicit in the notion of a helpless humanity dependent on the mercy of an inscrutable God. Educated, rational free-thinkers who largely shape social mores and ultimately decide the fate of belief systems, are no longer willing to abide such primitive nonsense in an age of increasing religious madness. They have lost patience with a religion mired in infantile notions of creationism and gender discrimination while teeming millions cry out in vain for justice and deliverance from horrific evil.

Some Christians might recoil at their institutions being shifted so squarely into the political arena. But they are already there both by design and default, and losing ground daily. Unlike the fractious, secular controversies Christians are now often embroiled in, Christian Humanism would be canvassing 'motherhood' issues. Christianity is at its best when it is tolerant and inclusive inclusive and engages with suffering humanity. It is the inspiring, sometimes heroic, humanitarian work of the churches—not their 'God bothering' rituals and Easter fixations—that gives Christianity its lingering cachet. A dynamic Christian humanist alternative to religious naval gazing and hypocrisy, should find strong resonance amongst those thirsting for some coherent spirituality, idealism, moral leadership and life purpose.

While not providing any simple solutions or roadmaps to utopia, Christian humanism could be at least a partial antidote to the nauseating waves of despair and guilt that surface almost daily with news of the latest disgusting act of viciousness and inhumanity. At its most basic level, this recast Christianity would be stimulating, investing parenthood with a new significance. By focusing on this and other mega issues like unemployment, corporate responsibility and youth in crisis, it may be possible to spur oncoming generations to new levels of compassionate awareness, optomism and creative inspiration. This would ensure a more robust response to extremities of suffering, invigorating public policy generally by setting new benchmarks for morality and human aspiration. These positive energies could permeate and revitalise our free societies at all levels of public and personal behaviour, giving democracy and the West a salutary boost.

In a sane and rational world, all the major religions would move in this direction, seeking to go beyond primitive faith, reconstituting themselves and converging in an ecumenical, spiritual humanist alliance. If Christianity took the lead here, Judaism should logically be the first to come on board. It should have little problem identifying—if not merging[5]—with a Christianity stripped of its 'Messiah complex' and steeped in the Judaic humanism of *hesed*. Muhammad as well as Christ drank from the well of Judaic ethics and that could become the basis of a desperately needed Islamic reformation. Buddha, whose teachings have been shown to be closely aligned with Christ's, drew heavily on Hindu humanism, otherwise known as dharma.[6] Such convergences could inaugurate a 'one world' dream scenario—a new world religion of spiritual humanism—where large swathes of humanity would be making a concerted push for fraternity, peace and justice. The transformative impact of such coordinated moral force could scarcely be overstated. As a new international theology of liberation, it would put the old Christian-Marxist version in the shade.

Unlike Marx's Communist Manifesto, this Christian Humanist one does not claim any scientific basis. There are probably no 'historical' forces like 'dialectical materialism' that will bring it to fruition, although there are some powerful existential reasons why it might gain some traction. Something similar to Marx's projection of a 'final stage of capitalism' may now be approaching as both corporate greed and robotic technology continues to dislocate economies, shredding the middle classes and creating a mass underclass of the unemployed. Moreover, rampant consumerism, the real mass religion of our time, may have run its course. As well as boosting global warming, it requires an unlimited plundering of natural resources that is unsustainable. Environmentalist Paul Gilding is not alone in seeing looming food and water shortages driving a revolutionary reappraisal of lifestyles and values throughout the world over the next few decades.[7] If secular humanism is left to plot a course through these minefields, it is just a matter of time before one of the mines explodes in a mushroom cloud.

Christian Humanism would not be doctrinaire like other ideologies and theologies. It has clear humanist values but no fixed positions and would be responsive to all ideas and rational arguments. Any faith it might profess would be a work in progress and entirely provisional. The final truth about Christ is shrouded in antiquity and swayed by subjectivity and ontological preconceptions. Atheists are obviously right in asserting there is no clear evidence for the existence of God—let alone definite knowledge of his nature and intentions. But that should not preclude our idealisation of

5. Christ predicts this reunion will eventually happen in Matthew 23:37–39.
6. Sharma S.K, 2000. *Dharma and Universal Values of Humanism*.
7. Gilding P, 2011. *The Great Disruption*.

Conclusion

God as human perfection and cherishing the hope of Hosea and Jeremiah that we can increasingly 'know' God through *hesed*, a hope that God exists independently and lovingly created humanity in his/her image, to fulfil a purpose and with the help of messengers like Christ, guide us towards it.

Marx's contemporary, the German philosopher Ludwig Feuerbach argued that God, enshrined in such spiritual aspirations, was the epitome of wishful thinking. Whether it may be more than that, can only be assessed by how those aspirations play out in the real world where they can be tested against the reality of human experience. As James said, 'faith without works is dead' because it is completely baseless without some hard evidence or tangible 'fruits', to use Christ's metaphor.

But sporadic good works, acts of individual charity and good intentions, will never constitute real evidence. *Hesed* may be the only epistemic key to theosis, as the Axial prophets and Jesus affirmed. If so, only a concerted commitment to change this benighted world could ever give faith substance, with some progress in that direction perhaps providing the visible 'fruit' of faith. Christian orthodoxy, preoccupied with personal immortality and convoluted faith abstractions, can never rise to this challenge. It is completely out of kilter with what Jesus taught and practiced and unless it changes and becomes animated by the Holy Spirit of *hesed*, it will continue to grow increasingly irrelevant and ultimately wither on the vine. Christian Humanism can prune that vine for "greater strength and usefulness" (Jn 15:3).

Immediately before his crucifixion Jesus declared: "Your strong love for each other will prove to the world that you are my disciples" (Jn13:35); and in expressing that love as *hesed*, he affirmed he would "be there amongst" us (Mt18:20 & 25:40), augmenting our efforts (Jn 15:8). Over the past two thousand years, Judeo-Christianity has achieved only a minimal fulfilment of that promise. The flickering flame of *hesed* has brought some love and hope into the dark recesses of the world and at times, 'ascended the brightest heavens of invention'. But more often it has been eclipsed by the quietism of faith, often enabling hatred, bigotry and violence to flourish.

With both Christianity and Western civilization in decline and the Damoclean sword of nuclear obliteration hanging over us, it is past time to excise bad faith and bring Christ's vibrant humanism to the fore. Compassionate empathy must intensify and proliferate and engage much larger numbers of people if Christ's expectations of humanity are to be met. Judeo-Christianity must now become the "world's light . . . for all to see"

(Mt 5:16), inspiring other religions to follow suit and chalking up ongoing, significant victories against human misery and despair. Then it might be possible to finally glimpse Christ's 'Kingdom of Heaven' breaking into our world as *hesed*, bringing tangible, lasting improvements to societies, families, and the human condition. Christ's spiritual humanism might then gain an unstoppable momentum as the first religion to have found some kind of empirical basis for its faith.

Bibliography

Aaronovitch D. "Jihadi Link for Amnesty Poster Boy." *The Australian,* February 10, 2010
———. "The Menace of Men who Hate Women." *The Australian,* August 16, 2010.
ABC News. *Bullying in Australian schools among worst in world: survey.* December 1, 2008. <http://www.abc.net.au/news/stories/2008/12/14/2445879.htm.>
Adams T.M.. *Chronic Violence and its Reproduction: Perverse Trends in Social Relations, Citizenship and Democracy in Latin America.* 2011
<https://www.wilsoncenter.org/sites/default/files/Chronic%20Violence%20and%20 its%20Reproduction%20-%20Adams%20FINAL.pdf>
Adegoke Y. *Nigeria's anti-corruption unit finds $43 million cash in Lagos apartment.* 2017. <http://edition.cnn.com/2017/04/13/africa/efcc-recovers-funds-nigeria/index.html>
Adetunji J. "Forty-eight women raped every hour in Congo, study finds." *The Guardian.* May 13, 2011.
Agence France-Presse "Belgian priest tells of 300 sexual abuse cases." *Sydney Morning Herald.* April 14, 2010.
Akbar A. *Germany has yet to rid itself of its guilt over the Nazis, says Schlink.* 2010. <http://www.independent.co.uk/arts-entertainment/books/news/germany-has-yet-to-rid-itself-of-its-guilt-over-the-nazis-says-schlink-2082712.html>
Akers K. *The Lost Religion of Jesus: Simple Living and Non-violence in Early Christianity.* New York. Lantern. 2000.
Akers K. *Was Jesus a Vegetarian?* 2001.
<http://www.compassionatespirit.com/wpblog/2015/12/01/was-jesus-a-vegetarian/>
Albrechtsen J. "Sticklers for labels tagged as groupthink suckers." *The Australian.* March 12, 2014
Ali A.H. *Nomad: A Personal Journey Through the Clash of Civilizations.* New York. Simon & Schuster. 2010.
Allen C. *The Human Christ: the Search for the Historical Jesus.* Oxford. Lion. 1998.
Alves M. *Hate speech and the rhetoric against criminalization in homophobic discussion by religious leaderships in Brazil.* 2012. <http://paperroom.ipsa.org/papers/paper_18212.pdf>
American Psychological Association's annual meeting in San Francisco. *Sexual Abuse of Boys.* 1998 <http://www.menstuff.org/issues/byissue/abusedboys.html#top>
Amersfoort J. "James the Just and Christian origins." *Vigiliae Christianae,* 60(1). 2006.

Bibliography

Amnesty International Report, 2018. *Syria: Relentless bombing of civilians in Eastern Ghouta amounts to war crimes.* <https://www.amnesty.org/en/latest/news/2018/02/syria-relentless-bombing-of-civilians-in-eastern-ghouta-amounts-to-war-crimes/>

Anand Y.P. *Mahatma Gandhi and Buddhism.* 2004. <http://www.iop.or.jp/0414/anand.pdf>.

Andrews D. *A Divine Society: The Trinity, Community and Society.* Oregon. Wipf & Stock. 2008.

Appleyard B. "Life after Life." *The Australian,* January 19.2009.

Archer, G.L. *Encyclopedia of Bible Difficulties.* Grand Rapids, Mich.: Zondervan Pub. House. 1982.

Argubright J. "The Search for Truth." *Bible Believer's Archaeology.* Volume 2. 2003.

Armstrong K. *The Great Transformation: The world in the time of Buddha, Socrates, Confucius and Jeremiah.* London. Atlantic. 2006.

———. *In the Beginning: a New Interpretation of Genesis.* London.Vintage. 2011.

Askew E & O. Wesley Allen Jr. *Beyond Heterosexism in the Pulpit.* Oregon. Cascade. 2015.

Aslan R. *Zealot: The Life and Times of Jesus of Nazareth.* New York. Random House. 2013.

Astor Y. *Does Judaism Believe in Reincarnation?* 2003. < http://www.aish.com/jl/kc/48943926.html>

Astell, A. W & Goodhart S. *Sacrifice, scripture, and substitution: Readings in ancient Judaism and Christianity.* Notre Dame. University of Notre Dame Press. 2011.

Ateek N.S. *A Palestinian Christian Cry for Reconciliation.* New York. Orbis. 2008.

Austin P. *Lovingkindness—Definition of Hesed.* 2015<http://preceptaustin.org/lovingkindness-definition_of_hesed.htm>

Auvinen V. *Jesus' Teaching on Prayer.* Åbo. Åbo Akademi. University Printing House. 2003.

Averbeck R.E. "Worshipping God in Truth" in Bateman H.W (ed) *Authentic Worship: Hearing Scripture's Voice, Applying Its Truths.* Grand Rapids. Kregel Publications. 2002.

Baker P., 2017. *Get ready for the next financial crisis.* <https://www.afr.com/markets/equity-markets/get-ready-for-the-next-financial-crisis-20170410-gvhvul>

Baldwin P. *Regressive Left puts bigotry and militant Islam on a pedestal.* 2016. <http://www.theaustralian.com.au/news/inquirer/regressive-left-puts-bigotry-and-militant-islam-on-a-pedestal/news-story/c42df8a48a1e2da5f33311f4a3303919>

Baron-Cohen S. "The Science of Evil." *The New York Times.* June 6, 2011. <http://www.nytimes.com/2011/06/07/science/14evil-excerpt.html?mcubz=0>

Barnett P. *Jesus & the rise of early Christianity: A history of New Testament times.* Downers Grove, Ill: InterVarsity. 1999.

Barton J. *Isaiah 1–39.* Sheffield. OTG. 1995.

Bates S. "Church of England parish sings battle hymns as it plans move to Rome." *The Guardian.* October 18, 2010.

Bauckham R. *Jesus and the God of Israel: God Crucified and Other Studies on the New Testament's Christology of Divine Identity.* Michigan. Eerdmans. 2009.

———. "The Origin of the Ebionites". In Tomson, P. J.& Lambers-Petry D. *The Image of the Judeo-Christians in Ancient Jewish and Christian Literature.* Tubingen. Brill. 2003.

Baugh S.M. *God's Purpose According To Election: Paul's Argument in Romans 9.* 1998. <https://www.monergism.com/thethreshold/articles/onsite/unconditional_baugh.html>

Bibliography

Baxter M. "Flesh and Blood: Does Pornography Lead to Sexual Violence?" *New Scientist*. May 5. 1990 <http://www.newscientist.com/article/mg12617154.200-flesh-and-blood-does-pornography-lead-to-sexual-violence.html?page=1>. BBC News. *MPs attack Greer on female circumcision*." November 25, 1999 <http://news.bbc.co.uk/2/hi/uk_news/politics/535488.stm>.
Beaton R. *Isaiah's Christ In Matthew's Gospel*. Cambridge. Cambridge University Press. 2002.
———. "Messiah and Justice : A Key to Matthew's Use of Isaiah 42.1–4?". *Journal For The Study Of The New Testament*, (75). 1999.
Beckstrom E.A. *Beyond Christian Folk Religion: Re-grafting into Our Roots*. Oregon. Resource Publications. 2013.
Bedard S.J. *Josephus, John the Baptist and the Historical Jesus*. 2008. <http://1peter315.wordpress.com/2008/03/05/josephus-john-the-baptist-and-the-historical-jesus/>.
Beer, F. *Women and Mystical Experience in the Middle Ages*. Suffolk. Boydell. 1992.
Ben Zion Bokser. *Judaism and the Christian Predicament*. New York. Knopf. 1967.
Berg C. "Secular world has a Christian foundation." *Sydney Morning Herald*, April 15, 2012.
Berkovits E & Hazony D. *Essential Essays on Judaism*. Jerusalem. Shalem. 2003.
Berkovitz J.R. *Encyclopedia of Children and Childhood in History and Society*. 2008. <http://www.faqs.org/childhood/In-Ke/Judaism.html>
Bernstein R.L. "Rights Watchdog, Lost in the Mideast." *The New York Times*, Oct 20,2009.
Bernstein E & Jakobsen J.R, *Sex, secularism, and religious influence in U.S. politics*. 2010. <http://www.opendemocracy.net/5050/elizabeth-bernstein-janet-r-jakobsen/sex-secularism-and-religious-influence-in-us-politics>).
Bethge E (ed). *Dietrich Bonhoeffer: Letters and Papers from Prison*. New York, Macmillan. 1974.
Bible.org, *What did Jesus mean when he said, "Upon this rock I will build my church"*? 2001:.<https://bible.org/question/what-did-jesus-mean-when-he-said-%E2%80%9Cupon-rock-i-will-build-my-church%E2%80%9D>*The Hidden Effects of Divorce on Children*
Bible Study Tools: *Pistis*. <https://www.biblestudytools.com/lexicons/greek/kjv/pistis.html>
Bilotta L. *The Hidden Effects of Divorce On Children*. 2007. <http://ezinearticles.com/?the-hidden-effects-of-divorce-on-children&id=405168>.
Bird M.F. *Jesus Is the Christ: The Messianic Testimony of the Gospels*. Illinois. Inter Varsity. 2012.
Birmingham M. *Word and Worship Workbook for Year C*. New Jersey. Paulist. 2000.
Bobosh T. *St. Paul: Christ is the Suffering Servant Exalted*. 2011. <https://frted.wordpress.com/2011/01/05/st-paul-christ-is-the-suffering-servant-exalted/>
Borg M.J. *Jesus: A New Vision: Spirit, Culture, and the Life of Discipleship*. San Francisco. Harper & Row. 1987.
———. *Jesus and Buddha: the parallel sayings*. Berkley. Ulysses.1997.
———. *Jesus: Uncovering the Life, Teachings, and Relevance of a Religious Revolutionary*. San Francisco. Harper. 2006.
———. *Meeting Jesus Again For the First Time*. San Francisco. Harper.1995
Borg M.J &Wright N.T. *The Meaning of Jesus: Two Visions*. New York. Harper Collins. 2006.

Bibliography

Botterweck J.G, Ringgren H, Fabry H.J. *Theological Dictionary of the Old Testament, Volume 12.* Michigan. Eerdmans. 2003.

Boulding M (Trans). *Augustine. The Confessions.* New York. New City. 2012.

Boundless World History. *Religion Under the Tang Dynasty.* 2016. <https://www.boundless.com/world-history/textbooks/boundless-world-history-textbook/chinese-dynasties-997/the-tang-dynasty-998/religion-under-the-tang-dynasty-1001-17605/>

Bowman J. "Mercy: Hosea 6:6." *The Expository Files.* 2006. <http://www.bible.ca/ef/expository-hosea-6-6.htm>

Boxall, I. *Discovering Matthew : content, interpretation, reception.* London. SPCK. 2014.

Boyce J. *Born Bad. Original Sin and the Making of the Western World.* Collingwood. Black Inc. 2014.

Brackley D. *Divine Revolution: Salvation and Liberation in Catholic Thought.* Oregon. Wipf & Stock. 2004.

Brandon S.G.F. *Jesus and the Zealots.* New York. Scrobner's Sons. 1967.

Buchanan P, *The Decline of Christian America.* 2015. <http://townhall.com/columnists/patbuchanan/2015/05/26/the-decline-of-christian-america-n2003650/page/full>

Buck C. *Illuminator vs. Redeemer: Was Ebionite Adam/Christ Prophetology "Original," Anti-Pauline, or "Gnostic"?* 2012. <http://christopherbuck.com/Buck_PDFs/Buck_1982_Illuminator.pdf>

Buddha Space: *Buddha & Eckhart: On Nothingness.* <http://buddhaspace.blogspot.com.au/2011/05/buddha-eckhart-on-nothingness.html>

Burke G, *May a Christian Believe in Reincarnation?* 2018.<https://ocoy.org/original-christianity/may-a-christian-believe-in-reincarnation/>

Burke K. "Anglican church doors open for divorcees to remarry." *Sydney Morning Herald.* 2002.

Butz J.J.. *The Brother of Jesus and the Lost Teachings of Christianity.* Vermont. Inner Traditions. 2005

Buxbaum Y. *The Life and Teachings of Hillel.* Plymouth. Rowman & Littlefield. Maryland. 2004.

Card M. *Matthew: The Gospel of Identity.* Illinois. InterVarsity. 2013.

Carlson A. "Why we need a renewed culture of natural marriage." *News Weekly*, Sept 4.2010.

Carmody D.L. *Women and World Religions.* Nashville, Abingdon. 1979.

Carroll V & Shiflett D. *Christianity On Trial: Arguments Against Anti-Religious Bigotry.* San Francisco. Encounter. 2002. <http://www.catholiceducation.org/en/culture/history/christianity-and-progress.html>

Carson D.A. "Matthew" in Tremper Longman III & Garland D.E (ed). *The Expositor's Bible Commentary.* Zondervan. Grand Rapids. 2010.

Carter H. "Stress, abuse damages childhood genes." *ABC Science,* Monday, 23 February, 2009. <http://www.abc.net.au/science/articles/2009/02/23/2498511.htm>

Cassian J. *Conferences.* New Jersey. Paulist. 1985.

Catholic Education Resource Centre.2000. *Christianity and Progress.* <http://www.catholiceducation.org/en/culture/history/christianity-and-progress.html>

Catholic Encyclopedia. *Permission of Sin and Remedies.* <http://www.newadvent.org/cathen/14004b.htm>

———. *Original Sin.* < http://www.newadvent.org/cathen/11312a.htm>

CBC News. *Crisis Caused 5.4 Million Deaths in Congo, Report Says.* 2008. <http://www.cbc.ca/world/story/2008/01/22/congo.html>.

Bibliography

Chadwick H. *The Church in Ancient Society: From Galilee to Gregory the Great.* Oxford. Clarendon. 2000.

———. *The Early Church.* London. Penguin. 1967.

Chidester D. *Christianity: a Global History.* London. Penguin. 2000.

Child Trends Databank. 2015. *Family structure.* <http://childtrends.org/?indicators=family-structure>

Christianity Today. *1536 John Calvin Publishes Institutes of the Christian Religion.* 1990. <http://www.christianitytoday.com/history/issues/issue-28/1536-john-calvin-publishes-institutes-of-christian-religion.html>

Christison K & B. *Does the Israeli Tail Wag the American Dog?* 2007. <http://www.informationclearinghouse.info/article17217.htm>.

———. *The Power of the Israeli Lobby.* 2006. <http://www.counterpunch.org/christison06162006.html>.

———. *The Rise of the Israeli Lobby. A Measure of its Power.* 2006. <http://www.paolobarnard.info/docs/Art.1%20CounterPunch%20sulle%20Lobbies%20israeliane.pdf>.

Cimperman M. *Social Analysis for the 21st Century.* New York. Orbis. 2015.

Clark K. *Civilization.* London. BBC.1977.

Cohen N. *Self Censorship and the BBC.* 2008. <http://standpointmag.com/television-august?page=1%2C0%2C0%2C0%2C0%2C0%2C0%2C0%2C0%2C0%2C3>

Collins J.J. *Introduction to the Hebrew Bible.* Minneapolis. Fortress. 2014.

Collins J.J and Harlow D.C. *Early Judaism: A Comprehensive Overview.* Cambridge. Eerdmans. 2012.

Coogan M.D. *A Brief Introduction to the Old Testament: The Hebrew Bible in Its Context.* New York. Oxford University Press. 2009.

Cortright C.L. *"Poor Maggot-Sack that I Am": The Human Body in the Theology of Martin Luther.* Marquette University Dissertation. 2009. <http://epublications.marquette.edu/cgi/viewcontent.cgi?article=1101&context=dissertations_m>

Crossan J.D. *The Birth of Christianity.* San Francisco. Harper. 1998.

———. *The Historical Jesus: the Life of a Mediterranean Jewish Peasant.* San Francisco. HarperCollins. 1991.

———. *Jesus: A Revolutionary Biography.* New York. Harper Collins.1994.

———. *Who Killed Jesus? Exposing the Roots of Anti-Semitism in the Gospel. Story of the Death of Jesus.* San Francisco. Harper Collins. 1995.

Crossan J.D. & Reed J.L. *Excavating Jesus: Beneath the Stones, Behind the Texts.* San Francisco. Harper. 2002.

Currie I. *You Cannot Die.* Shaftesbury. Element. 1978.

Danizier D. *Paul vs. Jesus (and James).* 2011. <https://danizier.wordpress.com/2011/04/22/paul-vs-jesus-and-james/>

Dauermann S, *New Perspectives on Paul and Why They Matter (4)—N. T. Wright.* 2012. <http://www.messianicjudaism.me/agenda/2012/03/04/new-perspectives-on-paul-and-why-they-matter-4-n-t-wright/>

Davidson J. *The Gospel of Jesus: In Search of His Original Teachings.* Shaftesbury. Element. 1995.

Davies S. *The Feminine Reclaimed: The Idea of Woman in Spenser, Shakespeare, and Milton.* University of Kentucky. 1986.

Dawkins R. *The God Delusion.* London. Transworld. 2006.

Bibliography

Dearden L. *Pope Francis 'to take 12 refugees on his plane back to Italy' after visit to Greek island where thousands trapped*. 2016. <http://www.independent.co.uk/news/world/europe/pope-francis-to-take-10-refugees-on-his-plane-back-to-europe-after-visit-to-greek-island-where-a6986946.html>

deClaissé-Walford N. *Commentary on Psalm 118:1-2, 14-24*. 2015. <https://www.workingpreacher.org/preaching.aspx?commentary_id=2380>

De Gruchy J.W. *Confessions of a Christian Humanist*. Minneapolis. Fortress. 2006.

Del Giorgio J.F. *The Oldest Europeans. Who Are We? Where Do We Come From? What Made European Women Different?* A.J Place. 2006.

Democracy Index. *Democracy in Retreat. A Report from the Economist Intelligence Unit*. 2010 <http://graphics.eiu.com/PDF/Democracy_Index_2010_web.pdf>.

Dhammika B.S. 2016, *Self-sacrificing Love*. <http://www.bhantedhammika.net/like-milk-and-water-mixed/self-sacrificing-love>

Dickerson J. 2012. "The Decline of Evangelical America." *New York Times*. December 15, 2012.

Doering L. "Sabbath Laws in the New Testament Gospels," in Bieringer R, Martinez F.G, Pollefeyt D & Tomson P.J (eds). *The New Testament and Rabbinic Literature*. Leiden. Brill.2010

Domhoff G.W. "Who Made American Foreign Policy, 1945-1963?" in Horowitz D. (ed). *Corporations and the Cold War*. New York. Monthly Review. 1969.

Donne A. "The Quest of the Historical Jesus: A Revisionist History through the Lens of Jewish-Christian Relations." *Journal for The Study Of The Historical Jesus*, 10(1).2012.

Donnelly S.B. *Saving Somalia*. 2007. <http://www.time.com/time/magazine/article/0,9171,1576842-3,00.html>.

Drazin I. *Philosophers reject the concept of grace*. 2013. <http://booksnthoughts.com/philosophers-reject-the-concept-of-grace/>

Dubay E. *The Truth About Reincarnation*. 2017. <http://www.ericdubay.com/?p=647>

Dubov N.D. *Reincarnation*. 2009. <http://www.chabad.org/library/article_cdo/aid/361889/jewish/Reincarnation.htm>

Dunn D.G. *Beginning from Jerusalem: Christianity in the Making*. Grand Rapids. Eerdemans. 2009.

Dupont C. *Jim crow, civil rights, and southern white evangelicals: a historians forum*. 2015. <https://blogs.thegospelcoalition.org/justintaylor/2015/02/10/jim-crow-civil-rights-and-southern-white-evangelicals-a-historians-forum-carolyn-dupont/>

Durland W. *God or Nations: Radical Theology for the Religious Peace Movement.*. Oregon. Wipf & Stock. 2010.

Easterly W.R. *The White Man's Burden: Why the West's Efforts to Aid the Rest Have Done So Much Ill and So Little Good*. London. Penguin. 2006.

Echegaray H. *The Practice of Jesus*. New York. Orbis.1980.

Edin M.H."Learning What Righteousness Means : Hosea 6:6 and the Ethic of Mercy in Matthew's Gospel." *Word & World*, 18(4).1998.

Edwards B. *Adam and Eve—the First Humans*. 2009. <http://birteedwards.hubpages.com/hub/Adam-and-Eve#lastcomment>

Eisenman R.H. *James the Brother of Jesus: The Key to Unlocking the Secrets of Early Christianity and the Dead Sea Scrolls*. New York. Penguin. 1993.

Eisenman R. *Paul as Herodian*.1996. <https://depts.drew.edu/jhc/eisenman.htm>

Eisler R. *The Chalice and the Blade: Our History, Our Future*. San Francisco. Harper & Rowe. 1987.

BIBLIOGRAPHY

Elazar D. *Deuteronomy as Israel's Ancient Constitution: Some Preliminary Reflections.* 1992. <http://www.jcpa.org/dje/articles2/deut-const.htm>

Elazar D. *Covenant as the Basis of the Jewish Political Tradition.* Jerusalem Center for Public Affairs. 1996. <http://www.jcpa.org/dje/books/kincon-ch1.htm>

Elliott L. *World Poverty Reduced by Growth in India and China.* 2007. <www.guardian.co.uk/business/2007/apr/16/china.india>.

Elliott L. *Modern slavery affects more than 35 million people, report finds.* 2014. <http://www.theguardian.com/world/2014/nov/17/modern-slavery-35-million-people-walk-free-foundation-report>

Ellis G & Kolchyna V. *Putin and the 'triumph of Christianity' in Russia.* 2017 <https://www.aljazeera.com/blogs/europe/2017/10/putin-triumph-christianity-russia-171018073916624.html>

Ellis P: *3 Reasons Why I Don't Preach on Repentance.* 2011. <http://escapetoreality.org/2011/11/28/3-reasons-why-i-dont-preach-on-repentance/>

Eskola T. "Paul, predestination and "covenantal nomism"-re-assessing Paul and Palestinian Judaism." *Journal for the Study of Judaism.* XXVIII, 4.1997.

Evans C. *Jesus' Action in the Temple and Evidence of Corruption.* 1989. <https://www.academia.edu/11940525/Jesus_Action_in_the_Temple_and_Evidence_of_Corruption_English_>

Evans C.A (ed) *The Historical Jesus.* Volume 2. London. Routledge. 2004.

Evans D.A. *Mark 8:27–16:20, Volume 34B.* Grand Rapids. Zondervan. 2018.

Ewart D. *Holy Textures.* 2018. <https://www.holytextures.com/2009/10/mark-10-35-45-year-b-pentecost-24-29-sermon.html>

Falk, H. "The Halakah of Jesus of Nazareth according to the Gospel of Matthew." *Journal Of Ecumenical Studies,* 27(2). 1990.

———. *Jesus the Pharisee: A New Look at the Jewishness of Jesus.* Oregon. Wipf & Stock. 2003.

Federow S. *G-d hates human sacrifice.* 2012. <http://www.whatjewsbelieve.org/explanation4.html>

Ferguson J. *Pelagius: A Historical and Theological Study.* Cambridge. W Heffer & Sons. 1956.

Fiensy, D. *The Social History of Palestine in the Herodian Period. The Land is Mine.* New York. The Edwin Mellen. 1991.

Finkle A. *Biblical, Rabbinic, and Early Christian Ethics.* 1994. <https://works.bepress.com/asher_finkel/40/ >

Finkelstein L.. "The Pharisaic Leadership after the Great Synagogue," in *The Cambridge History of Judaism: The Hellenistic Age, Volume 2.* Cambridge. Cambridge University Press. 1989.

———. *The Pharisees: The Sociological Background of their Faith.* Philadelphia. The Jewish Publication Society of America. 2002.

Finlan S. *Problems with Atonement.* Minnesota. Liturgical. 2005.

Fitzgerald A.D & Cavadini J. *Augustine through the ages : an encyclopaedia.* Michigan. Eerdmans. 1999.

FitzSimons-Allison C. *Trust in an Age of Arrogance.* Cambridge. Lutterworth. 2011.

Foster P. "Paul and Matthew: Tw strands of the early Jesus mvmt with little connection" in Bird M.F & Willitts J (eds) *Paul and the Gospels : Christologies, Conflicts and Convergences.* London. T&T Clark. 2011.

Forster W. *Palestinian Judaism in New Testament Times.* London. Oliver &Boyd. 1964.

Bibliography

Freke T & Gandy P. *Jesus and the Goddess: The Secret Teachings of the Original Christians*. London. Harper Collins. 2002.
Fredriksen P. *Jesus of Nazareth*. London. Macmillan. 2000.
———. *Augustine and the Jews: A Christian Defense of Jews and Judaism*. New York. Yale University Press. 2010.
Freedom House: *Freedom in the world, 2016:* <https://freedomhouse.org/report/freedom-world/freedom-world-2016 >
Freeman C. A. *A New History of Early Christianity*. New Haven. Yale University Press. 2009.
Freedman, D. N, Myers, A. C, & Beck, A. B. *Eerdmans dictionary of the Bible*. Michigan: W.B. Eerdmans. 2000.
Freyne S. *Galilee, from Alexander the Great to Hadrian, 323 BCE to 135 CE: a Study of Second Temple Judaism*. Indiana. University of Notre Dame. 1980.
Fricke C (ed). *The Ethics of Forgiveness: A Collection of Essays*. New York. Routledge. 2011.
Gale T. *Pentecostal and Charismatic Christianity*. 2005. <https://www.encyclopedia.com/environment/encyclopedias-almanacs-transcripts-and-maps/pentecostal-and-charismatic-christianity>
Garcia J. *Matthew 19:20: What Do I Still Lack?"Jesus, Charity, and the Early Rabbis*. 2015. <http://booksandjournals.brillonline.com/content/books/b9789004305434_004>
Gerecht R.M & Dubowitz M. "To Pressure Iran, Squeeze Russia and China." Wall Street Journal, 9 September, 2010.
Ghose T. *Animal Sacrifice Powered Ancient Jerusalem's Economy*. 2013. <https://www.livescience.com/39307-jerusalem-animal-sacrifice-found.html>
Gilding P. *The Great Disruption: How the climate crisis will transform the global economy*. Bloomsbury. USA. 2011.
Glatzer N. *Essays in Jewish Thought*. Alabama. Alabama University Press. 2009.
Gledhill R. *Churchgoing on its Knees as Christianity Falls Out of Favour*. 2008. <http://www.timesonline.co.uk/tol/comment/faith/article3890080.ece.>.
Global Issues. *Poverty Facts and Stats*. 2009.
<http://www.globalissues.org/article/26/poverty-facts-and-stats>.
Goetz J. *Conditional Futurism: New Perspective of End-Time Prophecy*. Oregon. Wipf & Stock. 2013.
Good E.M. *Genesis 1–11: Tales of the Earliest World*. Stanford University Press. Stanford. 2011.
Goodman L.E. *Love Thy Neighbor as Thyself*. New York. Oxford University Press. 2008.
Goodman M.A. *The Military-Industrial Complex's Win, Part II*. 2010. <http://www.truth-out.org/the-military-industrial-complexs-win-part-ii61187>.
Goodman M.A. *Rome and Jerusalem: the clash of ancient civilizations*. London. Penguin. 1987.
Gottwald N.K. Review of Stevens M.E. "Temples, Tithes, and Taxes: The Temple and the Economic Life of Ancient Israel," in *Catholic Biblical Quarterly*,70, 1, 2008.
Gottwald N.K. *The Hebrew Bible*. Minneapolis. Fortress. 2009.
Grant M. *Jesus*. London. Phoenix. 1977.
Grant T. *The Great Decline: 60 years of religion in one graph*. 2014. <http://tobingrant.religionnews.com/2014/01/27/great-decline-religion-united-states-one-graph/>
Greer G. "Half the Sky: how the other half suffer." *The Guardian*, Saturday 31 July, 2010.
Grof S. *The Cosmic Game: Explorations of the Frontiers of Human Consciousness*. New York. State University Press of New York. 1998.

Bibliography

Gruber E.R & Kersten H. *The Original Jesus: the Buddhist Sources of Christianity*, Shaftesbury. Element. 1995.

Gruber M.I. "An appreciation and precis of Jacob Neusner's theology of the oral Torah: Revealing the justice of God" in Neusner J (ed). *The documentary history of Judaism and its recent interpreters: Studies in Judaism*. New York. University Press of America. 2010.

Guijarro S. "The family in the Jesus movement." *Biblical Theology Bulletin*. 34.3. Fall 2004.

Hägerland T. *Jesus and the Forgiveness of Sins: An Aspect of his Prophetic Mission*. Cambridge. Cambridge University Press. 2011.

Hagin K. *The Coming Restoration*. 1985. <http://www.rhema.org/PDFs/ebooks/TheComingRestoration.pdf>

Ham C. "The Last Supper in Matthew." *Bulletin for Biblical Research* 10.1, 2000.

Hamblin W. "'Before Abraham was I AM' John 8:48–59." 2011. <https://www.academia.edu/685972/_Before_Abraham_was_I_AM_John_8_48–59>

Hamilton V.P. *The Book of Genesis, Chapters 1–17*. Michigan. Eerdmans. 1990.

Hamperton-Kelly R.G. *Sacred Violence: Paul's Hermeneutic of the Cross*. Minneapolis. Augsburg Fortress. 1992.

Hann R.R. "Judaism and Jewish Christianity in Antioch: Charisma and Conflict in the First Century." *Journal of Religious History*. December, 1987

Hanson P.D. *Isaiah 40–66*. Louisville. Westminster John Knox. 2012.

Hari J. 2008. *How we fuel Africa's bloodiest war*. 2008 <http://www.independent.co.uk/opinion/commentators/johann-hari/johann-hari-how-we-fuel-africas-bloodiest-war-978461.html>.

Harrington D.J & Landau Y. *The Synoptic Gospels Set Free: Preaching Without Anti-Judaism*. Mahwah. Paulist. 2009.

Harris M. *Prepositions And Theology In The Greek New Testament : An Essential Reference Resource For Exegesis.*. Grand Rapids. Zondervan. 2012.

Hayes J.H. *Interpreting Ancient Israelite History, Prophecy and Law*. Eugene. Cascade. 2013.

Hebrew Interlinear Bible. <http://www.scripture4all.org/OnlineInterlinear/Hebrew_Index.htm>

Hegesippus. Book 5. *Fragments from the Acts of the Church; Concerning the Martyrdom of James, the Brother of the Lord*.

Hezekiah 4. *Jesus the Pharisee*. 2010 <http://hezekiah4.xanga.com/2010/02/11/jesus-the-pharisee/>

Hick J. *The Metaphor of God Incarnate: Christology in a Pluralistic Age*. Louisville. John Knox. 2006.

Hill D. "On the Use and Meaning of Hosea vi. 6 in Matthew's Gospel." *New Testament Studies*, 24. 1977.

Hilton Danan J. *Do Jews believe in the Holy Spirit? 2010*. <https://www.beth-elsa.org/Worship/Sermons/Guest_Speakers/Do_Jews_Believe_in_the_Holy_Spirit_01_15_10>

Hirsch E.G, Cornill K.H, Schechter S, Ginzberg L. *Jewish Encyclopedia*: "Ezekiel." 1906. <http://www.jewishencyclopedia.com/articles/5950-ezekiel>

Hitchens C. *God is Not Great: How Religion Poisons Everything*. New York. Hachette. 2007.

———. *Hitchens vs. Blair debate: 'Be it resolved, religion is a force for good in the world'.* 2010. <http://www.newstatesman.com/blogs/the-staggers/2010/11/christopher-hitchens-tony-blair>.

Bibliography

Hobbes T. *The Leviathan*. http://oregonstate.edu/instruct/phl302/texts/hobbes/leviathan-c.html

Hogan R.C. *Yeshua Before 30 CE*. 2006. <http://30ce.com/paulinechristianity.htm>

Hooper J. "Vatican makes attempted ordination of women a grave crime." *The Guardian*, July 15, 2010.

Hooper R (ed). *Jesus,Buddha, Krishna, Lao Tzu: The Parallel Sayings*. Sedona. Sanctuary Publications Inc. 2007.

Hopler W. *How Does Archangel Chamuel Represent Geburah (Strength) in Kabbalah?* 2017. <https://www.thoughtco.com/archangel-chamuel-geburah-strength-kabbalah-124037>

Horsley R.A.. *Bandits, prophets & messiahs: popular movements in the time of Jesus*. Minneapolis. Fortress. 1999.

———. *Scribes, visionaries, and the politics of Second Temple Judea*. Louisville. Westminster John Knox. 2007.

———. "Jesus and the Politics of Roman Palestine." *Journal for the Study of the Historical Jesus*. 8, 2010.

Horsley R & Thatcher T. *John, Jesus, and the Renewal of Israel*. Grand Rapids. Eerdemans. 2013.

Hossein-Zadeh I. *The Political Economy of US Militarism*. New York. Palgrave Macmillan. 2006.

Houston W.J. *Social Justice and the Prophets*. 2018. <https://www.bibleodyssey.org/en/passages/related-articles/social-justice-and-the-prophets>

Howker E. *All in a good cause?* 2009. <https://www.spectator.co.uk/2009/12/all-in-a-good-cause/>

Hsiao A. *Is Darfur's Peacekeeping Chief Overly Optimistic?* 2010. <http://www.enoughproject.org/blogs/peacekeeping-chief-darfur-overly-optimistic>.

Hunger Notes: *World Hunger and Poverty Facts and Statistics*. 2015 <http://www.worldhunger.org/2015-world-hunger-and-poverty-facts-and-statistics/>

Huie B.T. *Who Were the Pharisees and Sadducees?* 1997. <http://www.herealittletherealittle.net/index.cfm?page_name=Pharisees-Sadducees>.

Hunt M. *Is "hesed" the same as "agape"? God's love defined by covenant in the old and new testaments*. 2007. <http://www.agapebiblestudy.com/documents/is%20hesed%20the%20same%20as%20agape.ht>

Ignatieff M. *Is identity politics ruining democracy?* 2018. <https://www.ft.com/content/09c2c1e4-ad05-11e8-8253-48106866cd8a>

Ilan T. *Integrating Women into Second Temple History*. Tübingen. Mohr Siebeck. 1999.

Ingram P.O. *Wrestling With the Ox: A Theology of Religious Experience*. Oregon. Wipf & Stock. 2006.

International Crisis Group. *A Way Forward for Zimbawbe*. 2010. <http://www.crisisgroup.org/en/key-issues/a-way-forward-for-zimbabwe.aspx>.

International Review of the Red Cross. 2005. <http://www.icrc.org/Web/eng/siteeng0.nsf/htmlall/review-858 p311 $File/irrc_858_Ferris.pdf>

Jacobs J & Broydé I *Free Will*. . 1906. <http://www.jewishencyclopedia.com/articles/6337-free-will>

Janowski B. "He Bore our Sins." In Janowski B & Stuhlmacher P (eds) *The Suffering Servant: Isaiah 53 in Jewish and Christian Source*. Michigan. Eerdemans. 2004.

Jenks D.F. *First Things First*. Fairfax. Xulon. 2002.

Bibliography

Jones J.W. *Catholic Church to welcome 50 Anglican clergy.* 2010. <http://www.telegraph.co.uk/news/religion/8131063/Catholic-Church-to-welcome-50-Anglican-clergy.html>

Josephus. *The Wars of the Jews.* http://www.ccel.org/j/josephus/works/war-pref.htm

Jacobs J & Blau L. *Jewish Encyclopedia: Gnosticism* <http://www.jewishencyclopedia.com/articles/6723-gnosticism>

Jacobson S.2017. *Daily Omer Meditation.* < http://www.aish.com/h/o/t/48969716.html>

Jastrow M & Mendelsohn S. *Jewish Encyclopedia.* "Bet Hillel and Bet Shammai."2002. <http://www.jewishencyclopedia.com/articles/3190-bet-hillel-and-bet-shammai>

Jenkins S. *Blame the identity apostles—they led us down this path to populism.* 2016. <https://www.theguardian.com/commentisfree/2016/dec/01/blame-trump-brexit-identity-liberalism>

Jett D. *The Mysterious Melchizedek: Genesis 14:18–20.* 2015. <http://webcache.googleusercontent.com/search?q=cache:http://crossgates.tv/wp-content/uploads/2015/10/2015-10-28-Genesis-14-18-20-The-Mysterious-Melchizedek.pdf&gws_rd=cr&ei=gn26VtzrOoTK0ASMvISgCg>

Johnson L.T. *The Letter of James.* New Interpreter's Bible. Nashville. Abingdon. 1998.

Jones D.M. *Dismissing Jesus: How We Evade the Way of the Cross.* Oregon. Cascade. . 2013.

Josephus F. *Antiquities of the Jews.* <http://www.sacred-texts.com/jud/josephus/ant-20.htm>.

Journeaux T. *The Gnostic paradox in the Gospel of Judas.* 2012. <https://thirdmillennialtemplar.wordpress.com/2012/06/06/the-gnostic-paradox-in-the-gospel-of-judas/>

Julian of Norwich. *Revelations of Divine Love. (c.1393).* <https://en.wikiquote.org/wiki/Julian_of_Norwich>

Kalimi I. *The Historical Uniqueness and Centrality of Yom Kippur.* 2017. <http://thetorah.com/historical-uniqueness-and-centrality-of-yom-kippur/>

Kasser R, Meyer M, Wurst G & Gaudard F. *Gospel of Judas.* 2006. <http://southerncrossreview.org/49/gospel-judas.htm>.

Kaufmann W. *Critique of Religion and Philosophy.* New Jersey. Princeton University Press. 1958.

Kaufmann E.P. *Shall the Religious Inherit the Earth? Demography and Politics in the Twenty-first Century.* London. Profile. 2010.

Keenan J.P. *The Wisdom of James: Parallels with Mahāyāna Buddhism.* New York. Newman. 2005.

Keizer L. *The Kabbalistic Teachings of Jesus in the Gospel of Thomas.* 2010. <https://www.academia.edu/11423212/The_Kabbalistic_Words_of_Jesus_in_the_Gospel_of_Thomas_Recovering_the_Inner-Circle_Teachings_of_Yeshua>

Kelly P. *Blair sees the real power in faith.* 2011. <http://www.theaustralian.com.au/news/inquirer/blair-sees-the-real-power-in-faith/story-e6frg6z6-1226102974094>

———. *Main parties are divided because we are divided.* 2018. <https://www.theaustralian.com.au/opinion/main-parties-are-divided-because-we-are-divided/news-story/0e5c63dd757b92c0b5f375b8587a7fe2>

———.*New progressive morality rapidly taking over from Christian beliefs.* 2017. http://www.theaustralian.com.au/opinion/columnists/paul-kelly/new-progressive-morality-rapidly-taking-over-from-christian-beliefs/news-story/c5f0c19f4f73d088f546fbd6b884befe>

Kelly R.H. *The Gospel and the Sacred: Poetics of Violence in Mark.* Minneapolis: Fortress. 1994.

Bibliography

Kennedy R.F. *Day of Affirmation Speech. Cape Town, June6, 1966.* <http://www.rfksafilm.org/html/speeches/unicape.php>

Keyser J.D. *Dead Sea Scrolls Prove Pharisees Controlled Temple Ritual.* 1996. <http://www.hope-of-israel.org/i000117a.htm>.

Kido I. *The Spirit of Buddha.*< http://shorinkutsu.com/_userdata/spirit.pdf>

Kinzer M. *Postmissionary Messianic Judaism: Redefining Christian Engagement with the Jewish People.* Brazos. 2005.

Klijn A.F.J. "2(Syriac Apocalypse of) Baruch, a New Translation and Introduction," in Charlesworth J (ed). *The Old Testament Pseudepigrapha.* Vol. 1, 1983.

Knowles M.P. *The Unfolding Mystery of the Divine Name: The God of Sinai in Our Midst.* Illinois. Intervarsity. 2012.

Knox N. *Religion takes a back seat in Western Europe.* 2005, <http://www.usatoday.com/news/world/2005-08-10-europe-religion-cover_x.htm>.

Koestner R, Franz C, & Weinberger J. "The Family Origins of Empathic Concern: a 26-year longitudinal study." *Journal of Personality Social Psychology.* 58: 709–717, 1990.

Kohler K. *Atonement.* 1906. <http://www.jewishencyclopedia.com/articles/2092-atonement>

Köstenberger A.J. "'What is truth?' Pilate's question in its Johannine and larger biblical context." *Journal of the Evangelical Theological Society.* 48/1. March, 2005.

Kristof N. "Farm Subsidies That Kill." *New York Times,* July 5, 2002.

Kristof N & WuDunn S. *Half the Sky: Turning Oppression into Opportunity.* New York. Vintage. 2010.

Kubler-Ross E. *On Life After Death.* 1991.

Lacocque A & P.E. *The Jonah Complex.* Atlanta. John Knox. 1981.

Ladwig J. *Brain can be trained in compassion, study shows.* 2013. <http://news.wisc.edu/brain-can-be-trained-in-compassion-study-shows/>

Lancaster D.T."Yeshua's New Wine: The Double Parable of Luke 5:33–39 Re-examined." *Bikurei Tziyon,* Issue 76, 2003.

Lawder D. *IMF: Global corruption costs trillions in bribes, lost growth.* 2016. <http://www.reuters.com/article/us-imf-corruption-idUSKCN0Y22B7>

Leiberman S. *Kabbala #10: Chesed—The World is Built on Kindness.* 2000. <http://www.aish.com/sp/k/Kabbala_10__Chesed_-_The_World_is_Built_on_Kindness.html>

———. *Kabbala #12: Chesed and Gevurah: The Two Sided Approach.* 2000. <http://www.aish.com/sp/k/Kabbala_12_Chesed_and_Gevurah_The_Two_Sided_Approach.html>

Lewis H. *Lenten Refelections 5: Compassion as integrative love-force.* 2017. <http://mattersindia.com/2017/03/lenten-refelections-5-compassion-as-integrative-love-force/>

Lezard N. *Inventing the Individual: the Origins of Western Liberalism by Larry Siedentop —review.* 2015. <https://www.theguardian.com/books/2015/jan/27/inventing-individual-origins-western-liberalism-larry-siedentop-review>

Lobe J. *Conservative Christians Biggest Backers of Iraq War.* 2002. <http://www.commondreams.org/headlines02/1010-02.htm>.

Lodge G.C. *Multinational Corporations: A Key to Global Poverty Reduction—Part I.* 2006. <http://yaleglobal.yale.edu/content/multinational-corporations-key-global-poverty-reduction-%E2%80%93-part-i>

Lomborg B. *Climate change: Paris Agreement makes too little difference.* 2017.

Bibliography

<http://www.theaustralian.com.au/news/inquirer/climate-change-paris-agreement-makes-too-little-difference/news-story/2a375b85f996e169611d2aafd81bcbee>

———. *Climate-change policies may be making world hunger worse.* 2018. <https://www.theaustralian.com.au/opinion/columnists/bjorn-lomborg/climatechange-policies-may-be-making-world-hunger-worse/news-story/1731c0124e3b89c57001afcd84c9537c>

———. *Does Helping the Planet Hurt the Poor?* 2011. <http://www.wsj.com/articles/SB10001424052748703779704576074360837994874>

Long P.J. *Acts 12:1–2—Why Did Herod Kill James?* 2013. <http://readingacts.com/2013/02/19/acts-121-2-why-did-herod-kill-james/>

Lúcás Chan Y.S. *The Ten Commandments and the Beatitudes: Biblical Studies and Ethics for Real Life.* Maryland. Rowman & Littlefield. 2012.

Ludwig T.M *Sacred Paths of the West.* New York. Routledge. 2016.

Marcion. *Gospel of the Lord.* < http://www.wendag.com/marcion/Marcion.html>

Marlowe M.*The Kingdom of God Is Within You.* 2011. <http://www.bible-researcher.com/luke17.21.html>

Marshall T. *Sirach: About a Biblical Book Rejected by the Reformation.* 2010. <http://www.calledtocommunion.com/2010/11/sirach-about-a-biblical-book-rejected-by-the-reformation/>

Maston J. *Divine and Human Agency in Second Temple Judaism and Paul.* Tubingen. Mohr Siebeck. 2010.

Mattison M. *A Summary of the New Perspective on Paul.* 2009. <http://www.thepaulpage.com/a-summary-of-the-new-perspective-on-paul/>

McCartney D.G. *James.* Grand Rapids. Baker Academic. 2009.

McConville J.G. *Exploring the Old Testament: A Guide to the Prophets.* Illinois. Inter Varsity. 2002.

McGarry P. *Mass attendance in Dublin to drop by one-third by 2030.* 2016. <http://www.irishtimes.com/news/social-affairs/religion-and-beliefs/mass-attendance-in-dublin-to-drop-by-one-third-by-2030-1.2504351>

McGrath A.E.(ed). *The Christian Theology Reader.* Chichester. Wiley-Blackwell. 2011.

McGreal C. "War in Congo kills 45,000 people each month." *The Guardian.* Jan 23, 2008.

Mckenzie J.L. *The Dictionary Of The Bible.* New York. Simon & Shuster. 1995.

McKnight S. *Jesus and His Death Historiography, the Historical Jesus, and Atonement Theory.* Waco. Baylor University Press. 2005.

Mcleod D. *Indigenous PM for Australia.* 2013. <http://theinspirationroom.com/daily/2013/indigenous-pm-for-australia/>

McNamer E. *The First One Hundred Years of Christianity in Jerusalem.* 2009. <http://www.bibleinterp.com/articles/mcnamer.shtml>

May R. *Putin: From Oligarch to Kleptocrat.* 2018. <http://www.nybooks.com/daily/2018/02/01/putin-from-oligarch-to-kleptocrat/>

Mearsheimer J.J & Walt S.M. *The Israel Lobby and U.S. Foreign Policy.* New York. Farrar, Straus and Giroux. 2007.

Meier J.P. *A Marginal Jew: Rethinking the Historical Jesus,Vol. 4.* New Haven. Yale University Press. 2009.

Michael R. *Holy Hatred: Christianity, Antisemitism, and the Holocaust.* New York: Palgrave Macmillan. 2006.

Miller M. *Chesed, Gevura, & Tiferet.* 2012. <http://www.chabad.org/kabbalah/article_cdo/aid/380796/jewish/Chesed-Gevura-Tiferet.htm>

Bibliography

Millett M.G. *Reincarnation and Christianity*. 2015. < https://elevatedtherapy.org.uk/reincarnation-and-christianity/>

Mills W.E (ed). *Mercer Dictionary of the Bible*. Macon. Mercer University Press.1997.

Moland L (ed). *Complete Works of Voltaire*. Vol10. Paris. Garnier. 1877–1885.

Molnar M.R. *The Star of Bethlehem: The Legacy of the Magi*. New Jersey. Rutgers University Press. 1999.

Moore C.E. *Pandemic Love* <http://www.plough.com/en/topics/faith/discipleship/pandemic-love>

Morris J. *Revival of the Gnostic Heresy: Fundamentalism*. New York. Palgrave Macmillan. 2008.

Moule, C. F. D. *The Origin of Christology*. Cambridge.Cambridge University Press. 1977.

Murawski J. "N.T. Wright Asks: Have Christians Gotten Heaven All Wrong?" *The Huffington Post*. 17 May, 2012

Murphy F.J. *Early Judaism: the Exile to the Time of Jesus*. Michigan. Baker Academic. 2010.

Myers C. *Binding the Strong Man: A Political Reading of Mark's Story of Jesus*. New York. Orbis. 1988.

National Center for Fathering. *The Effects of FatherFULLness*. 2007. <http://www.fathers.com/content/index.php?option=com_content&task=view&id=396>.

Needleman J. *Lost Christianity: a Journey of Rediscovery to the Centre of Christian Experience*. Shaftesbury. Element. 1990.

Neiman S. *The Rationality of the World: A Philosophical Reading of the Book of Job*. 2016. <http://www.abc.net.au/religion/articles/2016/10/19/4559097.htm>

Nemoianu V. *Teaching Christian Humanism*. 1996. <http://www.firstthings.com/article/1996/05/003-teaching-christian-humanism>

Neusner J. *The Rabbinic Traditions About the Pharisees Before 70, Part III: Conclusions*. Oregon. Wipf &Stock. 2005.

Neusner J (ed). *The documentary history of Judaism and its recent interpreters: Studies in Judaism*. New York. University Press of America. 2010.

Nichols B. *Reincarnation Quotes*.<http://www.ivymag.org/subsclub/reincarnationquotes.html>

Nietzsche,F. *The Gay Science*. 1882. <http://markandrewholmes.com/godisdead.html>

———. *The Antichrist*. 1888. <http://en.wikisource.org/wiki/The_Antichrist>.

Nolan A. *Jesus Before Christianity: the Gospel of Liberation*. .London. Darton, Longman and Todd. 1991.

Novak R. "Hesed: Its Significance and Impact on Jonah in His Mission to Nineveh as Recorded by the Prophet." *Encounter: Journal for Pentecostal Ministry*. Summer Vol. 11, 2014.

Nunnally W.E. "G'meelut Chasadin (Deeds of Kindness)" in Palmer M.D & Burgess S.M (eds) *The Wiley-Blackwell Companion to Religion and Social Justice*. Chichester. Blackwell. 2012.

Oderberg I. M. *Reincarnation as Taught by Early Christians*. 1973. <http://www.theosophy-nw.org/theosnw/reincar/re-imo.htm>.

Olar J.L. *Ecclesiasticus: the Wisdom of Ben Sirach*. 2001. <http://graceandknowledge.faithweb.com/sirach.html>

Oliver I.W. *Torah Praxis after 70 C.E.: Reading Matthew and Luke-Acts as Jewish Texts*. 2012. <https://deepblue.lib.umich.edu/bitstream/handle/2027.42/93865/ioliver_1.pdf?sequence=1https://www.google.com.au/webhp%3fgws_rd=ssl>

Bibliography

O'Loughlin M. *Pew survey: Percentage of US Catholics drops and Catholicism is losing members faster than any denomination.* 2015. <http://www.cruxnow.com/church/2015/05/12/pew-survey-percentage-of-us-catholics-drops-and-catholicism-is-losing-members-faster-than-any-denomination/>

Olson R.E. *The Dark Side of Pentecostalism.* 2016. <http://www.patheos.com/blogs/rogereolson/2016/10/the-dark-side-of-pentecostalism/>

———. *A Christian Humanist Manifesto: God Is Most Satisfied with Us when We Are Most Glorified by Him.* 2012. <http://www.patheos.com/blogs/rogereolson/2012/11/a-christian-humanist-manifesto-god-is-most-satisfied-with-us-when-we-are-most-glorified-by-him-part-1/>

O'Malley N. *Democracy under threat as young people warm to authoritarian rule.* 2016. <http://www.smh.com.au/world/democracy-under-threat-as-young-people-warm-to-authoritarian-rule-researchers-say-20161201-gt1usr.html>

Omnilexia: *Eleos.* <http://www.omnilexica.com/?q=eleos>

Online Encyclopedia. *Marcion.* 1911. <http://encyclopedia.jrank.org/MAL_MAR/MARCION.html>

Ong S.H. *A Strategy for a Metaphorical Reading of the Epistle of James.* Maryland. University Press of America. 1996.

Oriel J. "The Pope Caves in to Church's Old Enemies." *The Australian,* February 23, 2018

Osborne G.R. *Exegetical Commentary on the New Testament: Matthew.* Michigan. Zondervan. 2010.

Oxley A. WWF Concocts its Own Beautiful Set of Numbers." *The Australian,* Feb 11, 2010.

Packer G. *The Moderate Martyr: A radically peaceful vision of Islam.* 2006. <http://www.newyorker.com/magazine/2006/09/11/the-moderate-martyr>

Pagels E. *The Gnostic Gospels.* New York. Random House. 1979.

———. *The Gnostic Paul: Gnostic Exegesis of the Pauline Letters.* New York, Continuum.1992

———. *Beyond Belief: The Secret Gospel of Thomas.* New York. Random House. 2003.

Palley T.I. *Lifting the Natural Resource Curse.* 2003. <https://www.globalpolicy.org/the-dark-side-of-natural-resources-st/water-in-conflict/40112.html>

Pearson N. *Drone footage shows Putin's 'secret island mansion.* 2017. <http://www.9news.com.au/world/2017/09/01/10/52/vladimir-putin-secret-island-mansion-villa-alexei-navalny-drone-video>

Pelagius, "On the Christian Life," in Rees B.R. *The Letters of Pelagius and his Followers.* Boydell. Woodbridge. 1991.

Peterson D. *Atonement in Paul's Writings.* 2009. <http://davidgpeterson.com/atonement/atonement-in-pauls-writings/>

Pew Research Center—Religion & Public Life.*Pentecostalism.*2014. <http://www.pewforum.org/2014/11/13/chapter-4-pentecostalism/>

Pierard R.V. "The Lutheran two-kingdoms doctrine and subservience to the state in modern Germany." *Journal of the Evangelical Theological Society.* June, 1986.

Pierce C. *The Process of Restoration: "The Holy Spirit."* 2012. <http://www.elijahlist.com/words/display_word.html?ID=10647>

Plantinga A. *God, Freedom, and Evil.* Grand Rapids. Eerdmans. 1977.

Poppick S. *Corporations Dodge $200 Billion in Taxes Each Year.* 2015. http://time.com/money/3934642/corporation-tax-avoidance/

Bibliography

Powell F.F. *Robbing Peter to Pay Paul: The Usurpation of Jesus and the Original Disciples.* Bloomington. iUniverse. 2009.
Powell M.A. *Introducing the New Testament: A Historical, Literary and Theological Survey.* Grand Rapids. Baker. 2009.
Premnath D.N. *Eighth Century Prophets: a Social Analysis.* Massachusetts. Chalis. 2003.
Price R.M. *Deconstructing Jesus.* New York. Prometheus. 2000.
Prophet E.C & Prophet E.L. *Reincarnation: The Missing Link in Christianity.* Summit University Press. Massachusetts.1997.
Prophet E.C, Spadaro P.R & Steinman M.L. *Kabbalah: Key to Your Inner Power.* Montana. Summit University Press. 1997.
Ramkumar V. *The Good News in Brazil's Two-Headed Crisis.* 2016. <http://www.usnews.com/news/best-countries/articles/2016-04-22/the-good-news-in-brazils-two-headed-crisis>
Regan L & Kelly L. *Rape: Still a Forgotten Issue.* 2003. <http://www.rcne.com/downloads/RepsPubs/Attritn.pdf>.
Regev E. "The Temple in Mark: A Case Study about the Early Christian Attitude toward the Temple," in D. Jaffé (ed.) *Studies in Rabbinic Judaism and Early Christianity. Text and Context, Ancient Judaism and Early Christianity.* Series 74, Leiden; Brill. 2010.
Reid L. *She Changes Everything: Seeking the Divine on a Feminist Path.* New York. T&T Clark. 2005.
Reiss M. "Jesus the Jew." *Christianity: A Jewish Perspective.* 2003. <http://www.moshereiss.org/christianity/03_hillel/03_hillel.htm>.
Rich A. "Trailing the Class: Sole Parent Families and Educational Disadvantage," in Marquardt E. *Between Two Worlds.* Centre for Independent Studies Issue Analysis. No 11. 6 June, 2000.
Rich T.R. *Mashiach: The Messiah.* 2011. <http://www.jewfaq.org/mashiach.htm>
Richards L & Richards L.O. *Bible Teacher's Commentary.* Colorado. Victor. 2004.
Robertson B. *Jesus' Death: Ransom or Sacrifice?* <http://christianmystics.com/contemporary/BrianRobertson/RansomorSacrifice.html>
Robinson B.A. *Religious Identification in the US: How American Adults View Themselves.* 2009. <http://www.religioustolerance.org/chr_prac2.htm>.
Robotham J. "Childhood abuse may change stress gene." *Sydney Morning Herald*, February 23, 2009.
Rocha J.L. *The Third Horseman of Neoliberalism: The Neo Pentecostals.*
<http://www.envio.org.ni/articulo/4624>
Romer J. *Testament. The Bible and History.*.Sydney. ABC. 1988.
Rose G.B. "The Feminine Soul of the Renaissance." *The Sewanee Review.*Vol. 14, No. 4. Oct., 1906.
Rosenberg B.H. *Theological and Halakhic Reflections on the Holocaust.* Hoboken. KTAV. 1992.
Ross T. "Sex abuse 'humiliation' is a fault of the Church and the times, says Pope." *The Daily Telegraph* (UK), December 21, 2010.
Roth M. *Isaiah 53: The Suffering Servant: Cutting through the distortions and mistranslations of this enigmatic text.* 2011. <http://www.aish.com/sp/ph/Isaiah_53_The_Suffering_Servant.html>
Routledge, R. L. "Ḥesed as Obligation : A Re-Examination." *Tyndale Bulletin*, 46(1). 1995
Ruscillo L. *The Primacy of Christ and Wisdom Literature.* 2007.

<http://www.faith.org.uk/article/january-february-2007-the-primacy-of-christ-and-wisdom-literature>

Sacks J. *To Heal a Fractured World: The Ethics of Responsibility.* New York. Random House. 2005.

———. *Yitro (5774)—A Nation of Leaders.* 2014. <http://rabbisacks.org/yitro-5774-nation-leaders/>

Safrai S. "The Era of the Mishnah and the Talmud (70–640)," in Ben-Sasson HH, (ed), *A History of the Jewish People.*.Tel Aviv. George Weidenfield and Nicholson Ltd. 1969.

Sammut J. "Interventionist child protection policies are right." *The Australian*, Oct 2/3, 2010.

———. *Reaping the whirlwind: The 'new silence' about broken families and child sexual abuse.* 2014. http://www.abc.net.au/religion/articles/2014/02/04/3937917.htm

Sanders E.P. *Paul and Palestinian Judaism: A Comparison of Patterns of Re\ligion.* Philadelephia. Fortress. 1977.

———. *The Historical Figure of Jesus.* London. Penguin. 1993.

Sandmel S. *We Jews and Jesus.* New York. Oxford University Press. 1965.

Sarfati J.D. *Was God's finished creation perfect?* 2013. <http://creation.com/creation-perfect>

Schiffman, L. "New Light on the Pharisees: Insights from the Dead Sea Scrolls." *Bible Review.* June, 1992

Schussler Fiorenza E. *In memory of Her: A Feminist Reconstruction of Christian Origins.* New York. Crossland. 1985.

Schwartz S. *International Engagement with Somalia.* 2010. <http://www.usip.org/resources/international-engagement-somalia>.

Seidensticker B. *What Did Paul Know About Jesus? Not Much.* 2012. <http://www.patheos.com/blogs/crossexamined/2012/12/what-did-paul-know-about-jesus-not-much/>

Segovia F.F. "Reading the Bible Ideologically: socio-economic criticism;" in McKenzie S.L & Haynes S.R(eds). *To Each its Own Meaning. An Introduction to Biblical Criticisms and their Application.* Louisville. John Knox. 1999.

Semkiw W. *Reincarnation, Jesus, the Bible, New Testament & Christian Doctrine* <http://www.iisis.net/index.php?page=semkiw-reincarnation-past-lives-christianity&hl=en_US>

Severance D. *Jesus Loved Children.* <http://www.christianity.com/church/church-history/timeline/1-300/jesus-loved-children-11629553.html>

Severance M. *Vatican's Colloquium on Marriage.* 2014. <http://www.catholicworldreport.com/item/3524/vaticans_colloquium_on_marriage_focuses_on_universal_right_complementarity_anthropology_and_strategy.aspx>

Shapiro R.M. *Amazing Chesed: Living a Grace-filled Judaism.* Vermont. Jewish Lights. 2013.

Shariff A.F &Rhemtulla M. *Divergent Effects of Beliefs in Heaven and Hell on National Crime Rates.* 2012. < http://journals.plos.org/plosone/article?id=10.1371%2Fjournal.pone.0039048>

Sharma S.K. *Dharma and Universal Values of Humanism.* 2000. <http://www.peoplefirstindia.org/6dharma.htm>

Sheridan G. *Is God Dead?* 2017. <https://www.theaustralian.com.au/news/inquirer/is-god-dead-western-has-much-to-lose-inbanishinchristianity/news>story/b1dcbeabbd5776307debc9ddcb845539>

Bibliography

Sherwin B.L. *Kabbalah: An Introduction to Jewish Mysticism*. Maryland. Rowman Littlefield Inc. 2006.

Sherwood H. "Mutiny fear in Israeli army as religious Zionists gain influence." *The Guardian*. 12 July, 2012.

Shevchenko V. *Russian Orthodox Church lends weight to Putin patriotism*. 2015. <http://www.bbc.com/news/world-europe-33982267>

Shields J. *Lawyers accuse Catholic Church of 'push back' against victims of child sex abuse*. 2015. <http://www.abc.net.au/radionational/programs/breakfast/lawyers-accuse-catholic-church-of-pushing-back-against-victims/6979112>

Shirer W.L. *The Rise and Fall of the Third Reich: a History of Nazi Germany*, New York. Simon & Schuster. 1960.

Shorto R. *Gospel Truth*. New York. Riverhead. 1997.

Shulman M. *The Zohar on Isaiah 53*. 2003.< http://judaismsanswer.com/zohar.htm>

Sicker M. *Between Rome and Jerusalem: 300 Years of Roman-Judaean Relations*. Westport. Praeger. 2001.

Sider R (ed). *The Early Church on Killing : a Comprehensive Sourcebook on War, Abortion, and Capital Punishment*. Grand Rapids, MI. Baker Academic. 2012.

Sigal G. *Did Jesus fulfill the role of the asham, "guilt-offering?* <https://jewsforjudaism.org/knowledge/articles/did-jesus-fulfill-the-role-of-the-asham-qguilt-offeringq/>

Simmans G. *Jesus after the Crucifixion: From Jerusalem to Rennes-le-Château*. Rochester. Bear &Co. 2007.

Singer T. *Does Judaism believe in original sin?* <http://outreachjudaism.org/original-sin/>

———. *Who is God's Suffering Servant? The Rabbinic Interpretation of Isaiah 53*. <http://outreachjudaism.org/gods-suffering-servant-isaiah-53/>

———. *Sin and Atonement.*<http://outreachjudaism.org/sin-and-atonement/>

Sniegocki J. "Neoliberal Globalisation: Critiques and Alternatives." *Theological Studies*. June, 2008.

Souvay C. "Isaias." *The Catholic Encyclopedia*, Vol. 8. 1910. <http://www.newadvent.org/cathen/08179b.htm 26 Nov, 2009>.

Spaulding M. *What about Jesus and literal interpretation of Isaiah 9:6?* <https://carm.org/literal-interpretation-isaiah>

Spencer F. S. "Scripture, hermeneutics, and Matthew's Jesus." *Interpretation*. 64 no 40. 2010.

Spong J.S. *Liberating the Gospels: Reading the Bible with Jewish Eyes*. San Francisco. Harper. 1996.

Sprinkle P. *Paul & Judaism Revisited: A Study Of Divine And Human Agency In Salvation*. Illinois. Academic. 2013.

Stark R. *The Victory of Reason: How Christianity Led to Freedom, Capitalism, and Western Success*. New York. Random House. 2005.

Stedman E. *Basics of Bible Interpretation*. 2009. <http://www.raystedman.org/leadership/smith/ch10.html>

Stern D.H. *Jewish New Testament Commentary*, Jewish New Testament Publications, Clarksville, Maryland. 1992.

Stern M. "The Period of the Second Temple" in Ben-Sasson H.H. *A History of the Jewish People*. Tel Aviv. Dvir. 1969.

Steyn M. *The slow death of free speech*. 2014. <http://www.spectator.co.uk/australia/australia-features/9187741/the-slow-death-of-free-speech-2/>

Stinger C.L. *The Renaissance in Rome*. Indiana. Indiana University Press. 1998.

Bibliography

Strassel K. *The Liberal Hypocrisy of Free Speech*. 2016. <http://time.com/4379501/liberal-hypocrisy-of-free-speech/>

Swidler L. *Jesus Was a Feminist: What the Gospels Reveal about His Revolutionary Perspective*. Plymouth. Sheed & Ward. 2007.

Tabour J.D. *Ebionites & Nazarenes: Tracking the Original Followers of Jesus*. 2015. <https://jamestabor.com/ebionites-nazarenes-tracking-the-original-followers-of-jesus/>

Tadmor H. "The Period of the First Temple, the Babylonian Exile and the Restoration," in Ben-Sasson HH, (ed), *A History of the Jewish People*. .Tel Aviv. George Weidenfield and Nicholson Ltd. 1969.

Taylor G and Dinan S. *Violence surges in Central America, threatening new refugee flood*. 2016. <http://www.washingtontimes.com/news/2016/jan/10/el-salvador-honduras-guatemala-violence-surges-thr/?page=all>

Tetlow E.M. *The Status of Women in Greek, Roman and Jewish Society*. 1980. <http://www.womenpriests.org/classic/tetlow1.asp>.

The Apocryphon of John. <http://www.gnosis.org/naghamm/apocjn.html>.

The Complete Jewish Bible < http://www.chabad.org/library/bible_cdo/aid/16160>

The Economist. *Luther's Reformation*. 2017. <https://www.economist.com/essay/2017/11/04/the-stand>

———. *Pentecostals: Christianity reborn*. 2006. <http://www.economist.com/node/8401206>

———. 2014. *The Catholic church and child abuse: Looming shadows*. <https://www.economist.com/international/2014/05/17/looming-shadows>

———. *The world's next great leap forward: Towards the end of poverty*. 2013. <https://www.economist.com/news/leaders/21578665-nearly-1-billion-people-have-been-taken-out-extreme-poverty-20-years-world-should-aim>

The Essene Gospel of Peace. <http://academysounds.blogspot.com/2009/08/gospel-of-peace.html>.

The Gospel of Judas. <http://www.nationalgeographic.com/lostgospel/_pdf/GospelofJudas.pdf>

The Gospel of the Holy Twelve. <http://reluctant-messenger.com/essene/gospel_1.htm>

The Guardian. *Is empowering women the answer to ending poverty in the developing world?* 2013. <http://www.theguardian.com/global-development-professionals-network/2013/mar/26/empower-women-end-poverty-developing-world>

Theissen G. *Sociology of Early Palestinian Christianity*. Philadelphia. Fortress. 1977.

Theissen, G & Merz, A. *The Historical Jesus : a Comprehensive Guide*. Minneapolis . Fortress. 1998.

The Mosaic or Old Covenant. <http://internetbiblecollege.net/Lessons/THE%20MOSAIC%20OR%20OLD%20COVENANT.pdf>

Theosopedia: *Jehova*. <http://theosophy.ph/encyclo/index.php?title=Jehovah>

Thompson J.A. *The Book of Jeremiah*. Michigan. Eerdmans. 1980.

Thurston J. *The 9 Devastating Effects Of The Absent Father*. 2015. <https://thefathercode.com/the-9-devastating-effects-of-the-absent-father/>

Tickle L, *Free speech? Not at four in five UK universities*. 2015. <https://www.theguardian.com/education/2015/feb/02/free-speech-universities-spiked-ban-sombreros>

Torah 101. <https://www.mechon-mamre.org/jewfaq/qorbanot.htm>

Torrance T.F. *The Doctrine of Grace in the Apostolic Fathers*. Eugene. Wipf & Stock. 1996.

Bibliography

Torretto R.R. *A Divine Mercy Resource: How to Understand the Devotion to Divine Mercy.* Bloomington. University Press. 2010.

Torrey C. "James the Just, and his name 'Oblias'". *Journal Of Biblical Literature*, 63(2), 1944.

Tucker J. *Life Before Life: a Scientific Investigation of Children's Memories of Previous Lives.* New York. St. Martin's. 2005.

Tuckness A & Parrish J.M. *The Decline of Mercy in Public Life.* New York. Cambridge University. Press. 2014.

Tverberg L. *Why did Jesus Call Himself the "Son of Man?* 2001. <http://www.egrc.net/articles/director/articles_director_1101.html>

Tzadok A.B. *Israel: the Mission.* 2013. <http://www.koshertorah.com/PDF/vethanan2013.pdf>

UNICEF. "State of the World's Children: Excluded and Invisible". 2006. <http://www.unicef.org/sowc06/press/who.php>.

Unterman A. *Forgiveness.* 2008. <https://www.jewishvirtuallibrary.org/jsource/judaica/ejud_0002_0007_0_06619.html>

Valantasis R. *The Gospel of Thomas.* London. Routledge. 1997.

Vearncombe, E.K. "Redistribution and Reciprocity: A Socio-Economic Interpretation of the Parable of the Labourers in the Vineyard (Matthew 20.1-15)." *Journal for the Study of the Historical Jesus.* Vol. 8 Issue 3. 2010.

Vermes G. *Christian Beginnings from Nazareth to Nicea.* Allen Lane, Penguin. 2012.

———. *The Changing Faces of Jesus.* London. Penguin. 2000.

Viola F. *Shocking Beliefs of John Calvin.* 2015. <http://www.patheos.com/blogs/frankviola/shockingbeliefsofjohncalvin/>

Virginia Youth Violence Project, School of Education, University of Virginia. *Parent Statistics.* <http://youthviolence.edschool.virginia.edu/prevention/parent-statistics.html>.

Viviano B.T. *God in the Gospel According to Matthew.* 2010. <http://int.sagepub.com/content/64/4/341.abstract>

Voltaire. *Epistle to the Author of the Book, The Three Impostors.* 1768. <http://oldpoetry.com/opoem/29767-Voltaire-Epistle—to-the-author-of—The-Three-Impostors->.

Vosper G. *With or Without God: Why the way we live is more important than what we believe.* Toronto. Harper Collins. 2008.

Wachob W.H. *The Voice of Jesus in the Social Rhetoric of James.* Cambridge. Cambridge University Press. 2004.

Wallestein, J.S. *The Unexpected Legacy of Divorce: A 25 Year Landmark Study.* New York. Hyperion. 2000.

Wallis J. *Seven Ways to Change the World.* New York. HarperCollins. 2008.

Wallmann J. "The Reception of Luther's Writings on the Jews from the Reformation to the End of the 19th Century." *Lutheran Quarterly.* 1. Spring, 1987.

Wan, Sze-Kar. "Mercy, Merciful," in Sakenfeld K.D (ed) *The New Interpreter's Dictionary of the Bible, I-MA, vol3.* Nashville. Abingdon. 2008.

Watkins B. *Renewing the Wineskins.* 2016. <http://www.beverleywatkins.com/single-post/2016/07/22/Renewing-the-Wineskin>

Weissman R. *Privileges, Prerogatives and Power: Corporate Power Since 1980.* 2007. <http://www.counterpunch.org/weissman06012007.html>.

Bibliography

Wellman J. *What Is The Difference Between New Wine And Old Wine In The Bible?* 2015. <http://www.patheos.com/blogs/christiancrier/2015/08/22/what-is-the-difference-between-new-wine-and-old-wine-in-the-bible/>

Werner D. *The Two Gospels—Paul & Jesus.* 2017.

West J.K. *Introduction to the Old Testament.* New York: Macmillan. 1981.

Westerman P.A. *.Jesus & Kabbalah: The Hidden Treasure.* 2017. <http://www.lulu.com/shop/http://www.lulu.com/shop/paul-a-westerman/jesus-kabbalah-the-hidden-treasure/paperback/product-23346158.html>

White L.M. *From Jesus to Christianity.* San Francisco. Harper One. 2004.

White P. *The Doctrine of the Trinity.* 2014. <http://www.antipas.org/books/pwhite_trinity/sec1_chap1.html>

Williams D. *Treating Pedophiles.* <http://www.abovehisshoulders.com/treating-pedophiles/>

Williams K. *Jesus as the Reincarnation of Adam.* 2014. < http://www.near-death.com/reincarnation/jesus/adam.html >.

Williams S. *The Origins of Christian anti-Semitism.* 1993. <http://www.sandrawilliams.org/ANTI/anti-semitism.html>

Wills L.M & Wright B.G. *Conflicted Boundaries in Wisdom and Apocalypticism.* Atlanta. Society of Biblical Literature. 2005.

Wilson A.N. *Jesus.* London. Sinclair-Stevenson. 1992.

Wilson M & Daly M. "The Risk of Maltreatment of Children Living with Stepparents," in Gelles R.J & Lancaster J.B (eds). *Child Abuse and Neglect: Biosocial Dimensions, Foundations of Human Behavior.* New York. Aldine de Gruyter. 1987.

Wimborne B. "The Roots of Green Politics in German Romanticism." *Quadrant.* July-August, 2012.

Wippler M.G. *The Christian Kabbalah.* 2018. <http://www.llewellyn.com/journal/article/724>

Wiseman E. *Casualty was right to take on female genital mutilation.* 2013. <http://www.theguardian.com/society/2013/apr/21/casualty-was-right-female-genital-mutilation>

Witherington III B. *The Indelible Image: The Theological and Ethical Thought World of the New Testament: Volume 1, The Individual Witnesses.* Illinois. IVP Academic. 2009.

Wolfe G. "Is culture more powerful than politics?" *News Weekly.* October 15, 2011.

Wolff H.P. *Hosea: A Commentary on the Book of the Prophet Hosea.* Philadelphia. Fortress. 1974.

Wright N.T. *The Early Christian Letters for Everyone: James, Peter, John, and Judah.* London. SPCK. 2011.

———. *New Perspectives on Paul.* 2003. <http://ntwrightpage.com/files/2016/05/Wright_New_Perspectives.pdf>

———. *What St Paul Really Said: Was St Paul the Real Founder of Christianity?* Michigan. Eerdmans. 1997.

Wright T. *The Meal Jesus Gave Us: Understanding Holy Communion.* London. SPCK. 2014.

Your Total Health. *Child Sexual Abuse More Likely in Single-Parent Homes.* 2007. <http://yourtotalhealth.ivillage.com/child-sexual-abuse-more-likely-in-singleparent-homes.html>.

Youth Insearch Annual Report, 2016–17. < https://youthinsearch.org.au/latest-news/tags/annual-reports >

Bibliography

Zavada J. *Melchizedek—Priest of God Most High.* 2017. <http://christianity.about.com/od/oldtestamentpeople/a/Melchizedek.htm>

Zion N. *Biblical and Rabbinic Hesed.* 2013. <https://www.academia.edu/8357389/Hesed_and_Maternal_Love_in_Maimonides_and_Erich_Fromm>

Zobel H.J. "Hesed" in Botterweck G.J & Ringgren H (eds), *Theological Dictionary of the Old Testament, Vol V.* Michigan. Eerdmans. 1986.

Zwartz B. "*Losing our Religion.* 2009. <http://www.smh.com.au/opinion/blogs/the-religious-write/losing-our-religion/20090922-g0o8.html>.

Index

Adam
adam, Adam Kadmon 97, 101
    androgynous, 97,101
    not fully aware of consequences of his choice for mortality, 99–100
    prototype of humanity, 97
    as both *YHWH* and Jesus, 95–105.
Apostles
    Ebonites, successors of, 83
    hesed priority, 20, 22
    Paul at odds with regarding Messianic role, 22
    see Jesus as a future Messiah, 69
    use Temple to prozelitize, not worship, 83.
Arianism, 24
Augustine
    his idea of an invisible church contradicts Jesus, 99
    Luther, 29
    negative influence of, 25–26
    Paul's faith doctrines refined and extended, 24–25.
Australian Indigenous Education Foundation (AIEF), 135.
Axial age, 2.
Bad faith, 12,14,26,50,57,58–9,91,92,106, 137,143,144.
Beatitudes, 48.
Benedict, St
    monasteries basis for universities, 27.
Borg Marcus, 39.
Buddhism, 2
    distortion of, 12

    parallels with Jesus teachings and actions, 106–7, 109.
Capitalism
    essential restructuring, 133–4
    redressing unemployment, 133–34
    tax evasion, 134.
Cassian, John, 25, 28.
Christian humanism, 3
    empirical basis, 149–50
    and Western civilization, 9, 28 (see also spiritual humanism).
Christianity
    anti-Judaism and anti-Semitism, 12, 22–26, 29–30,32
    child abuse cover up, 11
    decline of in the West, 10, 34, 147
    ethical confusion
    flawed theology, 15
    needs to show leadership, 143, 146
    mysteries of faith, 14
    slavery abolition, 31. (see bad faith).
Commandments
    compressed into *hesed*, 55, 118.
Compassion
    alien to ancient world, 65
    centrality of to Christ's mission and the world, 15
    daunting, 120
    ephemeral nature of, 119–120
    family vital to nurturing of, 132
    needs the assistance of grace, 126
    teaching and learning compassion, 125–6.
Covenant, 4

Index

covenantal nomism, 50.
Crossan, J.D.
    critique of his perspective on Jesus, 59–62
    postmodern view of Jesus, 39, 58–59,.
Democratic Republic of the Congo (DRC), 135.
Divorce (see Jesus)
Donatism, 24.
Elohim, 96–7. (see also *YHWH*).
Empathy, 2, 142
Emunah, 5,6–8,20,23,32,118,122,123.
Enlightenment, 2
    and Christianity, 31
    hesed and Judeo Christian influence in Britain and France, 30–31.
epistemology of God (see theosis)
Erasmus, 28
Evil
    derived from self preservation, 114–15
    detachment, 114
    humility, 127
    the human ego as Satan, 115,127–8.
Faith
    absence of the word in John's gospel, 55–6, 123
    anti-semitism (see Christianity)
    as a temporary expedient, 123
    bigotry and atrocities, 9,20, 27
    breeds complacency, 9,114
    conducive to hierarchies, 121
    criteria for any it to be viable, 14
    'doubting Thomas' story in John's gospel, 122
    expressed as faithfulness, 6
    Jesus comparative disinterest in, 92–3
    modernism and War boost faith, 33
    neo-orthodoxy, 33
    smokescreen for evil, 114
    theology of faith, 16
    versus works, 6.
Faithfulness, 5–6
    eclipses faith in early Judaism, 16–17
    Jesus appeals to faithfulness, not faith, 71 (see *emunah*)
Family
    breakdown and remedies, 4,131–33
    as origin of *hesed*, 40,50,68,132.
'Feminine principle'
    and Renaissance, 28.(See also Jesus)
Forgiveness
    adversity seen as sign of sinfulness, 44
    crucial importance of, 16
    culture of guilt, 44, 46,117
    danger of vindictiveness, 113
    human forgiveness as an enabler of *hesed*, 55,114
    need to balance with *geruvah*, 116
Free will, 3,6
    basic assumption of Judaism, 80, 85–93
    Jesus endorses, 91, 92
    precludes divine intervention, 98
    scriptural basis of, 91.
Genesis, 4, 5
    reinterpreted, 95–105
    two different creation stories, 96.
Geruvah (see *hesed*).
Girard, Rene
    Jesus negates scapegoat trope, 76
    flaws in theory, 76.
Global warming, 128.
Gnosticism, 24.
Gospels
    flawed methodology, 37–38, 57
    hesed is the central theme, 41,42, 48–56
    integrity of, 35–39, 61–2
    Jesus scholars questionable deconstructions of, 35–37
    John's emphasis on truth, 56
    Matthew emphasis on *hesed*, 48–50
    misconception of Christ's mission, 37
    not anti-Semitic, 58–9
    not supersessionist, 57
    sacrificial atonement idea absent in all, 67–9.
Grace, 6.
Hasidim
    hesed, men 41
    Isaiah suffering servant a *hasid*, 72–3.
Hesed
    Apostles committed to, 22
    as the Holy Spirit, 28, 40, 42,48–56,52

Index

as righteousness, 52
as the New Covenant, 53
as worship, 82
asymmetry, of 8
best understood as *tiferet, 15–16*
critical importance of forgiveness, 16, 44
expressed as *emunah*, 6
and humility, 115
imitatio dei, 5
in Epistle of James, 52
in Mark, & Luke, 51
in Matthew, 49–51, 53–55
in John, 55–6
Jesus citation of *hesed* in Jonah, 54
Judaism infused with in 1st century, 21–22, 91
justice imperative, 8
juxtaposed against Temple cruelty, 48,49
meaning of, *4–5*
more than works of charity, 8
Mosaic Law, 40
necessary to control human egotism, 105,114
need to be balanced with *geruvah*, 15,116, 137–38
potential to transform world, 147
prophets endorse, 80
theosis, 5
unique in ancient times, 40
Western civilization, 20, 27–28.(See also Renaissance, Enlightenment).

hesed e'meth
the essence of God, 51

Hell and judgment
based on ethical behaviour, not beliefs, 112
based on individual capacity, 117–18
danger of marginalizing, 112,114
importance of *hesed*, 113
positivity of *hesed* based soteriology, 118
unfashionable, 112.

Hillel, 21,45,49,55,58–9,90,91,131
Hinduism, 2
distortion of, 12

Holy Spirit (see *hesed*)
Hosea 6:6
explicit centrality of hesed, 49–51
Humanism (see also secular and spiritual, Christianity and Judaism)
Irenaeus
patristic tradition, 23, 123
Isaiah
suffering servant, 71–4
Islam, 2
distortion of, 12
Israel-Palestine conflict, 138–39
James, brother of Jesus
identifies with the *hesed* prophets, 52.
Jesus
acclamation of children, 92,130–32
and women's rights, 28,130
aligned with the prophets, 79
appeals to faithfulness, not faith, 71, 92–3
as Adam, 99–101
as child of *Sophia*, 101
as Hillite pharisee, 45,90, 107
as Isaiah's suffering servant, 71–4
as Messiah, 3–4
as a messianic teacher, 3–4, 69–71
as Son of God, 100
as Son of Man, 99–101
as *YHWH*, 17, 95–105
cites and affirms Book of Sirach, 91
divinity, 3–4
first feminist, 130
forgiveness and repentance negated sacrificial atonement, 78
negative historical depictions, 31,34–35, 39
opposed to divorce, 130
rabbi and Hasid, 41
reasons for giving his life, 104–5
refutes Messiah having Davidic lineage, 70–71
saw infidelity as both cheating and violence, 13fn
threat to Temple, 45
transcends political categories, 130
vegetarianism, 82–3

INDEX

worship as *hesed,* 82–3. (See also
    Buddhism, Crossan J.D).
Jews
    as moral exemplars, 102.
John the Baptist, 45
Judaic humanism, 2.
Judaism
    importance of free will and individual
        repentance, 80–81
Kabbalah, 5
    and Renaissance, 28
    geruvah, 116
    hesed highest virtue, 97,104
    sefirots, 97, 101
    tikkun olam, 145.
Knowledge of God (see theosis).
Liberation theology, 8, 33–34.
Life purpose, 100,103, 105–111,119.
Luther, Martin
    anti-Semitism and Nazism, 29–30
    negative influence, 29–30.
Melchizedek, 100.
Merkel A,137.
Modernism, 33.
Muntzer T, 29.
New Covenant
    extends Old Covenant to all humanity, 54.
new perspective on Paul (NPP), 13
    claims Judaism was mainly based on
        faith, not works, 84.
Nietzsche, 4, 32.
Original sin
    alternative rational interpretation of
        Genesis, 95–105
    anomalies and contradictions, 13
    not a sin but a brave quest for
        freedom, 97–8
Paul
    anomalies of his doctrine of original
        sin and atonement theology,
        12–14
    anthropomorphic pessimism, 64
    a Shammaite, 63
    co-opts Judaic sacrificial conventions, 74
    Corinthian embarrassment, 65
    differences with Jerusalem Christians, 86
    disinterest in prophets, 65–6
    discordance with Gospels, 19
    ethical behaviour 'boasting', 65
    faith rather than faithfulness, 6–7, 20
    grace needed for genuine ethics, 65–6
    ignorance of human *hesed,* 20, 66
    influenced by Isaiah, 71–2
    Jesus and apostles at odds with, 22, 64
    Jesus personality cult, 4
    manipulation of Scripture, 91
    minimizes importance of repentance, 80
    misunderstands Jewish sacrificial
        offerings, 75
    out of step with Judaic belief in free
        will, 85–93
    pattern of religion same as
        Shammaites, 89–90
    predestination, 84.
Pelagius
    Augustine debates, 24–25
    Celtic Christianity, 26,27,30, 31
    Jewish Christianity and, 24–5
    faith versus *hesed,* 24
    hesed legacy, 24–25,31
    regards original 'sin' as a choice for
        freedom, 98.
Pentecostalism
    negativity of, 8, 10, 136–37.
Pilate, Pontius
    exaggerated fear of Pentecost unrest, 60–61
    role of in death of Jesus, 60.
Pistis
    Greek word used to denote *Emunah,* 6–7.
Political alignments
    akin to faith delusions, 130
    faults of the Left and Right, 129
    Jesus and, 130
    Kabbalah wisdom and, 129
    need to transcend left/right
        allegiances, 128–130
Pope Francis, 34,132,138.
Prayer

Index

complex teachings on, 124
hesed is main purpose of, 124-5
humanist dimension of the Lord's Prayer, 125.
Prioritization, 135-38, 142.
Prophets
  disdained sacrificial offerings, 79-80
  exultation of *hesed*, 79
  Jesus strongly identifies with, 42,79.
Ptochos
  and prioritization, 9
  Jesus aligns with, 8-9, 145
  land dispossession, 43-44, 114.
Quietism, 9.
Reincarnation, 17
  clinical psychology case histories, 109-10
  early Christian believers, 107-8
  integral to divine justice, 105
  in the Gnostic gospels and Kabbalah, 107
  Jesus confirms reality of, 107
  linguistic evidence, 107
  well established in Judaism in first century, 107.
Renaissance, 2
  hesed revived and inspires creativity, 27-28
  humanism, 28.
Reformation
  Calvin, 29
  negative and positive impacts, 29 (see Luther M)
Refugees, 137-38.
Repentance
  more important than sacrificial rites, 76
  through *hesed*, 81
  through prayer, fasting and charity, 81
  through suffering, 81.
Routledge, R.
  misunderstanding of Judaic sacrificial rites, 77.
Russia
  Orthodox Church, 11-12,136,144,
  tyranny of Putin, 11-12.
Sacrifice

Christ's disdain for, 54.
Sacrificial atonement
  asham ritual symbolic and secondary to repentance and reconciliation, 77-8
  Ebonite contempt for, 82
  eclipsed by repentance, 76
  Jesus misconstrued on in Matthew, 68-9
  prophets disdain for, 79
  valorization of savagery, 75.
Salvation
  only through *hesed*, 56.
Schweitzer, Albert, 33.
Secular humanism
  captive to human ego, 127-28
  failure of, 1-3, 119, 148.
Shammaite pharisees
  active in Gallilee, 47
  Christian historians tend to ignore, 21, 58-9
  exclusivity, 46
  fanaticism, 21,58 60
  links with Zealots, 45
  Paul a Shammaite, 63
  power and influence of, 46,54
  purity rules, 46-47.
Sirach, book of (See Jesus)
Social justice, 5, 134-6
Sophia
  divine wisdom and compassion, 98.
Sprinkle, P.
  claims prophets relied of God's grace, 86-89.
Spiritual humanism
  and *Kabbalah*, 145
  essence of *hesed*, 139
  imitatio dei, 5
  humanity in charge of its destiny, 105
  latent in major religious traditions, 17,141, 147-48
  positivity of *hesed* based soteriology, 118
  superior to secular humanism, 2,143
  way forward, 131. (see also Christian humanism).
Temple of Jerusalem

Index

central to issues of justice, 145
connections with Herod, 45
corrupt, 42–43
criticism of not anti-Semitic, 57–62
Jesus laments its lost tradition of
  hesed, 82
Jonah critique, 82
land dispossession, 43–44
murders three Apostles, 52
opposition to, 45
scribes, 49fn
responsible for Christ's death, 43
Shammaites dominate, 47
venal priests, 43–45
Theodicy, 13, 93–104
  freedom and compassion override mortality and suffering, 98
  free will precludes divine intervention, 98
  inexorability, 99
  natural disasters, 98–9
  unintended consequences of divine choice for mortality, 99–100.
Theosis
  God glorified through *hesed*, 51
  God known through *hesed*, 2,5,50,55–56,89
  Paul says not humanly possible, 66
  Plato's idealized God, 65.
Vermes. G.
  divisions between Paul and Jerusalem Christians, 64, 86
  Jews could never represent themselves as God, 75
  Judaic emphasis on works more than faith, 86

'schizophrenia' regarding Jesus attitude to gentiles, 37
sees John's gospel as anti-Semitic, 59.
Wesley, J., 31.
West, the
  achievements of, 9, 14,20,27,31 137–38, 141
  crucial importance of *hesed*, 128, 131,142,147
  decline of, 1–3,17, 133
  linked to the decline of Christianity, 144, 149
  negative attitudes towards, 129, 132,137,141
  responsibilities, 137–41,144
  world security and development, 134–35.
Women (see Jesus)
Worship
  as a temporary expedient, 122
  as *hesed*, 82, 122
  Jesus deprecates, 122
  primitive origins of, 121.
Wright, N.T.
  applies Jewish sacrificial trope to Jesus, 75
  misconstrues core Judaic religious conventions and beliefs, 67, 92
  sees Paul as an erstwhile Shammaite, 90.
YHWH
  adam becomes, 101–103
  anthromorphic and errant, 96–7
  Jesus as an incarnation of, 101–103.
Youth Insearch, 135.
Zakkai, Rabbi Yohanan ben, 22
  prioritized *hesed*, 90.

www.ingramcontent.com/pod-product-compliance
Lightning Source LLC
Chambersburg PA
CBHW051931160426
43198CB00012B/2107